Making Houses,
Crafting Capitalism

EARLY AMERICAN STUDIES

Daniel K. Richter, Director,
McNeil Center for Early American Studies,
Series Editor

Exploring neglected aspects of our colonial, revolutionary, and early national
history and culture, Early American Studies reinterprets familiar themes and
events in fresh ways. Interdisciplinary in character, and with a special emphasis on
the period from about 1600 to 1850, the series is published in partnership with the
McNeil Center for Early American Studies.

A complete list of books in the series is available from the publisher.

Making Houses, Crafting Capitalism

BUILDERS IN PHILADELPHIA, 1790–1850

Donna J. Rilling

UNIVERSITY OF PENNSYLVANIA PRESS   •   Philadelphia

10 9 8 7 6 5 4 3 2 1

Published by
University of Pennsylvania Press
Philadelphia, Pennsylvania 19104-4011

Library of Congress Cataloging-in-Publication Data
Rilling, Donna J.
Making houses, crafting capitalism : builders in Philadelphia,
1790–1850 / Donna J. Rilling.
p. cm.
ISBN 0-8122-3580-0 (cloth : alk. paper)
1. Building—Pennsylvania—Philadelphia—History.   I. Title.
TH24.P4 R55 2000
338.4'76908'0974811—dc21   00-062859

Contents

Introduction

I'm a contractor when the economy is good, and a carpenter when the economy is bad. Right now I'm a carpenter.
— Construction worker, early 1990s

HOUSE BUILDERS in early nineteenth-century Philadelphia would have readily identified with their twentieth-century peer. They, too, exercised flexibility in their occupations in order to make a living. When credit flowed, they competed for contracts to build twelve, thirty, even forty houses at a time. With business at a standstill, they ferreted out small jobs, repairs, and renovations. But they also possessed a critical third option: early nineteenth-century Philadelphia artisans built on speculation. They made building in the expectation of quickly selling completed houses a central strategy for attaining independence. The practice drew them deeply into a competitive and volatile economy. Those who amassed fortunes often did so through well-calculated advance building. Others secured a modest living, and plenty paid a high personal and financial price for their decisions. Insolvency lurked around every corner, but it could not dissuade builders from the possibility of gain—or the imperative of keeping even—that the market in real estate offered.

Men in the Philadelphia construction trades were aggressive and ingenious operators who plunged wholeheartedly into the dangers and rewards of capitalism. They anticipated markets for housing, wagering that they would find buyers for their products. They organized credit so that they could build, and, when money dried up, they sought out other means to meet obligations. By maneuvering financial and property instruments in inventive ways, craftsmen influenced the development of real estate law and practice. In their strategies to secure independence, novice as well as veteran masters were also active agents in reorganizing production within crafts, exploiting piecework, subcontracting, and specialization. Building tradesmen developed new materials that warranted new skills and new technology to extract, harvest, transport, and fashion supplies for use in Philadelphia houses. They employed local and craft knowledge to make decisions in the face of ever-changing information about costs and material availability. And they worked and prospered in an unpredictable economy that was subject to a myriad of unknowables—labor supply, weather, war, consumer taste, and cost of credit, to name a few.

House building was a business of crucial importance in the expanding metropolis of the nineteenth century. Between 1790 and 1850, the population of Philadelphia's "city and suburbs"—the built-up sections of Philadelphia County—grew from 44,000 to 389,000 residents. To meet this increase, tradesmen added more than 52,000 new residences to the housing stock.[1] Construction provided employment to one-fifth of the urban mechanic (i.e., craft) population (and one-tenth of the entire male labor force). Any one construction project required the collaboration of no fewer than twenty men of diverse specialties (subcontracting artisans, journeymen hands, and material suppliers). Factoring in unskilled laborers and small capitalists allied to the trade, nearly one-quarter of all male workers in Philadelphia depended on the building economy for their livelihoods.[2]

Slightly more than half of all building craftsmen in the first decades of the nineteenth century were carpenters. The proportion reflected the prevalence of framing and woodworking labor captured in the brick houses typical of Philadelphia. Owing to their productive importance, house carpenters became "master builders" much more frequently than other artisans in construction trades. Carpenters, consequently, take center stage in this narrative.

Builders set Philadelphia's housing economy in motion by exploiting the city's unique ground-rent system of property tenure. Ground-rent transactions put building parcels and credit for advance construction within the reach of artisans, making Philadelphia a promising and even rewarding venue for small producers. As long as the economy beckoned with cycles of growth and optimism, real estate development invited young men to take chances and become masters, and to anticipate great gains in the business.

House carpenters particularly, but bricklayers, plasterers, and other building mechanics as well, bet their futures on selling row houses to the expanding residential market. The row (or "separate") house system, transmitted with the city's English immigrant craftsmen, epitomized Philadelphia since its colonial youth. These brick structures, usually two and one-half or three stories high, were visually alike houses built in alignment. Visitors to the Quaker City found their uniformity and architecture monotonous, but these brick dwellings came to distinguish Philadelphia as the "City of Homes." [3] The persistence of the row house in Philadelphia meant that shelter for workingmen's families changed only modestly between 1790 and 1850. No precise contemporary architectural survey exists to ascertain the size of living space, but evidence suggests that dimensions of the residences intended for the "lower sort" varied little throughout the period. Dwellings constructed in the heart of Philadelphia for white-collar residents also continued to follow the basic ideals of the row house. These structures were more grand, rose higher, had more square footage, sported more marble or granite, and boasted central heating and indoor plumbing. They incorporated diverse architectural conceits such as the Italianate styles that influenced design at midcentury. Despite new-fashioned façades, however, middle-class and elite city residences continued to evoke the Philadelphia tradition and the artisans behind it.

*   *   *

"Making houses"—producing parts and assembling them into buildings—and "crafting capitalism"—grasping the opportunities and grappling with the challenges of the expansive economy of the young nation—are the central topics of this study. This book examines how journeymen, masters, and entrepreneurs reorganized production in the building trades and how they set limits to organizational and technological change. It also examines the relations of capital and credit in construction, and the ways in which an increasingly sophisticated industry, an assertive cadre of professionals, and a fledgling American legal system mediated those relations. Furthermore, *Making Houses, Crafting Capitalism* recognizes the small producers who were central to the economy of early America.

This book does not, however, explore labor conflict in the building trades, the formation of craft associations, or the ethnocultural composition of the construction business. These topics have been investigated by other scholars and are important in documenting the lives of workingmen and placing them in the narrative of early American history. [4] Labor associations and strikes, however, do not constitute the sum total of the artisan experience. They are by nature too episodic to capture the day-to-day as well as the career experiences of most small producers in the early republic. In addition, the recent focus on labor conflict has actually shifted attention away from work and productive behavior more generally. This book thus applies a broad definition to men's activities; it is both a study of labor and a study of business. It examines manual processes situated in craft establishments, but also investigates the nonmanual tasks (for example, managing, financing, designing, and marketing) that small capitalists executed and refined in the dynamic business climate of early America.[5]

By highlighting the conflicts between employers and employees, and the clashing conceptualization of republican and worker ideology, artisan studies have diverted attention from the many ways that journeymen and small masters actively transformed their crafts with a mind to participating in the nation's competitive economy. Historians have underestimated the critical role both young and established mechanics played in shaping capitalism.[6] *Making Houses, Crafting Capitalism* opens up the everyday world of independent artisans and reveals their centrality in exploiting and creating opportunities in the expanding metropolis. Legal institutions, credit markets, geography, and the diversity of Philadelphia's economy enabled men of humble origins to gain a foothold in the mid-nineteenth-century construction industry. As late as the 1850s, workingmen in the Philadelphia building trades continued to exploit avenues out of employee status. Subcontracting and specialized production frequently led to greater prospects—in building, in ancillary fields, or in quite divergent manufacturing ventures. Ironically, the erratic nature of the economy and the frequency of failure in construction also kept opportunities fluid. Entry into independent building often hinged more on cyclical movements in the economy, than on linear transformations of the business. Bigger risks also paved the way for spectacular failures, of course, but the very instability of the economy beckoned to entrepreneurs.

The revised view presented here emerges from close scrutiny of primary sources that have yet to draw attention from most historians of the artisan world. I have relied intensively on deeds, mortgages, and mechanic lien records to reconstitute the financial and productive strategies of builders. Case papers filed in several courts revealed accepted trade practices and new innovations; testimony in especially contentious suits added human dimensions to the men who practiced in construction, and insolvency petitions and bankruptcy cases aided in chronicling goals, fleeting triumphs, and insurmountable disappointments. Many of these inscrutable documents were still bundled in the legal red tape of nineteenth-century prothonotaries and warehoused in municipal and county archives that lack the resources to organize and preserve them. Of the records more readily available and more typically consulted by scholars, account books, diaries, and letters have proven invaluable. In examining these diverse and often remarkable records, one cannot help but be struck by the deep involvement of building artisans in the capitalist economy.

What can the experiences of building mechanics tell us about other men—and about women—in early America? This study provides insight into the ways Americans dealt with and thought about the inconstancies of the nineteenth-century economy. The impact that its capriciousness had on craftsmen and small businessmen enables us to better understand the lives of many individuals in early America. Precariousness of fortune may have been more pronounced in construction, but the experiences of other small capitalists undoubtedly were similiar to those of builders. The fact that the market for housing was local and construction dependent on weather should not mask parallels to manufacturing. For many industries, supply of materials was regional, nature continued to affect production, and hiccups in the international economy reverberated locally.

Philadelphia shaped the creativity of building artisans, but was their innovative propensity peculiar to their environment? The work of a number of historians has distinguished the mid-Atlantic city and its inhabitants. Thomas Doerflinger finds a "fabric of adversity" that called forth a "vigorous spirit of enterprise" among merchants in the revolutionary city. Philip Scranton stresses the importance of proprietary workshops, skilled craftsmen, and flexible specialization. Thomas Heinrich also places small enterprises central to the organization of skill and capital in shipbuilding. Did Philadelphia breed a uniquely spirited proprietary capitalist? I suggest that what we now know about Philadelphia may well be a more widespread phenomenon that deserves closer scrutiny, even in regions known for large-scale manufacturing enterprises.[7] Knowledge of the tenacity and creativity of artisan producers and their role in crafting capitalism promises to be increasingly important to a complex understanding of nineteenth-century America beyond the City of Homes.

* * *

On my numerous trips between New York and Philadelphia, I am always transfixed by the northeastern part of the latter city visible from the commuter rail. Streets and streets of row houses alternate with the seemingly abandoned remains of Philadelphia's manufacturing past. The stamp that Philadelphia builders left on the urban landscape is evident. They proffered to nineteenth-century Philadelphians a recognized architectural form. Builders varied size, comforts, and style to fit a diversity of consumers—

laboring and mechanic owners, white-collar households, elite families, and landlord-investors among them. The basic building style persisted into the twentieth century. But in the booming economy of 2000, housing values in sprawling suburbia have risen rapidly, while the demand for compact urban row houses is much weaker. Complicating urban fortunes is the racially and economically homogenous character of the neighborhoods dotted with row developments. Today's conceptions of adequate space and comfort, moreover, have rendered the row house untenable for middle-class families in the metropolis. The housing form that was so vital to artisan entrepreneurs and working-class families has left an ambivalent legacy to the city that nurtured their fortunes and aspirations.

ONE

Men on the Make

Philadelphia Builders

THE EARLY CAREER of John Munday resembled that of many house carpenters in the new republic. Born around 1760, Munday apprenticed to the trade and was free from his training by 1782. For the next nine years, he wandered through Delaware, New York, and Philadelphia, working as a journeyman, doing skilled labor for various craftsmen, and getting paid by the day. He also worked occasionally as a master carpenter employing his own laborers. In 1785 he married, and by 1793, when he had finally settled in Philadelphia, he had incurred over £235 (approximately $630) in debts toward the support of his growing family. The sum was considerable, equivalent to what a journeyman carpenter might earn in two or three years of steady employment.[1]

During the post-Revolutionary depression of the 1780s, Munday had been unable to advance toward more stable master status. By 1792, however, when Munday examined his prospects, he found Philadelphia alive with activity. Rents and prices in the new nation's capital were rising sharply in 1792 and "it was considered . . . a good speculation to build houses for Sale." Though Munday owned only his tools and a few household items, "from this Period [he] resolved no longer to continue in the capacity of a Journeyman, but to try his fortune in the way of building."[2] Over the next decade, in the heady environment of the American political, social, and economic experiment, Munday would test "his fortune," craft skills, and business sense.

Like Munday, journeymen (employees), small producers, and masters in Philadelphia all aimed to accumulate wealth and live off of it in their retirement. They intended to gain from the difference between the cost of building and the sum commanded by the commodity made through their labor and supervision. If the market warranted, building mechanics did not hesitate to pocket profits in excess of a "good price" for their labor. The rewards of undertaking one's own project enticed both journeymen and mas-

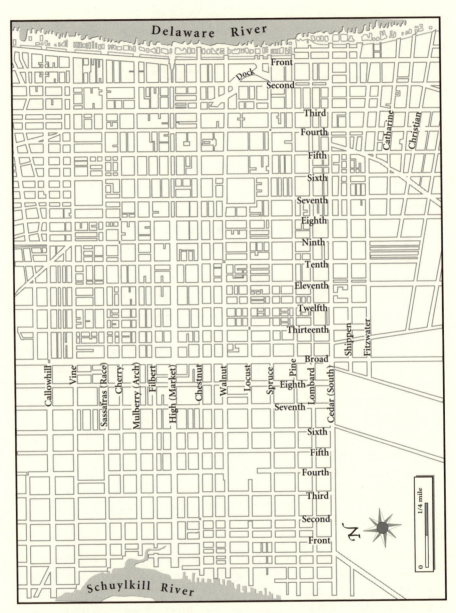

Delaware River

Front
Dock
Second
Third
Fourth
Fifth
Sixth
Seventh
Eighth
Ninth
Tenth
Eleventh
Twelfth
Thirteenth

Catharine
Christian

Shippen
Fitzwater

Broad

Eighth
Seventh
Sixth
Fifth
Fourth
Third
Second
Front

Callowhill
Vine
Sassafras (Race)
Cherry
Mulberry (Arch)
Filbert
High (Market)
Chestnut
Walnut
Locust
Spruce
Pine
Lombard
Cedar (South)

N

1/4 mile

0

Schuylkill River

1 Philadelphia's early nineteenth-century development continued to reflect the city's colonial reliance on Delaware River maritime traffic. Residents crowded near the river and carved up the original grid of William Penn's town into small alleys and courts. After J. Simons, Philadelphia, 1835.

ters. Many factors influenced intent: the quest for larger income to support a family, the aspiration to improve one's social prominence, and the lag between custom or contract jobs. Similarly, many elements affected outcome: the stage in one's career, national economic cycles, personal circumstances, and luck. The urge to build with the prospect of selling quickly, however, was ubiquitous.

* * *

Crucial to entrepreneurial activities were the places where construction tradesmen worked and the times in which they lived.[3] Place is a sum of its history, and John Munday and his peers encountered a city whose characteristics shaped them while they, in turn, molded their environment. Decades before Munday's appearance, Philadelphia had already bulged beyond the legal boundaries that William Penn had established in 1682. In 1682, the plan for the Quaker City seemed a grand vision: a distance of two miles between the Delaware River on the east and the Schuylkill River on the west, and one mile north to south. Nomenclature reflected Penn's hope that settlement would develop inward from both banks and converge at the midpoint. Designating the north-south byways by their proximity to Philadelphia's rivers, he named the adjacent ones "Delaware Front Street" and "Schuylkill Front Street." He numbered inward from each river until Delaware and Schuylkill streets met in the middle at Broad Street.[4]

From the start, Philadelphians rejected Penn's neat grid, spacious lots, and wide streets (Figure 1). Their response was merely logical. Crowding along the Delaware River and stretching beyond the official municipal northern and southern bounds, commercial and residential establishments testified to the city's colonial maritime prowess.[5] From the Delaware piers, Philadelphia exported local products. Agricultural yields conveyed from the hinterlands by regional waterways as well as overland roads overwhelmed the urban warehouses with their fecundity and awaited shipment to ports near and far. Philadelphia's vessels engaged in continuous traffic with Great Britain, Ireland, Iberia, Madeira, and the Caribbean. The city dominated the reexport business and the West Indies trade. In the British empire, Philadelphia ranked second only to London as an entrepôt. After American independence, maritime trade with China, India, and North Africa added to the commercial reputation of the port.[6]

Property near the Delaware River, the market, and the primary commercial section commanded premium rents. Major east-west streets—Mulberry (later Arch), High (later Market), Chestnut, and Walnut streets—and smaller byways attracted inns, taverns, boardinghouses, and other market services. Merchants directly involved in international trade and shopkeepers in retail sales joined the mixture. Marine crafts—sailmaking, cooperage, caulking, smithing, rigging, ropemaking, and assorted others—vied with commercial interests for waterfront. By the close of the eighteenth century, commercialization had squeezed shipbuilding, the keystone of the maritime economy, to the southern and northern extremities of urban settlement.[7]

A subsidiary tier of trades producing wares for local consumption also competed for land. Seeking large amounts of space and natural resources, industries established manufactories on the urban edge. For water outlets to dispose of dyes, liquids, and animal remnants, and to transport heavy finished products, noisome tanneries and stinking sugar refineries moved beyond congested neighborhoods. Brickyards, too, gravitated to the periphery, nearer to new construction, wood fuel, and raw material sources.[8]

Physical expansion accompanied the beginning of recovery from the War of Independence, and building accelerated. In the late 1780s the Pennsylvania commonwealth government, in an attempt to pay war debts, had auctioned off lots formerly held by the colony's proprietors. The dull economy of Philadelphia (and the nation generally) netted a disappointingly meager number of buyers.[9] But by the early 1790s, mercantile interests recovered from the disruption of the American Revolution. Profits from international trade poured into the metropolis, rejuvenating local production. When Congress selected Philadelphia for the country's capital, political functions and prominence buoyed the city's prospects.[10] Proprietary lots purchased in the 1780s promised handsome returns after all.

Excitement seized the Federal city. Individuals from a broad segment of society invested capital in western land schemes, manufacturing ventures, and local real estate and building construction. In 1792, Philadelphian Susanna Dillwyn wrote to her absent father that "the town increases surprisingly . . . thee wou'd hardly know the upper ends of Market, Chestnut, Walnut, and Arch Streets, they are so built up with new houses."[11] Exhibiting a similar faith in progress, residents (including several building tradesmen) lobbied for opening more streets in Northern Liberties township. Freemen proposed public thoroughfares to accommodate "the increasing population [and their] . . . several Buildings and Improvements . . . now erecting."[12] A 60 percent increase in the number of houses built by the end of the 1790s would even outstrip the concurrent rise in population.[13]

John Munday hastily grabbed the chance for financial and personal independence that the national economy and Philadelphia particularities promised. He had waited a long while to do so. In contrast to his nine years at journeywork, men much younger than Munday waited only months before the explosion of the 1790s boosted them to master status. No law barred any free man of majority (that is, the age of twenty-one) from declaring himself a master, which in effect is what Munday did when he announced his intention to build. Nor did guilds restrict admission to a craft. Voluntary associations or mutual aid societies, such as the Carpenters' Company of the City and County of Philadelphia, set standards and prices for workmanship and assisted widows and children of deceased members (all master craftsmen). But for the trade at large, the Company could neither prescribe the length or standard of training a man required before he could call himself a master carpenter nor limit the number of young men apprenticed to the trade. The guidelines that the Carpenters' Company advocated, moreover, bound only its own members, who never comprised more than a quarter of all masters active in the eighteenth-century city.[14]

Long-standing practices, and not legal restrictions, held American mechanics to an occupational hierarchy adapted from Europe. Boys bound as apprentices until adulthood filled the bottom tier of the craft. They learned the mysteries and mastery of the trade; in return, they provided cheap and generally pliant labor. Length of apprenticeship varied, but a white male in early national Philadelphia typically could anticipate a term of five to seven years terminating at the age of twenty-one.[15] At the completion of his indenture (the legal agreement of service), the apprentice was given his "freedoms." He then embarked on the relative autonomy—but uncertainty—of journeywork. Some young men performed stints with the same masters that they had served as apprentices. Others went to work with male relatives, benefiting from the tuition, artisanal connections, and trade opportunities opened by their seniors. Walking the town and inquiring at various shops and worksites offered other means of finding employment.[16]

From this stage as an employee, a craftsman calculated the optimal moment to launch his independence. For a house carpenter, autonomy connoted the privilege and responsibility of employing his own laborers and managing his own shop. It also meant dealing directly with a client who would engage him for custom work, that is, to design and erect a house. Another mode of building was by contract, whereby the craftsman agreed to finish several structures, usually at a stipulated price, for a paying customer. Alternatively—and significantly more lucrative—autonomy for the craftsman entailed speculative construction, that is, borrowing and spending money, contracting and subcontracting for workers and materials, and erecting one or more dwellings in anticipation of a buyer. For Munday, advance building meant having three to six houses in progress at any one time. Twenty years later, house carpenters were likely to increase that number to twelve or fifteen. By the 1830s, some artisan builders juggled the simultaneous construction of as many as fifty houses.

Of these three ways of going about their craft (that is, custom, contract, and "spec"), artisans repeatedly equated speculative construction with initiation into independence. Like Munday, they decided to "try [their] fortune in the way of building." Joshua Sharples, a contemporary of Munday, also deduced that construction on his own account was pivotal for social and economic advancement. Two dwellings that Sharples ventured to build marked his debut as master and received self-conscious notice by the fledgling house carpenter. Sharples tabulated precisely the "[a]mount what they cost including what I p'd for the Lot and allowing a good price for my own work." He cleared more than $1,450 "[b]y the purchase & Sale" of the properties. Above the wage he paid himself, he tallied a 31 percent return on the sums spent. For the two- and one-half years of intermittent work on the houses, punctuated by labor on other projects, Sharples earned a generous income, enlarged by the profits from his undertaking. Independent construction netted Sharples more than twofold the amount he could hope to get as a fully employed journeyman house carpenter.[17]

Beneath the occupational sobriquet of "carpenter" in the early republic lay a diversity of activities, some fluidity among specialties, and a transferability of basic woodworking skills. One man, for example, called himself a "Carpenter," describing his labor at making "looking Glass Frames."[18] Another made "weaving machines on a New Construction," but asserted otherwise that he was a "House carpenter."[19] Still a third mechanic stated that he was a house and ship carpenter. He shifted between the two areas during starts and stops in maritime commerce.[20]

Carpentry as a designation, then, ranged across a spectrum of skills from making looking-glass frames to building houses. Frequently, carpentry was simply a convenient term used in lieu of a more specialized or comprehensive word. Alphonso Ireland, for example, was identified as a "Carpenter" within the same indenture that apprenticed a boy to him to learn "house carpentry."[21] But distinctions and specialization, normally masked by general language, did surface occasionally. Although Jehu Robinson initially tendered a bill for "services done and performed as a house carpenter," upon reflection he (or another) struck through the word "house" to describe his work simply as carpentry.[22] House carpentry intimated that he had "appl[ied] timber in the construction of buildings" and framed the windows, built the staircases, floored the rooms, and hung the doors and windows.[23] Instead, Robinson likely finished inside the rooms, or performed miscellaneous tasks throughout construction, and associated the work with general carpentry.

Within the crafts, journeymen outnumbered masters by a small margin. Unfortunately, tax lists, censuses, and city directories—the sorts of records historians use to sketch a general view of Philadelphia's population—provide no certain means of distinguishing between the two groups. One scholar has estimated boldly that 55 percent of the craft force labored as journeymen and 45 percent as masters.[24] Arriving at rough figures, however, is not solely an evidentiary quandary. Fluidity between the two craft ranks also clouded distinctions. A master of a small enterprise might find the craft or manual work he did identical to that of a journeyman. Many masters did not regularly retain journeymen but made do with the labor of themselves and an apprentice or two—this was most likely John Munday's approach before he arrived in Philadelphia. A mechanic even interspersed journeywork on one construction site, with management as a master builder on another. The difference between the two craft levels lay in the independent status of the master, which garnered him respect among artisans, as well as a measure of standing within the larger polity. Independence required oversight of all aspects of a small business. It linked a young craftsman to the rewards and losses of the concern.

Lack of capital—a "want of funds"—did not bar John Munday from building. Landed men and women, brokers, and investors eager to enrich their estates by lending money at interest made the decade's real estate takeoff particularly alluring to journeymen poised for their leap into independence. The upper tenth of Philadelphia's inhabitants—mostly merchants and landed elite—owned approximately half of all taxable wealth. Several of the wealthiest men and women lived not from lucrative mercantile investments, but off the profits of rents and mortgage loans derived from property acquired in the colonial and Revolutionary periods.[25] Landowners wanted their parcels developed, and they attracted venturesome builders with the offer of long-term credit to pay for improvements.

Filling the need for short-term capital was, nonetheless, an ongoing challenge for a young builder. Munday's lack of cash, for example, repeatedly forced him to "sell his houses in an unfinished State to raise money to compleat them." Buyers also often had empty pockets, and when Munday sold his first house (unfinished, with an agreement to complete), he accepted the purchase price of £600 ($1,608) in goods. He then was obliged to borrow cash to develop the adjoining lot, and also to run a small store to dispose of the goods. A few months later, he accepted £1,000 ($2,680) in dry goods to sell to raise immediate funds for construction. Munday identified himself subsequently as both a house carpenter and a shopkeeper, although his wife Elizabeth ran the store. Proprietorship was "used as the means of . . . aiding [Munday] in his [building] Business, [rather] than as an independant means of subsistance."[26]

To acquire lots for building, Munday quickly entered into "ground rent" arrangements that entailed long-term credit of thousands of dollars. Ground rent land transactions were unique to the Quaker City and used widely to develop property.[27] (I will discuss the complexities of ground rent more fully in Chapter 2.) Under this means of property holding, title to a lot was granted in perpetuity, subject to payment of an annual rent. A "ground lord" often advanced a mechanic money for construction on his lot. Advantages to a builder are obvious: he needed nothing for purchase and could expend capital erecting dwellings or workshops. Elimination of entry cost, moreover, gave an artisan builder access to the means of independence (one's own construction project), and even entry to buying and selling real estate. Upon completion, a builder could sell the dwelling and assign the rent obligation to another party.[28]

In light of brisk inflation, ground rent purchases did not work optimally for Munday's strategies. Rents for 1795 alone committed him to pay $2,225, a hefty sum even in diluted currency. Prices of materials and labor were also highly inflated. Fearing war in 1794, and with it a plunge in housing prices, Munday unloaded some properties at a loss. Nevertheless, other profitable deals kept him afloat. In 1793 and again in 1794 Edward Shippen, a judge of the Supreme Court of Pennsylvania and a prominent member of Philadelphia's elite, advanced Munday credit. The house carpenter applied the loans to two substantial houses on Chestnut Street near Eighth Street.[29] On one he gained approximately £1,000 ($2,680), but on the other property, Munday lost an undetermined amount. Fortunately, concurrent trading in undeveloped real estate netted him £1,000.[30]

An infusion of that sum, however, could not stem Munday's financial problems. If he followed the practice of most craftsmen, Munday contracted in the fall or late winter before the building season began, looking ahead to the spring. Based on prices, supplies, and wages of the previous year, he bargained with landowners, material producers, creditors, subcontractors, journeymen, and customers. He began to assemble stock in the winter and to dig foundations as soon as the ground thawed. But operating in the inflationary environment of the early republic, autumn estimations inevitably diverged sharply from spring realities. What sums Munday had to lay out overall exceeded the prices he could negotiate for his houses. Here, particularly, timing was critical because inflation did not always work against builders. Lucky was the speculator who sold all his houses while the market was up and paid for borrowed money in inflated currency. Munday, however, was not lucky.

To make matters worse, in 1795 Munday miscalculated the likelihood of war, relinquishing building opportunities. Then in 1796, he undertook "a large and elegant house with stables" for Samuel Fisher. Fisher promised Munday £1,600 ($4,288) and a fifty- acre farm valued at more than £1,600. Munday insisted afterward that he had contracted too cheaply for the job and blamed the expense of labor and materials "and [his] want of Cash" for a loss of £500 ($1,340). Perhaps Munday was right; Fisher immediately sold the finished property at a profit of $9,000.[31]

Undefeated, Munday turned again to Shippen. In exchange for a loan, the carpenter pledged to build a house for the judge for £2,500 ($6,700) and give Shippen a mortgage on the residence going up on an adjoining lot. The carpenter subsequently misappropriated part of the money ($600) to break ground on other structures. Similarly, in 1797 Munday received $400 from John Field to complete the dwelling he had sold him, only to apply the funds elsewhere and leave Field's property untouched. Munday justified the diversion as necessary to develop his remaining lots so that he could realize some gain (even by selling the new houses partially finished).[32]

Thereafter Munday's schemes to rob Peter to pay Paul unraveled swiftly. For his failures, he blamed "heavy Ground Rent" and his inability to procure sufficient cash through "Loans, and contracts of sale" for the several (six) houses he had under way. His "credit of consequence was lost & the business proceeded slowly & upon very disadvantageous terms." Munday was soon harassed by lawsuits. He struggled to get his dwellings "under Roof" and once again appealed to Shippen, who accommodated him with £1,000 ($2,680) on a mortgage of two other houses. To meet additional debts, he borrowed $900 on a short-term loan at the exorbitant rate of 2½ per cent interest *per month*, pledging goods worth $1,800. (The security was a portion of £3,500 — $9,380 in goods that Munday had received in payment for Field's house.) But he was unable to meet this latest obligation, and the sheriff seized the merchandise, auctioned it off, and apportioned the proceeds to judgments against Munday.[33]

During the next few years, Munday sank deeper. Speculation on a lot lost him $1,065 when he defaulted on the ground rent and the property was repossessed. Munday sold the last of his houses under construction to Edward Shippen in 1798, but the debts against it and "the depression in [the] Price of Real Estate" diminished the value. Meanwhile, he did "a variety of lesser work," probably subcontracting, repairs, and day labor. The small trade in dry goods that his wife Elizabeth managed also helped to keep Munday and his family going.[34]

Squeezed by creditors, Munday scurried for immediate solutions. He erected six small wooden (or "frame") houses and sold them all to a prospective landlord; tenants would likely come from the city's population of the "lower sort"—laborers, mariners, tailors, cordwainers—who had few means.[35] Frame houses were bleak, compared to Philadelphia's two-and-a-half-and three-story brick row houses. In 1798, for instance, Robert Thomas rented a dwelling similar to those Munday erected. It was a one story "frame plastered house," though in this case "very old."[36] Wooden construction was more vulnerable to the elements. Contemporary Charlotte Burns rented space that "was not quite so bad as to shake when the wind blew but the wind used to come in bad enough. [T]he kitchen roof leaked the most but it all leaked through at times in very wet weather."[37] Charlotte Burns's experience exemplified another disadvantage of frame buildings: their flammability. Her quarters burned down, though fortunately for her, after she had vacated them.

Abundant wooden structures hid behind principal arteries lined with impressive brick dwellings. Frame dwellings, secreted in narrow alleys or in backyards, or placed at the edge of settlement as Munday's were, comprised a major share of the cheapest housing (Figure 2).[38] As late as 1810, frame buildings accounted for 65 percent of the total housing stock. The proportion rose in peripheral neighborhoods where indigent residents congregated.[39]

After 1798, ordinances that prohibited construction in wood gradually encompassed the commercial and exclusive parts of the county.[40] In the poor and outlying neighborhoods which lacked restrictions, however, frame sometimes outpaced brick building. To the west of the city and beyond the ban—the areas where Munday was building—wood exceeded brick construction in a five to three ratio even in 1802.[41] Munday was not

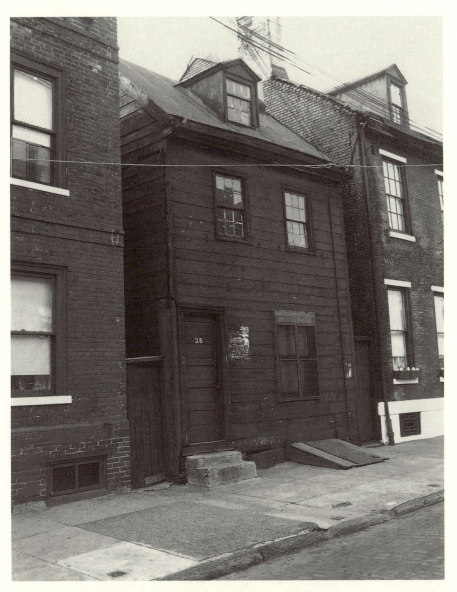

2 Captured in a 1960s photograph, this dwelling on Catharine Street near Third Street stands as a lone survivor of the city's frame housing stock. Wooden buildings accounted for much of Philadelphia's cheaper housing well into the nineteenth century. Courtesy of Independence National Historic Park.

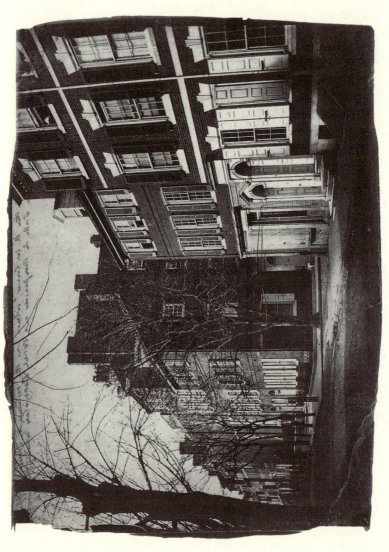

3 Philadelphia's elite could afford spacious and elegant dwellings situated on pleasant arteries, such as this location at Fourth and Locust Streets. Eighteenth-century residents of the houses pictured here included the eminent Dr. Casper Wistar and Louis-Philippe, later king of France. Courtesy of the Print and Picture Collection, The Free Library of Philadelphia.

alone among builders, nor his buyer alone among landlords, in generating cheap rental houses for profit.

Munday's career thus encompassed the two extremes of housing in the Federal city. On the high end, he produced for the city's elite. Shippen's new houses, for example, rose up on one of the main breezy and wide streets (Figure 3). They lay convenient to the commercial hub, but were sufficiently residential to attract President George Washington who lived nearby. The number and size of rooms, expanse of frontage, and Munday's attention to detail surpassed that of the vast majority of Philadelphia residences. Many of the city's other brick structures, such as the "bandbox" houses with one room on each floor, were very small (Figure 4).[42] Whereas Shippen, Washington, and their ilk enjoyed spacious and commodious lodgings, the median artisanal household inhabited a dwelling no larger than 648 square feet. That footage allowed for a two-and-a-half-story house roughly fourteen by thirteen feet, with a one-and-a-half-story back kitchen thirteen by ten feet.[43]

Catchpenny construction proved inadequate to prop Munday up. In 1798, Munday's recourses exhausted, creditors unsatisfied, the threat of "the [yellow] fever" hovering, and his household possessions seized by the sheriff, Munday moved his family to a heavily mortgaged farm in Chester County.[44] In the spring of 1799, "to avoid the Gaol" and following the advice of the eminent Dr. Benjamin Rush to restore his "very low State of Health," Munday traveled to the West Indies.[45] (Since many Philadelphians suspected that French- and African-Caribbean refugees had brought yellow fever to the Quaker City, this was indeed a startling recommendation to a man who tried to *avoid* the disease!) In St. Croix, Munday hatched yet another venturesome plan. The carpenter purchased sizable quantities of sugar and coffee and returned to Philadelphia more than a year later to sell his imports.[46]

In her husband's absence, Elizabeth Munday fought off legal suits and sustained the family by raising wheat, rye, and other market produce in Chester County. By the spring of 1801, John had returned. Back in Philadelphia, the couple once again traded dry goods, first out of the quarters they sublet from Elizabeth's sister, and subsequently from a rented shop. But continued bad health (exacerbated by a stay in debtors' prison) and a broken leg caused by a fall from a horse debilitated Munday. Discovery by old creditors of the carpenter's whereabouts compounded these hardships, creating obstacles Munday would never surmount. He died in 1803, leaving an estate worth less than $100. Having no rental properties or other annual income that the widow of a house carpenter might anticipate, Elizabeth

4 Bandbox houses with one room to a floor were respectable though tiny dwellings that housed many of Philadelphia's mechanic families. These properties on Christian Street in Southwark appealed to Philadelphians employed in the nearby maritime industries. Courtesy of the Print and Picture Collection, The Free Library of Philadelphia.

supported her family by keeping a boardinghouse until shortly before her death in 1812.[47]

* * *

Euphoria vanished in the late 1790s, as Munday's experiences testified. Threat of war with Europe and hostilities between European powers made merchants, investors, and even house builders nervous. Failure in the economy generally (exacerbated by the collapse of the house of cards raised by securities and land trader Robert Morris) caused a dramatic contraction of credit. A decline in housing prices followed.[48] Subsequent years hosted a series of national business depressions (1798 and 1802) and booms (1800–1801 and 1805) that affected the pace of construction in Philadelphia.[49]

In contrast to Munday, Moses Lancaster was one artisan who adapted resourcefully to the era's many economic fluctuations. Notwithstanding losses at junctures in his career, by the end of his working life Lancaster accumulated a small "competence." Competence was a slippery term in its day. Contemporaries applied it to the amassing of life's necessities, particularly with respect to mechanic incomes. Diligent manual labor meant ideally that an artisan, bolstered by the mutually interested pursuits of his wife, could provide for the family. Beyond the needs of every day, the household had to muster resources to usher children into an appropriate trade and maintain the household once the head of the family ceased working; the concept comprised a notion of "manly" independence as head of a thriving family. But the term described a wide array of living standards, from hardscrabble existence to commodious retirement. Respectability and contributing to the welfare of the larger polity also comprised the "social goals" of competence.[50] For Moses Lancaster, all his ingenuity, activity, longevity, and the employment of his household yielded only a modicum of wealth. Yet, the standing he achieved in craft, cultural, and religious communities as well as his ability to provide for his children into their adulthoods accorded him social respectability (Figure 5).

Born in 1783 in Bucks County, Pennsylvania, into a Quaker family of small means, Moses Lancaster moved to Philadelphia at the age of nineteen. He likely spent his early years working among Quaker building tradesmen. An active religious network between Bucks County and Philadelphia Monthly Meetings of the Society of Friends (Quakers) linked Moses immediately to the city's artisans. Quakers (and Anglicans of English descent) figured prominently in Philadelphia's more highly capitalized arti-

5 Moses Lancaster, 1783–1879. The master builder sat for this portrait to record his lengthy membership in the prestigious Carpenters' Company. Courtesy of The Carpenters' Company of the City and County of Philadelphia.

sanal occupations; connections to Friends would continue throughout much of Lancaster's career. Lancaster would continually tap this network for artisanal and mortgage credit.

Artisanal credit, or trade, which Lancaster utilized throughout his career, depended on trust acquired through longstanding association. Consequently, familiarity with an artisan's personal and financial situation that could be gained through community ties gave Friends explicit, though not exclusive, advantages over many nonQuakers. When rumor brought a member under suspicion "for want of adhering to the dictates of truth" or for having "contracted debts in a reproachful manner," the entire Monthly Meeting—masters, employees, and investors—discovered the transgression.[51] An interview with appointed visitors, and resulting communal sanction, frequently elicited the desired response by the debtor—and forbearance by lenders. A contrite party would concede his recklessness, "but [state] his intention of paying" his obligations in full if granted time.[52] Members, however, sometimes fell short of the Society's expectations. House carpenter Evan Lloyd, a contemporary of John Munday who also faltered in the 1790s, stubbornly refused to reform. The Philadelphia Southern District Meeting expelled him for moral and business misconduct, severely limiting Lloyd's access to credit.[53]

Unlike Munday, Lancaster pursued journeywork only briefly. The strong building economy of 1805 provided him with the chance to become a master. In 1806, when he was twenty-three, Lancaster married the daughter of a late member of the prestigious and predominantly Quaker Carpenters' Company. Marriage solidified his craft connections and brought a bit of property within his reach. The couple established an independent household; expenses were mounting and the family was expanding. The first of twelve children (including only two sons) was born in June 1807. Paternal concerns likely contributed to Lancaster's decision to supplement or replace his daily wage labor and small contract jobs with projects as a master carpenter. In addition to producing for clients, Lancaster undertook houses in anticipation of definite buyers.[54]

When Lancaster embraced in this move the vagaries of the market economy, he did so by availing himself of longstanding ethnocultural connections. In April 1807 he bought a lot from Samuel Middleton, a bricklayer and neighbor who, with Lancaster, attended the Society of Friends Green Street Monthly Meeting. In exchange, Middleton took Lancaster's mortgage. The sale marked the first of many transactions in Lancaster's early career that he would make with other craftsmen. In so doing, and in contrast to John Munday, Lancaster generally avoided financiers and big creditors as sources of capital. Perhaps he had no choice; Lancaster's independence did not coincide with a manic real estate market. But such personal contacts could also help him mitigate the effects of economic fluctuations. Over the next six years, Lancaster repeatedly used the lot from Middleton and the house that he completed on it (which he leased to tenants) as collateral for mortgages of incremental values. By paying each loan in full, Lancaster established his credit worthiness.[55]

Lancaster's operations and opportunities expanded further in about 1808. Once again, while he built houses on the expectation of selling them later, he resorted to traditional kinship ties by choosing his first cousin, John Lancaster, for a partner. The elder cousin brought to the business goodwill, credit, capital, and connections (as well as a share of the risk) beyond Moses' immediate reach.[56] Over the next few years, the cousins cooperated intermittently. Among their building ventures was a court that gained five houses for each partner. Their choice of product was a step above the residential frame dwellings John Munday built. Like Munday's project, the small structures—grouped around a common space, but likely sandwiched among backyards of more prominent dwellings—required minimal capital. They answered to a ready market, moreover, and the prospects for long-term income were not lost on Moses Lancaster. He owned his half of the dwellings for many years as rental units, yet he mortgaged and redeemed them repeatedly to raise money for further building.[57]

Concurrent with gradual improvement in his economic standing, Moses Lancaster made his mark in mechanics' organizations. In 1808 he joined one of Philadelphia's volunteer fire-fighting associations, the Reliance Fire Company, and regularly attended its frequent meetings. In the absence government-funded fire companies, the Reliance and similar groups provided a critical response to emergencies. At the time Lancaster joined the brigade, it was also a respectable cultural forum in which a middling artisan could test his mettle. The constituency of Reliance intersected with that of other networks through which Lancaster negotiated his upward career path. It drew from the Northern Liberties section of Philadelphia where many artisans and building material suppliers resided. Construction tradesmen swelled its ranks, and membership overlapped with Quaker Meeting affiliation. Participation in the Reliance Fire Company thus offered vital access to an intertwined social web of mechanics and small capitalists. Membership—by sponsorship—further affirmed Lancaster's distinction as a promising young master. In addition, the Carpenters' Company elected him to their association at the relatively young age of twenty-eight.[58]

By choice and by luck, Lancaster set up his own enterprise at a propitious moment. Throughout the nation, embargo and navigation acts (in 1807–1809) ushered in depression. But construction in Philadelphia exploded. American policy—and war—curtailed international commerce dramatically, and merchants investigated alternative outlets for capital. They found an option in real estate development and initiated a half dozen years of massive building. Expansion of bank currency in the period from 1811 to 1816 also fueled national credit supplies, inflated prices, and made mortgage loans cheaper to carry.[59] Building activity caused lawyer (and investor) Peter A. Browne to remark on the "astonishing progress in the improvement, and consequent rise in the value of real estate."[60] In one year alone, mechanics constructed 1,063 houses in the city and the "compactly built parts" of the surrounding districts.[61] For investors, it was one of the most profitable times in early nineteenth-century construction. Contemporaries confirmed the diminished severity of the embargo on Philadelphia's laboring population, "owing in a great measure to the buildings now erecting in the city."[62] Many journeymen and masters in the construction sector also enjoyed the boom. High employment, good wages (though accompanied by inflated prices), fast progress up the career ladder, and success in advance building characterized much of the period.

As in Munday's prime, the built city suddenly bolted outward. By the end of the thrust, row construction west of Thirteenth Street, undertaken in 1812, no longer marked the urban frontier. Series of six, twelve, and even fourteen two- and three-story brick houses pushed beyond the "built parts" of Philadelphia. Much of the expansion occurred north of the city in the district of the Northern Liberties. Moses Lancaster soon focused his efforts in that section and avoided the central commercial area to obtain cheaper land in bigger parcels.[63]

The projects Lancaster undertook required him to increase the number of his employees and, once engaged, to keep his hands steadily occupied. Throughout his career, Lancaster did what many masters did—he accepted apprentices as cheap and steady labor, but retained the more expensive journeymen under temporary wage arrangements. The practice gave him maximum flexibility. Lancaster varied journeymen hiring arrangements by the day, the task, or the piece fashioned. He minimized employment commitments outside the building season.[64]

Lancaster mixed practical business calculations with complex personal motives. He weighed charitable and craft factors in the selection of apprentices and journeymen. He also wove a web of obligations that might have heightened the stability of his work force and the loyalty of his employees and their kin. In 1813, for example, one of his three apprentices was the dependent of a man who was a former member of the Carpenters' Company and probably an alcoholic. Another was related to a prominent Quaker lumber retailing family.[65] Later, the master agreed to teach the son of John Lancaster's lumberyard partner the mysteries of the trade. He also employed several journeymen, one of whom was a member of the same Friends Meeting.[66]

Other steps cemented Lancaster's relationships with his journeymen while furthering the mutual interests of master and employees. In at least three instances over his career, he assisted former hands in gaining independence. The earliest recorded example occurred when Lancaster himself was midcareer, having been a master house carpenter for more than ten years. In 1816, he bought a lot on ground rent and built several houses on the parcel. Two years later, he subdivided the undeveloped parts of the lot and conveyed sections to journeyman Samuel Copeland, a former apprentice of his. Lancaster encouraged Copeland to build a house in anticipation of a buyer and provided the young man with jobs, referring business associates to Copeland for small contracts. Copeland agreed to complete portions of two houses, particularly to "lay the floors and finish the inside work." He also committed to "do all the Carpenter work in the 2nd [and] third story and garret of [Lancaster's] New house." Subcontracting enabled Copeland to test his capabilities as an autonomous mechanic. Similarly, Lancaster sold lots, made subcontracts, and referred work to two other journeymen embarking on their own.[67]

By conveying land, linking workers into the network of other building tradesmen, and advancing credit and access that contact with an established craftsman offered, Lancaster assisted novice carpenters in the transition from journeymen to masters. Lancaster won much in return. He cleverly unloaded undeveloped property that became a burden as the national economy adjusted to peace and the money supply contracted. He tactfully rid himself of expensive labor in a manner that promoted cohesion, not friction or dissent. (He could then replace seasoned men with younger, less costly apprentices and journeymen.) Lancaster also reaffirmed a commitment to upward craft mobility, and he replicated his own early struggle for independence. In doing so, he strengthened a critical alliance with masters of the next generation. Copeland and others proved loyal carpenters to whom Lancaster could turn when projects expanded beyond his own capacity. In their early careers, he sometimes subcontracted to them the interior work on houses he was building. By the mid-1830s, Copeland was at work developing forty houses on lots in Spring Garden, one of Philadelphia's rapidly urbanizing neighborhoods. Journeyman William Ellis became a very successful lumber merchant, and Lancaster bought from him. Another former employee later became Lancaster's partner in a lumberyard.[68]

Fiscal concerns were not secondary to Lancaster's tactics, and he exploited advantages over his subordinates. For example, when he promised to provide Ellis with orders on other building mechanics in exchange for carpentry work, Lancaster demanded a discount on the carpentry, but a surcharge on the other contracts. (This decreased the value of Ellis's work, but increased the price Ellis had to pay Lancaster for orders for other types of labor such as stonemasonry.)[69] Lot conveyances also represented shrewd planning by Lancaster. In the sale to Copeland, he created a new ground rent payable to himself. Shortly afterwards, Lancaster sold the title to the rent charge issuing out of the lot for a net gain of nearly $2,000. Testifying to his entrepreneurial talent, the senior carpenter succeeded in working the deals in 1818 (having bought the lot two years earlier) in spite of the downward direction of the business cycle. Neither Ellis nor Copeland appear to have been soured by Lancaster's gain at their expense. Both continued to deal with Lancaster as seasoned craftsmen.[70]

Subcontracts Lancaster made with his journeymen indicate a trend toward more ambitious building projects that he was unable to do solely with the labor of his shop. Nor could he supervise all work directly. By his late thirties he was probably doing little manual work himself, relying instead on his shop foreman to oversee and train apprentices. Without abandoning his identification as a master carpenter—rather by reinforcing it—he adapted to new challenges. Entrepreneurial opportunities helped to make Lancaster a manager, a businessman, and a trader in real estate. In the decade of the 1820s, he continued to strengthen his operations. He built on parcels that he had bought on ground rent in 1816, 1819, 1820, 1825, and 1826. As necessary and possible, he subdivided and mortgaged the lots, made new ground rents payable to himself, and sold the titles to raise money.

In addition to alliances with his laborers, Lancaster's achievements depended on associations with other masters. His network of material and labor exchange was labyrinthine, involving intricate third-party debts, often beyond the building community. Lancaster's emphasis on mutual reliance does not suggest that he was naïve or unaware of his financial interests. Contracts stipulating payment in trade held economic advantages. They cushioned a builder against increases in costs by locking in labor at current prices and redeeming the debt in a future market of higher prices. Orders drawn on other artisans might, at a later date, be pivotal in competing for skilled labor and meeting deadlines. Furthermore, payment pledged in trade carried the same legal privileges of mechanics' contracts made for cash.[71] An artisanal financial network based overwhelmingly on exchange rather than a cash-based system might even have added to a carpenter's chances for success. Less dependent on cash for payment, Lancaster may have avoided some of the problems other contemporaries experienced by virtue of their appetite for merchant financing.

Lancaster also used his religious ties effectively and distinguished himself within the Quaker community. He resisted militia duty during the War of 1812 and suffered his property to be seized for government fines. He worked in various ways to support education (and even paid the tuition of a free black "girl"). He, and later his daughters, joined Quaker charitable and reform activities including abolition efforts. When Orthodox and Hicksite Quakers divided in 1828, Lancaster chose — as the majority of artisans did — to adhere to the Hicksites, who endorsed a more radical and evangelical message.[72]

Through craft, religious, and civic channels, Lancaster had not only laid a solid financial base, but by his early thirties presented a figure of note. To enhance this position, he continued to secure his wealth and offset the perils of the building market through diversification of his business. By late 1821, he began dabbling in the grain trade. He patronized for his contacts a flour and commission merchant who was a former member of the Carpenters' Company, as well as a cousin (John Lancaster's brother) who was in the trade. Commodity purchases were a bold venture in the severely depressed agricultural market following 1819, the year that marked the young republic's most notorious downturn in the economy. But Lancaster had some success.[73] Playing the international commodities market was vastly different from building and selling houses. A dwelling — even a partially completed one — was a tangible result of artisan optimism. If Lancaster and his peers failed to sell their houses, they still might retain them for rental income. Speculative construction, then, was frequently an investment, whereas grain dealing was not.

Sometime prior to 1823, Moses Lancaster bought Jonathan Conard's interest in the lumber business of Conard & Lancaster (John Lancaster).

Even before he formally identified himself as a lumber merchant, Lancaster was buying stock in quantity, permitting him to control costs more closely. Payments to mechanics in lumber also decreased Lancaster's dependence on cash. With his share in the lumberyard, he was poised to benefit from the modest building recovery of 1824–25. Later, in April 1829, Lancaster began to take an interest in inventions related to construction. He considered investing in the latest in woodcutting technology and paid for the rights to a mortising patent. His attention to innovation would produce better rewards in the early 1830s when Lancaster's lumberyard employed a newly patented planing machine, built from his own design.[74]

During his time as a lumber merchant, Lancaster retreated intermittently from building. His activities in the 1820s corresponded to national business cycles. Reacting to a sluggish market precipitated by the panic of 1819 and subsequent depression, Lancaster suspended construction about 1821 when the trade hit its low point. In 1825 and 1826, responding to a brief economic upswing, Lancaster again bought land, subdivided it, built on several parcels, and sold others to tradesmen. That he took on an apprentice shortly before the building season of 1826 suggests that Lancaster anticipated continued recovery and thus reoriented his labor force for construction. In need of managerial assistance while his partner John prepared for retirement, Lancaster installed his carpentry shop foreman as building partner. Meanwhile, Lancaster probably continued to devote his attention to the lumberyard. In 1829, he bought John Lancaster's half of the concern. He then used some of the stock in a project he had under way by that year.[75]

In keeping with a master craftsman of his stature, Lancaster widened the physical and social distance between himself and his workers. In the early years Lancaster's household included some of his laborers. In 1810, Lancaster's family was still relatively small, and three of his employees lived with him. Apprentice Charles Conard, for example, boarded weekdays with Lancaster, although his own relatives lived two doors down the street. By 1820, although the family itself had grown to nine, six of Lancaster's employees lived with the master. In addition, journeymen who resided with protégé Samuel Copeland may have worked as well for Lancaster, extending the master's potential for discipline, paternalism, and patronage.[76]

A change in the Lancaster residence, however, mirrored a decline throughout urban America in master-employee household composition that had begun as early as the mid-eighteenth century. By 1830, Lancaster had surrendered some of the responsibility and authority that boarding and lodging his employees would have entailed, losing as well a familiarity with young men training for the craft. Contrasting with Conard's arrangement, apprentice Lewis Bitting received cash "in Lieu of clothing washing &c" which he would have expected in a master's household.[77] Lancaster arranged for another apprentice to live with a German immigrant carpenter he employed at day labor. Lancaster's own family had grown to twelve and the production of his own shop had shifted markedly in preference to subcontracting. These family and career considerations, and the advancement of Lancaster's economic and social status, contributed to the decision that he would no longer lodge or board his employees.[78]

Lancaster was at the peak of his career by the 1820s and by all indications was to fulfill the ideal of competence. He owned numerous income-producing properties. In 1827, his mortgage credit (exclusive of trade and other loans) was $19,000, comprised of eight loans secured by eighteen brick houses.[79] He had shaped an enviable craft and civic reputation. He provided amply for his many children and must have been gratified to see the eldest of his daughters marry a Quaker carpenter. (Lancaster had no grown sons who might have became partners in construction; his son-in-law briefly filled that void.) Surrounding Lancaster in his Northern Liberties home were symbols of his success as a master artisan. Mahogany dining and breakfast tables, parlor and stair carpets, a china tea set, silverware, table and bed linens, and glassware were among his household's many furnishings. Newspapers and books announced to visitors and clients that he was a man who kept current with commercial concerns and new ideas.[80]

Long-term gains in construction, however, were commonly punctuated by setbacks and revealed the dangers of risk-taking in the capitalist economy. Short-term losses tried even Lancaster's ingenuity. In 1828 or 1829, Lancaster became general contractor in a project funded by Dorothy Large, the widow of a merchant. This agreement was the most considerable Lancaster ever undertook in association with a single financier, and it represented a departure from his role as builder on his own account. Large consented to advance money for expenses and authorized Lancaster to draw orders payable on her credit. In compensation, Large probably contracted to convey several of the properties to Lancaster upon completion. Lancaster tendered Large a bond for $5,000 assuring his part in the plan. The bond carried a penal sum of $10,000 if Lancaster failed to follow through on his agreement.[81]

The site Lancaster and Large chose on George Street (now Sansom Street) west of Schuylkill Seventh (Sixteenth Street) aimed to benefit from recent urban expansion. The parcel lay at the very edge of development, however, and depended for success on continued growth. By 1828, the city and its "suburbs"—its bordering sections—had nearly 160,000 inhabitants.[82] Shifts in Philadelphia's residential and productive geography accompanied population growth and were vital to the plans of Lancaster and fellow builders. By 1828, economic diversification had inaugurated decentralized development around several nuclei. Dispersion relieved competition for space in Philadelphia's older wards and provided relatively inexpensive land in newer locations (Figure 6).

Lancaster and Large paid particular attention to the changing face of the Schuylkill River's east bank. Traffic through the Delaware port continued to fuel Philadelphia's economy, but a shift away from international toward intraregional trade showed in the location of new enterprises. The Schuylkill River provided a critical outlet to the interior, and beginning in the 1820s, wharves sprang up on the city's western edge. Jobs on its docks employed men who found housing for their families in the surrounding vicinity.[83]

Lancaster was forty-five years old in 1828, and for many years he had delegated manual labor, and even supervisory responsibilities, to others. His carpentry crew was likely quite small, if he kept steady hands at all. Moreover, he now was busy with management of the lumberyard. The career stage he had reached affected his decisions in handling Large's venture, but also dovetailed with trends that altered the organization of capital and of work throughout construction. He brought in two partners, including his soon-to-be son-in-law. Lancaster made the traditional contracts with tradesmen. He also subcontracted extensively with carpenters to complete parts of individual houses. Various men undertook "inside" work, constructed steps, and laid floors. In assembling the standardized parts, two mechanic partners made the largest number of doors (fifty-eight), and five other men produced a sizable quantity of doors, window sash, and fencing. Lancaster paid men by a daily wage, by the item they produced, and by measurement (an appraisal of the work after its completion); the choice of payment method depended on the task and on the progress each mechanic had made toward master status. Young Archibald Thomson, for example, covered the spectrum from employing his own crew at the site, to shaping his own piece work.[84]

Lancaster was unable to complete Dorothy Large's houses. The economy, already in an industrial depression, worsened in 1828 and 1829 with the dumping of British goods and a tight credit market. Money constriction was "so sudden and abrupt," observed one Philadelphian, "that it has caught

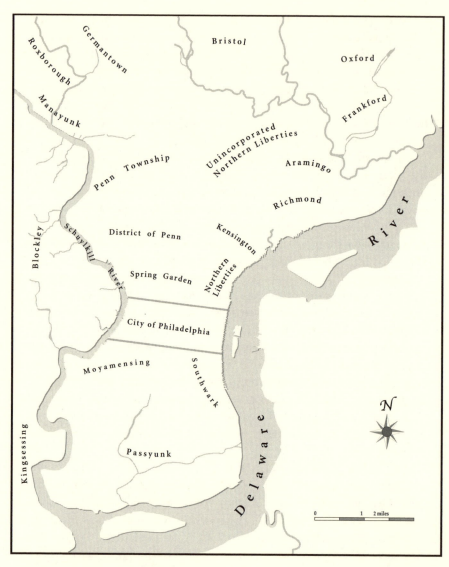

6 Philadelphia County, circa 1830.

even prudent men unawares." Locally, a brutal winter that strained charitable resources exacerbated the severity of the business lull.[85] Rapid decline
of real estate values in 1829 poleaxed many building tradesmen; Lancaster
stumbled dangerously. John Lancaster's withdrawal from the lumber partnership at this time—and the cash for his share—exacerbated Moses' personal discomposure. It is likely, however, that the location of this project,
which had anticipated the city's growth too enthusiastically, was particularly vexing. Consumers had more convenient housing options than the
block of Schuylkill Sixteenth and George Streets. Dorothy Large's involvement, moreover, did not render Lancaster invulnerable; reneging on the
contract, in fact, Lancaster forfeited the bond he had given her and stood
liable for its $10,000 penalty sum. Subcontractors sued, forcing the sale of
at least six of the partially finished structures. Public auctions brought between $250 and $270 for each property, sums which were likely much less
than Lancaster had extended in expenses and contracts.[86]

In meeting this crisis (and scrambling to compensate Large), Lancaster
protected certain properties, but surrendered others. In the process, the results of years of labor (and most of his insurance for old age) slipped through
his fingers. He parted with a house he had built in 1816. Three houses built in
1819 also had to be sold; they brought $3,000 less than interest and principal
due against them. When a creditor forced the auction of yet another dwelling, Lancaster, in desperation, "influenced the sale by his own bidding" and
misrepresented the amount of "rent annually rec'd from the property." In
all Lancaster lost eight houses and two undeveloped lots (in addition to six
of the houses built in connection with Dorothy Large) to sheriff's sales in
1829 and 1830.[87]

In spite of his financial difficulties, his selection of a few properties
to shelter left Lancaster with surprising resources. Tax assessments suggest
how far he had actually managed to climb before his misfortune. In 1830
(and again in 1831), Lancaster's payment was more than half that of 1824,
when he was at the height of his career. By 1834, Lancaster still commanded
enough funds to build several more houses on his own account. By the fall
of the same year he was drawing income from at least seven houses, each of
which rented for $120 per annum. And in the following spring, mortgage
lenders did not hesitate to extend him $10,000 with this new security.[88]

The stress and perils of these last projects, his age, and the hope of con-
solidating remaining wealth convinced Lancaster to withdraw from construction. He sold three developed properties (subject to mortgages) and
combined other assets to capitalize his final business venture, a manufactory

for oilcloth, a low-cost floor covering. By 1838 at age fifty-five, Lancaster had shifted the business and managerial skills amassed throughout his career to industry. Perhaps the manufactory was a desperate attempt to recoup his fortune, or an opportunity that was too enticing to ignore. Timing, however, was against Lancaster, as the depression that began in 1837 was long and deep. Lancaster was no neophyte in the face of economic stagnation. He might have thought that he could repeat his success of earlier cycles—dismissing the 1828–1829 problems as aberrant. A few years after commencing production, however, Lancaster abandoned the business without any significant improvement in finances. In fact, he incurred debts (likely from the oilcloth concern) that would lead to the loss of three more houses in 1841 and 1844.[89]

When Lancaster retired from business in 1841, he retreated to the relative peacefulness of his native Bucks County. In 1850, when the census enumerator found him, he was still clinging to his occupation of "Carpenter" though he was sixty-seven years old and inactive. Lancaster declared real estate of the negligible value of $100, but he ignored at least three rental houses in Philadelphia that were assessed at $1,100.[90] In 1860, in residence with his wife in the home of his daughter and son-in-law, Lancaster no longer identified himself by the craft he had pursued. His occupation is listed as "Gentleman," a sobriquet granted men living on accumulated assets, or old men living in genteel poverty. He represented his personal estate at the sum of $3,000; ten years later it had increased—perhaps through inflation—to $6,000 (though his real estate was valued at only $800). Unfortunately, no evidence remains to explain the nature of Lancaster's personal assets, but the sums would have accorded him a small annual income somewhere between $160 and $320.[91] The amount was insufficient for basic needs, and Lancaster was forced to apply to the Carpenters' Company for assistance. "Although an active business Man for many years, and quite enterprizing," Lancaster was "head on the list of Beneficiaries" of the Company's aid to members (for $200 per annum) for "a long series of years." He died intestate in 1879 at the age of ninety-six before the next census could add to the record. Lancaster worked throughout much of his long life, rose to the respectable status of master builder, and raised his large family in comfortable circumstances. At the end of his labors, however, he enjoyed but a small competence, passed only meager assets to the next generation, and relied in his final years on the charity of fellow craftsmen.[92]

* * *

Warnet Myers strived aggressively to accumulate wealth, but lost. In his efforts, he combined strategies used by numerous contemporaries, Lancaster among them. The extent to which Myers engaged in speculation and subcontracting and depended on ties with one financier, however, is striking. Myers's career illustrates one individual's rapid transition from artisanal production to contracting and, finally, to brokering. The man was an occupational chameleon and a recidivist insolvent, but his machinations are fascinating. They attest to a conception of independence that frankly placed a quick ascent to wealth above relationships with other craftsmen, social respectability, or concern for the public good.

Warnet Myers was born about 1793 in Philadelphia. His father died while Myers was a child. The family had slim resources, notably a small frame house in the Northern Liberties. (Myers's mother would later mortgage it, perhaps to raise money for her son.) Myers learned the trade of painting, and might have enjoyed connections to building mechanics through his mother's second husband. Throughout his career, Warnet Myers identified himself variously as a coach and sign painter, a house painter, or a painter and glazier. He would also later become an oilcloth manufacturer (like Lancaster), a real estate broker and, finally, an artist.[93]

In January 1818, Myers borrowed $260 from the Franklin Legacy, a fund established by Benjamin Franklin's estate to assist novice artisans. Sureties to the bond illustrate the network Myers was already developing among fellow tradesmen: Robert Wallace, a prominent lumber merchant, and John Saunders, a house carpenter (and possibly Myers's brother-in-law) guaranteed the loan.[94] As a young married man, Myers sought to set up his own shop and household. He likely spent the funds to open a coach and sign painter's shop on North Front Street and to begin a brick house on property he purchased on ground rent in December 1817. His new dwelling would soon provide him with security to obtain credit. Like Moses Lancaster and other artisans, Myers probably paid for much of the labor and materials on the house in orders redeemable in trade. By 1820 Myers had built three or four dwellings that he used for rental income and to raise money on second and third mortgages. Though he met his half-yearly interest payments on his houses, he defaulted on his debt to the Franklin Legacy, which pronounced him "Insolvent" in 1821.[95]

The 1820s presented no opportunities comparable to those Moses Lancaster enjoyed in the previous decade, or to those John Munday exploited in the 1790s. Consequently, Myers was slow to get on his feet. Precisely how Myers and his family earned a living during several years of a stagnant national economy is unclear. He gave up his shop and perhaps returned to journeywork, or scrambled to obtain contracts, piecework, and small jobs. The virtual standstill in local construction in the early 1820s would have strained the family's resources severely. More fortunate than many, Myers mortgaged his share of inherited property to leverage whatever small sums he could.[96]

Only in 1823 did the city begin to recover from depression. In an erratic, though frequently slack economic climate, the house painter gradually got on his feet. In 1825, as Lancaster had done, Myers responded to modest recovery. Over the next five years, the house painter enthusiastically bought and sold finished houses as well as undeveloped lots. He also embarked upon his own building projects. Joseph Reed, an established lawyer from a respected elite Philadelphia family, assisted him in these affairs. Reed was president of the American Fire Insurance Company, which invested its assets in loans and mortgages.[97]

From 1825 through 1828, at times independently and otherwise through Reed, Myers borrowed nearly $50,000. The American Fire Insurance Company, the estate clients of Reed, Reed's relatives, the University of Pennsylvania (whose financial affairs Reed supervised), and the lawyer himself underwrote Myers's and Reed's real estate ventures. Reed frequently acted illegally, making these loans without the direct knowledge of his clients. He lent Myers cash at interest, paid bills for building expenses, taxes, paving, ground rents, and court judgments against Myers. In addition, Reed provided legal expertise (for which he charged Myers's account). He drafted deeds and mortgages and supervised the official transcription of the documents, a procedure familiar to him in his role as a city recorder. Furthermore, Reed often paid interest due on Myers's mortgage bonds, and debited the painter's accounts accordingly.[98]

Myers, meanwhile, incurred additional obligations by assuming a half interest in properties purchased with the attorney. In October 1827, for example, Myers and Reed bought lots and houses for $2,300. Reed paid $800 in a note at ninety days, and charged Myers's account $400. The balance of $1,500 was taken by Myers in a mortgage. (The partners then leased the lots and houses on an annual basis.) Similarly, in February 1828, when Myers and Reed purchased a lot and its two brick buildings from William Hooven, Reed paid in notes endorsed by Myers. Subsequently, because Myers had no money, the parties agreed that "in lieu of the notes WM [Warnet Myers] w'd build 4 houses for $750 each on the lots taken by Hooven of WM on Germantown Road." When Myers and Reed bought yet another house and lot, Myers paid his share of the purchase price in notes to come due over the next ten months. In January 1828, the pair, with Robert Jardine, purchased property at public sale for $13,000. Myers held two-thirds interest in the deal (though mostly on mortgage), of which one third was actually Reed's. As in all these transactions, Reed confirmed that "my name does not appear—the settlement made with Jardine in Myers' [name.]" Availing himself of his clients' money, Reed used his assenting partner to hide his own involvement.

Hundreds of dollars Reed lent Myers each month (in addition to mortgages) had little chance of repayment by Myers's credits for "bills for sundry painting" and "by bill agst the University $332.70"—pocket change compared to Myers's outstanding obligation. At times, Myers acted as Reed's agent in collecting rents from their tenants and gained setoffs for his services. Presumably, the painter also investigated promising real estate and used his artisanal expertise to judge its potential.[99]

Myers was not, however, Reed's employee, nor was Reed his legal or exclusive partner. In spite of his role in financial ventures with Reed—or indeed, in light of the demand for cash the deals exacerbated—Myers continued as late as 1829 to perform jobs as a master craftsman. In June 1826, house carpenters Franks & Wagner paid Myers $305 in trade "for painting glazing and Glass," and again in August 1829 Wagner paid Myers for similar work. These amounts were a small portion of the business between the parties; Myers later felt sufficiently certain of his relationship with Wagner to plead for a loan of "[t]en or fifteen dollars on account." In addition, painting jobs Myers's shop performed for the University of Pennsylvania allowed him cash, trade, or credits for the short term.[100]

But Myers's compensation to Reed did not rest in the insignificant orders the painter transferred to his financier. Instead, Myers's principal contribution was twofold. First, as explained, Myers cloaked Reed's illicit activities. Second, the partners anticipated that the eventual profits from building would amply clear Myers's obligations. In 1827 and 1828, some Philadelphians thought that "more houses were erected than had been for many years previous," and Myers certainly was building his share. By 1828–29, he had multiple projects underway, including fourteen three-story brick houses in Spring Garden; six small three-story houses in the Northern Liberties; eighteen two-story brick houses in Kensington; another eleven in the Northern Liberties; and clusters of two dwellings each, mostly also in the Northern Liberties (Figure 7).[101]

The row of eighteen two-story brick houses in Kensington illuminates

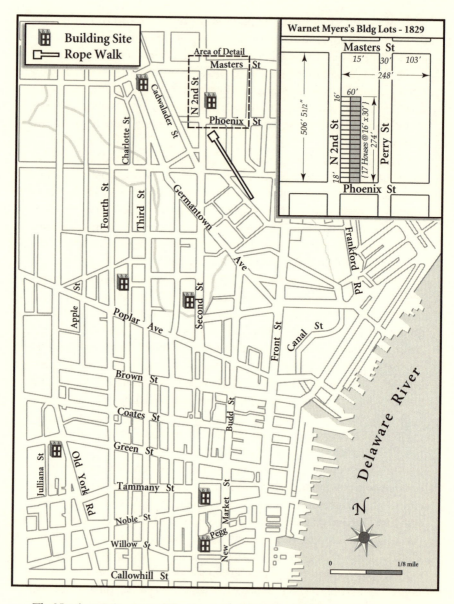

7 The Northern Liberties and Kensington building sites of Warnet Myers, 1828–29.
After the Kensington District Survey and Plan, Third Division, October 1829.

Legend and labels within the map:

Building Site
Rope Walk

Warnet Myers's Bldg Lots - 1829

Masters St

Area of Detail

N 2nd St

Masters St

Phoenix St

Cadwalader St

Charlotte St

Germantown Ave

Fourth St

Third St

Apple St

Poplar Ave

Second St

Brown St

Coates St

Budd St

Green St

Front St

Canal St

Frankford Rd

Delaware River

Julliana St

Old York Rd

Tammany St

Noble St

Pegg

Willow St

New Market St

Callowhill St

N

0   1/8 mile

Inset (Warnet Myers's Bldg Lots - 1829):
Masters St
15'   30'   103'
248'
506' 51/2"
16'
60'
N 2nd St
117 Houses @ 16' x 30'
274'
18'
Perry St
Phoenix St

the wager Myers made and the tactics he used in pursuit of his plan. The parcel he took on ground rent was about half the size of a city block, fronting on North Second Street and reaching in depth to another street that would shortly thereafter be opened. The site had only recently been made more accessible to urban Philadelphia. Pegg's Run, a navigable stream and marshy area on the northern edge of the town, had meandered between the city and the northern suburbs. Discouraged both by the swampy terrain and the steep descent from the north side of Callowhill Street to the low valley of the run, the city's progress at first circumvented the vicinity. Bridges over major north-south thoroughfares made the area passable after 1802 (barring occasional flooding from the Delaware River) and the population expanded into the Northern Liberties beyond the waterway. But in 1826, pollution problems and the lure of prime land led the county to fill the marshes. Officials leveled uneven terrain and raised it with refuse then laid a street. Builders hastened to take advantage of real estate in close proximity to the city's heart and vacant of structures.[102]

By 1828, cartographic renditions of Philadelphia extrapolated many of its streets northward and southward beyond actual settlement. In these depictions, Warnet Myers's row houses were even more remote. To reach his building site at Second and Phoenix, if one gave credence to the plans, required a healthy walk from the commercial center north up Delaware Second Street. On the ground, however, the muddy reality belied the exaggerated zeal of mapmakers, contractors, and other city boosters.[103]

While Myers expected the value of his project to reflect improved access into Kensington, he needed to consider additional virtues of the location. Who, after all, would buy his houses? Myers first looked east to Kensington's Delaware riverfront, rather than south to the city's core. Nearly touching Myers's site was an enterprise for producing rope (a "ropewalk"), and within a few streets there were two more. These manufactories supported a thriving shipbuilding nexus to the east. Shipwrights, caulkers, riggers, mastmakers, and engineers populated Kensington. Other industries, such as glass manufactories—one establishment would grow to three hundred employees by 1833—drew an abundance of glassblowers to work and settle in the area. James Gibson, John Naglee, and the Lehigh Coal & Navigation Company each ran steam sawmills, lumberyards, and wharves to facilitate shipments. Cotton factories, a steel furnace, and tanyards flourished in Kensington in the 1820s. In addition, taverns, victuallers, fishermen, and all manner of service and craft trades met the day-to-day needs of this northern suburb.[104]

Located several streets west of the heart of Kensington, Myers's un-assuming two-story dwellings did not attract the top tier of mechanics and small manufacturers. A decade after completion, owners included two shopkeepers, a carter (who held three houses), two cordwainers, a lamp-maker, a weaver, a tailor, and a manufacturer. Tenants of resident owners included a similar socioeconomic cross-section of laborers, craftsmen, and proprietors. By the area's standards, these were modest quarters that Myers had planned for laboring households—a mainstay of the district's popula-tion.[105]

Myers was to receive title to the parcel once he secured the ground rent with brick houses. In the winter of 1828, Myers designed plans for the row houses, began to subdivide the lot, and made contracts to build the requisite structures. Craftsmen expected to work on several dwellings, but be paid for labor and materials with a title to a house and lot. They also probably expected Myers to secure them credit and arrange orders in trade with other artisans. Myers, however, became insolvent in June 1829 and assigned all his estate to two of his creditors. Craftsmen who had begun work on the first six of the proposed eighteen houses, having dug the foundations and walled the cellars, then abandoned them.[106]

Although Warnet Myers was broke, he continued to conduct business through an associate, Samuel Hoover, and even made some contracts in his own name. Legal insolvency did not absolve Myers from previous obliga-tions, but it did afford the advantage of starting a clean balance sheet on new credits and debts. (It also kept Myers out of debtors' prison, once he turned his assets over for distribution among creditors.) The original build-ing agreement was assigned to Hoover, and Myers negotiated contracts for the additional twelve houses and completion of the original six. Again, however, he was only able to bring the houses under roof by the fall of 1829 before subcontractors suspended work; they resumed work once again in the spring of 1830. Finally, in July 1831, Horatio Pennock, a merchant who had lent money on mortgage, forced a sheriff's sale of the unfinished struc-tures. Though assessed at $10,800, the properties brought only $2,608. Mas-ter artisans and suppliers received no more than twenty-six cents on each dollar of their labor and materials.[107]

Had Reed sustained him, Myers could perhaps have weathered the 1829–1830 real estate depression (much as Moses Lancaster did) and the suits brought by his many creditors. Reed, however, became insolvent by 1829. His financial and fiduciary improprieties (he misappropriated funds of the University of Pennsylvania, as well as those of other clients) stripped him of assets and reputation. Moreover, Myers had alienated his fellow master artisans—less so by his aggressive building than by his vacant pledges and duplicitous practices. In October 1829, for example, Myers gave Pennock a bond, and in so doing endangered the interests of the mechanics at work on the Kensington properties. Myers insisted that the parties record the bond in the State Supreme Court (rather than the District Court of the City and County of Philadelphia, as was usual), so "that it might not be seen by many."[108]

Although subcontractors blamed Myers for their own financial crises, the real root of their demise was a general economic downturn. Their willingness to censure Myers, while ignoring the stable building concerns that teetered all around them, underscores their dislike of his extremes. (No doubt they also did not want to acknowledge their own overextended finances.) When carpenter James Shaw explained his failure, for instance, he pointed to deals with the house painter-builder that required him to borrow money at exceedingly high interest rates. Myers paid Shaw in old notes and debts for his labor, when he paid him at all; Shaw also endorsed $2,000 in notes for Myers. Shaw conveyed title to three houses to Myers in exchange for the promise to liquidate all claims against Shaw. Myers, however, cleared none of the debts, and Shaw's creditors seized all his remaining property.[109]

Persistent attempts to gain a foothold after 1829 failed, and Myers's prospects and standard of living declined. Remnants of his reputation shredded further when a dispute arose between Myers and a congregation whose church he had contracted to build.[110] The characteristic punctuated growth of the 1830s did little to boost him. Prosperity, accompanied by low interest rates, finally returned by 1833, but dramatic fluctuations continued to mark the economy: 1834—depression; 1835 to 1836—inflation and speculation; 1837—panic and severe depression. Business failures, worsened by overextension from 1835 to 1836, occurred throughout the building community and brought activity to a halt.[111]

As late as 1835–36 the city directory listed Myers's occupation as "painter" but he had no separate shop. In 1837, Myers manufactured oilcloth in a shop next to his home—by curious coincidence, a year before Moses Lancaster began his interest in the business and only a few streets away. By 1840, Myers assumed the title of "broker" in a real estate transaction, implying that he engineered deals between ground lords, mortgage creditors, and builders. Two years later, when he filed under the Federal Bankruptcy Act of 1841, he told the court he was "late [formerly] Painter now Real Estate Broker." Myers itemized more than $3,300 in recent obligations and an additional indebtedness by court judgments of nearly $75,500. Among these judgments were unpaid debts from his earlier construction activity that had not been cleared by sheriff's sales. Not until the late forties did builders enjoy renewed activity that the recovery of financial strength and investment capital provided. By that time, new modes of local transportation opened spacious sections of the county. But for Myers, opportunities had passed. After 1842, he scraped by, working as late as 1860—nearing the age of seventy—as an "artist."[112]

*   *   *

Munday, Lancaster, and Myers shared some characteristics, but diverged in several ways. Had they known each other (as is likely), they would have recognized similarities as well as distinctions among themselves.[113] Timing, sources of capital and credit, artisanal relationships, economic fluctuations and building cycles, cultural networks, scale of enterprise, career stage, and diversity of financial interests are among the many interrelated factors in their stories. Munday, Lancaster, and Myers show how artisans struggled to direct the course of their careers.

Moses Lancaster, in many ways, is a transitional figure who bridges the distance between the mechanic John Munday and the extensive builder Warnet Myers. Like Munday, Lancaster took an active role in the planning and actual construction of his houses, attended sites daily, and labored alongside his journeymen. The two house carpenters (Lancaster more than Munday) remained closely connected to other craftsmen, who counted among their principal creditors.

Munday overextended his finances and his projects, while Lancaster avoided most of these pitfalls until later in his career when he held sufficient assets to weather losses. Munday's activities responded to a spiraling real estate market, but the cycle came too early in the young man's career to find him with a secure base. Rapid increases in rents, labor costs, and material costs further exacerbated Munday's plight. He attempted to meet the economic challenges of the 1790s by constructing frame houses to sell for quick cash. Lancaster, too, built cheap dwellings, though brick made them more valuable as rental structures and as loan collateral than frames. Lancaster, who also encountered cyclical extremes, improved his financial position by decreasing reliance on new construction as his sole source of income.

Lancaster owed his good fortune to a confluence of factors. He was calculating—and lucky—in the timing of his entry into Philadelphia's building market. Personal networks were vital to his business start and growth by linking him to organizations that shared information, credit systems, capital sources, skilled personnel, and values. Lancaster met crises by protecting his most valuable properties, he exercised conservative strategies of borrowing, building, and accumulating, and he diversified his assets and business interests. He reduced and expanded operations in response to economic cycles, designing labor force flexibility into his production schedule. Lancaster used subcontracting to increase capacity, though he continued to manage building. In contrast to Myers's approach, Lancaster traded only modestly in land and quickly disposed of lots that he could not develop immediately. Nonetheless, the house carpenter exploited these opportunities to solidify relationships with other craftsmen and to make a cash profit. Myers went a step beyond Lancaster's arrangements and functioned principally as a broker. He attempted to pass on the risks of development to others by acquiring urban blocks, dividing them into lots, and contracting with master mechanics to build entire dwellings on the properties.

Like Munday, Myers precociously began building on his own account (and like Myers made inaccurate predictions about the direction of the market). In particular, Myers extended himself by simultaneously constructing nearly sixty houses before bracing projects with any foundation of assets. Remarkably, he did so without any of his own capital, relying on the advances of financiers; had he paid more attention to trade relationships, he might have faired better. Similarly, John Munday conducted extensive business with few assets, owing his opportunities to an ebullient credit market.

The risky strategy of building on one's own account also links these artisans. Both in Munday's day and forty years later, speculative construction was one of the keystones of achieving a competence. "Speculative" in this context should be understood as a descriptive term used by contemporary builders, and not as a moral judgment. All manner of mechanics in the trade—ethical, competent, circumspect, misguided, optimistic, fiscally conservative—"speculated" in the sense that they practiced their craft and anticipated customers for their products. Speculative building was one facet of doing business as an artisan in the early republic; it was often a lucrative one. As small producers, carpenters, painters, bricklayers, and their colleagues steeled themselves for the challenges of the nation's expanding economy.

Individual qualities—whether one craftsman was smarter, more shrewd, or more Quakerly (and ethical?)—should not mask the lessons offered in the biographies of Munday, Lancaster, and Myers. Equally crucial to their stories was timing. When a mechanic entered business, when

he exited it, and the myriad decisions he made during his career—to buy
land, build, hold, or sell—contributed enormously to chances for success.
Personal talents and experience counted, particularly in a builder's ability to
temper the impact of economic cycles. (Lancaster, after all, relied on three
decades of asset accumulation and artisanal and religious connections to
avoid insolvency, whereas Munday and Myers could not.) But national economic instability was no less disastrous for mechanics in Myers's heyday
than it was in Munday's; indeed, expansion and integration of the economy
in the later period—and builders' willingness to expand with it—might have
made their livelihoods even more precarious.

Differences among these craftsmen should not be overdrawn. Business
cycles forty years apart could elicit surprisingly similar strategies, even as
changes in the economy—availability and mobility of capital for financing
construction, for example—occurred over the antebellum period. Conditions in the 1790s matched at times the scenarios of 1833 and other prosperous seasons, more than they approximated a dull period closer in time.
In the aggressive methods builders employed in such climates, John Munday's business arrangements resembled those of Warnet Myers, more so
than Lancaster's; the comparison stands despite a greater chronological gap
between Munday and Myers.

What kept artisans reaching, when failure, or at best dramatic setbacks, frustrated many assays? While they could count numerous insolvent
peers, craftsmen could also name dozens who had overcome obstacles to
win—and retain—wealth and the social respectability it could purchase.
House carpenter Frederick Forepaugh, for instance, bequeathed real property valued at nearly $12,000 when he died in 1827. Forepaugh's contem-
porary William Garrigues left an estate worth nearly $25,000 after having
established several of his sons in artisanal and retailing businesses. Aspiring
mechanics saw the results of building ventures in the residences of enterprising men. House carpenter Horatio Melchior, in his prime in 1822, adorned
his home with ingrain carpeting, fancy chairs, mahogany card tables, and
a collection of Shakespeare's plays. Peter Berry, too, enjoyed his advanced
years surrounded with the accouterments of fortune: numerous mahogany
chairs and tables, five mahogany bedsteads complete with bedding, decant-
ers and tumblers, china, a sofa, and a bookcase among them.[114] Moses Lancaster and his family possessed similar material comforts and measures of
social standing for the greater portion of the house carpenter's career.

Building craftsmen gambled aggressively on the growth of the Quaker
City. National depressions, local business fluctuations, the fate of the city's

economy, the optimistic or pessimistic humors of the period—these factors shaped the experiences of Munday, Lancaster, Myers, and their contemporaries. Physical room and resources for growth and a multifaceted economic base influenced the opportunities of builders. Continuous struggle for craft and economic independence even encouraged dispersion of housing in the county. A consumer population of craftsmen, laborers, small proprietors, men of commerce and landed elite, and a suitable architectural tradition also affected the lives and decisions of families engaged in the industry.

The imperatives of construction often pushed craftsmen into ever more ambitious undertakings, often to pay off previous deals. Nevertheless, craftsmen were ready players, placing in jeopardy their own capital and that of their families, laborers, and creditors. Artisans did not resist the intrusion of an unfettered market or merely ride a tide caused by more powerful segments of society. Mechanics widely endorsed the marketplace and promoted the transformation of their trades.[115] They adapted tried-and-true methods to new conditions and made innovations to escape capital and production constraints. They manipulated property instruments and shaped the growth of capital and real estate markets. By their creative construction, entrepreneurial building artisans contributed to the dynamic reorganization and expansion of capitalism.[116]

T W O

By "Credit & Industry"

Financial and Legal Contexts

I
SAAC S. LOYD called himself a "merchant," but others called
him a "speculator." Purchases and sales of real estate in the years surrounding 1835 reveal Loyd's extensive interests in buying and selling
property. In 1833 he purchased a substantial piece of ground on the western edge of the city of Philadelphia. In subsequent years he made further
acquisitions in the neighborhood. As quickly as Loyd bought parcels, he
sold them to building mechanics, reserving to himself a perpetual rent on
the land. William Green—sometimes in partnership with his brother and
fellow house carpenter, and sometimes on his own—bought a dozen lots
(Figure 8). Loyd sold adjoining land to plasterers, painters, bricklayers, and
others. Perpetual payment on these lots—ground rent—reflected the size
of each parcel and ranged from $60 to $270 per annum. Few assiduous and
fortunate craftsmen needed to pay that amount, however, as Loyd set the
rent to begin nearly one year after the time of purchase. Artisans had the
first year rent-free to fulfill a provision of the conveyance—the construction
of a house—and to sell the house subject to the rent.[1]

Loyd expected to assist these men in their endeavors by providing
credit and capital as the dwellings progressed. Not all builders enjoyed the
outcome. Loyd "held out inducements . . . to take his Lots and build upon
[them] . . . assuring to advance funds," house carpenter Michael Barron recounted. Barron bought lots on a ground rent "far above their value and
built Houses upon them [but] . . . [t]he Houses are unfinished for want of
funds which [Loyd] failed to advance."[2] The onset of depression in 1837
could not have helped either Barron or Loyd. Whatever the truth of the arrangement between the merchant and the carpenter, Barron's predicament
emphasizes the promise as well as the uncertainty of residential building in
Philadelphia.

The methods by which building artisans William Green, Ealy Green,

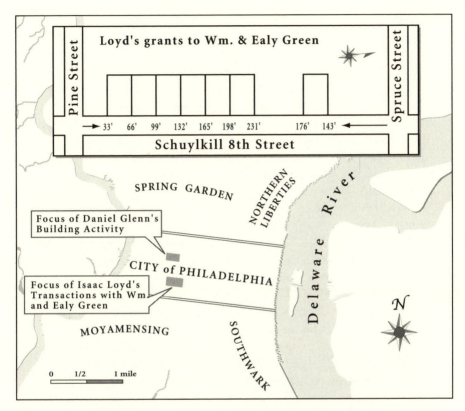

8 Landowners divided large parcels and sold individual lots to building mechanics who undertook to develop the properties and find buyers for the houses. In the 1830s, the location of William and Ealy Green's lots, as well as those of Daniel Glenn, reflected the spread of the city's productive enterprises beyond the riverfront.

and Michael Barron procured land and credit to practice their trade were widespread in antebellum Philadelphia. The strategies they employed, their engagement in speculative housing construction, and the credit they could command linked these builders to John Munday, Moses Lancaster, and Warnet Myers (see Chapter 1) and to the artisanal community throughout the city. Likewise, the participation of Isaac Loyd in selling undeveloped lots on ground rent and assisting with financing exemplified the role that many merchants assumed in construction.

Established and evolving practices, laws, and customs relating to land and credit affected mechanics in the building trades. Of these, ground rent assumed primary importance for real estate development. Ground rent was a pervasive form of land tenure in the urban sections of Philadelphia County. Virtually eliminating capital barriers, ground rent created an environment that encouraged builders to take chances. The property arrangement had dramatic consequences; it allowed artisans to pursue competence, security, and wealth. Access to financing put each mechanic in a position to be—simultaneously or alternately—craftsman, contractor, and developer. Able to build in advance, men of humble backgrounds could become real estate developers. Motivated by the prospect of profit and readily accepting risk, Philadelphia artisans found themselves in one of the most unfettered capital markets in the nation.

Credit practices were a second critical element that affected the building trades. Mortgages, notes, and trade credit—though not unique to Philadelphia—were important resources builders used to carry out their work. These mechanisms capture the interaction among financiers and artisan borrowers in the early nineteenth-century city. Increased reliance on merchant sources, in lieu of reciprocal craft credit networks, tied builders to a volatile economy that had few anchors. Here was a paradox: to achieve independence, builders had to become dependent on an unpredictable market economy. Use of merchant credit in lieu of trade credit was neither complete nor immediate, but cyclical and gradual. By midcentury, nevertheless, private and institutional mortgage credit became central to major development.

In the process, artisans adapted to institutions in constant flux. They availed themselves of whatever had worked traditionally: trade credit, labor exchange, book debt, kinship and craft networks. They added innovations: speculation in ground rent, exchanges in instruments of credit, loans from banks and insurance companies, and deals mediated by brokers. In their endeavors, craftsmen in the construction trades became highly leveraged entrepreneurs whose successes ebbed and flowed with economic tides, individual abilities, and personal misfortunes.

Men and women with capital embraced urban real estate as a conservative option within a larger investment portfolio. Old wealth chose investments that minimized risk and favored long-term dependable gains over short-term profits. In Philadelphia, staid investors abandoned untried ventures leaving them to more daring or desperate entrepreneurs. Cautiousness repelled merchant capital from many manufacturing undertakings. Local textile manufacture in particular relied principally on artisan resources and far less on merchant capital compared to ventures in the New England textile industry.[3]

Philadelphia merchants and financiers did direct large amounts of capital into development of the area surrounding the city. Especially after the 1820s, Philadelphians funded a canal system to bring anthracite coal from the north for local consumption and export. Investments in canal and coal stocks proved highly desirable, and profits from them showed up in mortgage loans and real estate purchases. Capitalists in turn put gains made from real estate back into a growing city, into stocks in the coal trade, or into projects to develop the hinterland.[4]

Compared to the picture historians have painted for New York City and Boston, Philadelphia merchant capitalists took a less active role than their northeastern peers in building up urban properties. Gentry in New York developed urban lots themselves and exploited the city's tight land market. Similarly, wealthy and established families dominated real estate construction in Boston.[5] In contrast upper-class Philadelphians rarely attempted to put up rows of houses on the land they owned. Instead, they encouraged artisans and small capitalists—who readily obliged—to undertake the risks associated with construction.

In New York, Boston, and other rival urban centers, building mechanics became employees of merchant developers and abandoned independent production for dependent wage labor. Craftsmen attempting to go it alone floundered in a real estate market that required access to ever greater sums to meet increasing land costs. Capital barriers undermined their independence as producers who designed, built, and marketed houses.[6]

In contrast, Philadelphia mechanics kept step with changes in labor and production processes, and as late as the mid-nineteenth century, retained control as master builders. They continued to erect dwellings on their own account. Nevertheless, craftsmen struggled to remain independent operators. In addition to continuous sparring with national economic fluctuations and a host of circumstantial problems that could cause disaster, artisan builders competed against one another. They contended, moreover, with entrepreneurs selling new expertise, among them real estate brokers, architects, conveyancers, and lawyers. Middlemen of a sort—neither manual nor craft workers, but intermediaries who acted as contractors of landowners—were found in Boston and New York and also emerged in Philadelphia. In the Quaker City, they did not replace master builders but shared the industry with artisan entrepreneurs, the latter of whom predominated.

Ground rent is key to explaining the evolution of property and capital in Philadelphia, though geography compounded its influence. This land-tenure form evolved from English law and custom and was peculiar to Phila-

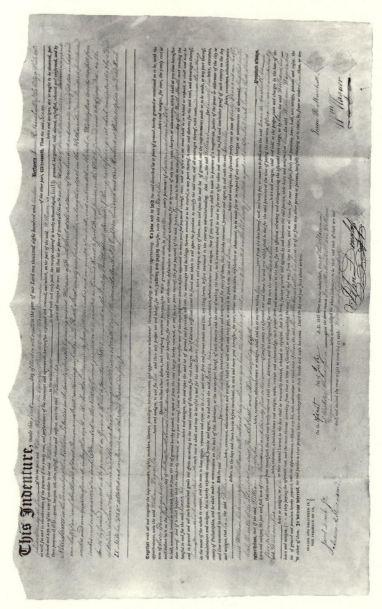

9 The strong real estate market in 1812 enabled house carpenter William Wagner to create a ground rent payable to himself when he sold this Northern Liberties property. Gift of Louise B. Beardwood to the author.

delphia among American cities. It appeared in the Quaker City in the earliest days of the colony. In the waning years of the American Revolution, the commonwealth's legislature sanctioned the continuation of the system. Over time, however, battles in the courts, not the legislature, defined the particulars of ground rent in Pennsylvania.[7]

The careers of John Munday, Moses Lancaster, and Warnet Myers (see Chapter 1) have already revealed how individuals manipulated ground rent in order to progress as builders. Ground rent also offered advantages to capitalists (those with money or land) and had ramifications for house ownership and the contours of urban development. Capitalists and craftsmen interacted to shape the practices emanating from ground rent. They tested the legal and practical boundaries of the system constantly, creating new ways to use ground rent for their own purposes. The evolution ground rent underwent because of these experiments and contestations perpetuated artisan entrepreneurship in antebellum Philadelphia.

Under ground-rent property arrangements, the ground lord or landowner (recall Isaac Loyd) sold the lot to a "grantee" or purchaser, subject to a rent that was to be paid "forever."[8] (People bought and sold, rather than rented or leased in ground-rent transactions.) The grantee gained all the rights of land held in "fee simple" (the absolute ownership of land) so long as he paid the rent. He also paid taxes and assessments on the property (Figure 9).[9] The purchaser, often a building mechanic (for instance, William Green), needed no initial outlay of capital. He therefore expended his funds improving the parcel. Most ground-rent deeds required the grantee to build a house within the first year. The dwelling was security for the rent, which was fixed at 6 percent of the value of the lot at the time the parties executed the deed. Six percent was the maximum legal interest and represented, in effect, a perpetual loan on the purchase price of the lot. While the calculation was applied consistently throughout the antebellum period, the value (i.e., price) of a property fluctuated according to the rhyme and reason of any given real estate market.[10]

Ground-rent conveyances were not the sole way to buy property; one could purchase land, albeit for a much larger sum, without the strings of a perpetual payment. Yet, throughout the mid-nineteenth century, ground rent remained the dominant method of transferring unimproved lots in the increasingly urbanized areas of Philadelphia County. The abundance of land, dispersed settlement, and historical developments contributed to the retention of ground rent and its form in the county. Philadelphia rentiers inherited a large proportion of their estates from William Penn's original grants to their ancestors. They and their predecessors also acquired lots at the time of the Revolution.[11] Peripheral land lacked an immediately lucrative market, so leases for a finite period (that is, in contrast to ground-rent transactions) often suited acreage for farming or pasturing. A landlord balanced the term of the finite lease against expected growth of the city since, upon expiration, he intended to convey the land on ground rent for urban improvement.[12] But as one contemporary expert recounted, "leases for 99 to 999 years"—the sort in force in London, for example—"are almost unknown" in Pennsylvania.[13]

Once in place, Philadelphians molded the customs, laws, and financial applications of ground rent and made it more attractive than the long-term leasehold. Whereas a landlord in a long-term lease could claim only one year's overdue rent and followed other creditors in priority, the law protected ground lords for all arrearages. Leases appeared less enticing to those in search of land as well. Tenants found long-term leases unappealing because all improvements reverted to landlords at the expiration of the lease.[14]

Protection of capital, historian Morton Horwitz asserts, became a premier aim of judicial bodies in the early days of the nation. The argument holds in several ways pertaining to ground rent. Throughout the antebellum period, the laws made bolstered the interests of ground lords and increased the security of their investments. In legal suits brought to recover debts, the owner of a ground-rent charge enjoyed distinct advantage over other creditors. In selling the property of a debtor to satisfy claims, proceeds first cleared ground-rent debts. When building craftsmen forced the sale of Ira Sibley's buildings in 1835, the ground lord received full payment for arrears before any of the mechanic creditors. Craftsmen divided remaining monies to net 21 percent of the value of their claims.[15]

Attracted by its legal and fiscal characteristics, most estates, institutions, and prominent families placed significant portions of assets into ground rent. They did so either by selling lots on ground rent and collecting the payments on a regular basis, or by buying (from other investors) the rights to collect already existing rents. (Title to the rent charge and title to the ground itself were two separable and independently transferable estates.) The University of Pennsylvania, churches, and charitable institutions accepted bequests in rent charges (that is, the claim on the annuity), and also sold properties on ground rent. Estate administrators and guardians of minors frequently bought rent charges and conveyed lots on ground rent for secure annuities. When the friends of a deceased sea captain raised $1,000 on behalf of his children, for example, their guardian bought a rent charge that would produce an annual income of $60.[16] While this was a modest amount, earnings mounted for those with extensive holdings. One ground lord, for instance, recorded a rent income of $1,543 in 1812 and $1,722 in 1822, while the gain of another totaled over $4,000 in 1832.[17]

Ground rent was not simply an elite investment tool. Because it was secure, long-term, local, and had only modest costs of transaction, "middling sort" individuals placed savings in ground rents. Addressing a landowner, an intermediary represented that "a Friend . . . wishes to purchase a Ground Rent of about 1000 $. If you have one to Sell please inform me."[18] A mechanic and his wife invested a similar amount, although they owned neither the house in which they resided nor the land that their craft shop occupied.[19] Widows, too, turned savings into rents. Investing on behalf of "An Old lady," Isaac Elliott sought a "Small ground Rent the principal of which . . . would be about $200."[20] Testators often made provisions for wives and daughters through ground-rent charges, which could be preserved as a woman's separate estate, protected by law from a husband's creditors. With the title placed in trust, ground rent proved a strategem when a husband's finances floundered. (Moses Lancaster tried this means of shielding assets in 1829, when his career faltered.)[21]

Builders learned about ground rent early in their careers. The method of sale between merchant Isaac Loyd and carpenters William Green, Ealy Green, and Michael Barron, for example, was routine among real estate transactions in the Quaker City. These builders bought the ground, subject to an annual rental payment to Loyd. The carpenters enjoyed all rights of ownership so long as they upheld the terms of the contract: payment of the rent and erection of a structure. In the next year, the Green brothers built on one lot—possibly quickly enough to avoid any payments to Loyd. They sold the house and lot (subject to ground rent) to a third party. The price— $4,200 paid to the Green brothers—reflected the improvements. The buyer of the newly completed house assumed the fixed annual ground rent of $108 due Isaac Loyd. The chain of obligation to Loyd and his heirs passed to any subsequent owner of the lot.[22]

Loyd could not sell the land to benefit from rising real estate prices; though, regardless of property depreciation or appreciation, he always claimed a dividend of 6 percent. Six percent was better or comparable to interest Loyd could expect from any other conservative investment.[23] He might, however, realize the value of the annual premium by selling or assigning his right to collect it. If he urgently needed cash, Loyd could look for a ground-rent buyer among his associates, advertise in a newspaper, or employ a broker to match him with an interested purchaser. For cash in hand, he might agree to a sum below the value set when he sold the lot to the carpenters. One merchant struck such a deal with a necessitous ground lord when he paid $693.33 for a yearly rent charge of $53—nearly $200 less than full redemption price. In general, however, buyers would not pay more than the original price; both land and rent charges were too abundant to justify doing so.[24] After 1854, when by law new perpetual ground rents ceased to exist, exceptions occurred. A late nineteenth-century commentator asserted that old rents, "by reason of their permanent character" and the "march of improvements," actually commanded premium prices, although the rents to the original ground lords remained unchanged.[25]

As transferable and valuable instruments, rent charges fueled a steady market in Philadelphia. They could be bought, sold, used to settle debts and—like securities or other valuable paper—offered to secure loans (i.e., mortgaged). In addition to long-term investment potential, negotiability promised short-term money-making possibilities. Philadelphians set about to adapt this formerly feudal tenure system to a dynamic capitalist economy. Consider one scion of an elite family, Henry Fisher, who quickly multiplied inherited wealth in a hot property market. In 1849 alone, he made $100,000 from "speculations in lots" using a *modus operandi* admired by his brother. Fisher "buys a lot for 40 or $50,000, cuts it up, [sells] it on ground rent sometimes at a profit of 2 or 300 per ct., &, as soon as the lots are improved, sells the grd. rents." Fisher's ground-rent purchasers had "150 houses building on various lots," from which the ground lord was sure to realize lucrative long-term annuities or windfall returns on quick sales of rent charges.[26]

Building artisans, too, lost few opportunities to participate in the speculative facet of ground rents, albeit generally on a more modest scale than Fisher. Builders often did so to rid themselves of undeveloped properties left over from construction projects or to make some cash in a good deal. Carpenter Moses Lancaster acquired a lot, subdivided it, and then made sales contingent on ground rents payable to himself. One week later, Lancaster sold the titles to the rent charges to another party. In his haste, he accepted more than $200 less than the full redemption sums stipulated in the deeds. The smaller amount was worth it: Lancaster netted nearly $2,000 for a few weeks' work in real estate transfers.[27] Similarly, house carpenters Alexander Hampton and Thomas Tompkins held an undeveloped lot on ground rent in 1810. They sold the lot, transferring the rent obligation to the buyer. Hampton and Tompkins took advantage of sharply rising real estate prices to create a second annual rent charge—on the very same land—

payable to themselves. Thus, upon selling the lot they incurred no further liability for the first ground rent nor for building on the lot, but looked forward to receiving an annuity from the buyer.[28]

But dealing in ground rents could also backfire. If the market was weak and the seller eager to part with the property, he might retain liability for the charge. In the depressed market of 1802, a desperate William McDonagh sold a lot "free and clear" of the $30 annual rent. The lot was adjacent to two other properties McDonagh had built on, and he identified these houses as security for the original ground rent—that is, he took the cash from the purchaser, but obligated himself or subsequent owners of the other lot to pay the rent forever. So creative (though foolish?) was McDonagh's attempt to mold ground rent to his needs, that his behavior anticipated legal interpretations. It was not until 1836 that the Pennsylvania Supreme Court ruled against such conveyances where rent was not set proportionally to divided lots.[29]

In spite of the adeptness of Philadelphians in manipulating ground rents and their familiarity with rapid price increases in real estate, existing rents did not keep pace with the market. They never reflected the increased value of the property, since ground lords failed to demand adjustments for increased land prices. (Additional rents, as Hampton and Tompkins illustrated, could be created by owners of the land—but not owners of the initial rent charge.) Isaac Loyd, for example, never proposed a gradual escalation of rent to capitalize on the improvements throughout the neighborhood (or to keep pace with inflation). In contrast, *rentiers* in New York City took measures to ensure augmented profits. That city had a property tenure called "ground rent," but it was actually a long-term lease method. In New York, lease terms (which were never perpetual) soon shrank from fifty to fourteen years. Rent escalation clauses, too, appeared in transactions. Investors in New York real estate refused to commit capital at fixed returns while land prices rose at phenomenal rates.[30]

Why, in view of the graduated rent clauses their New York neighbors favored, did Philadelphians initially look like reluctant capitalists? The explanation rests on a combination of factors, geography and land availability (which determined what the market would bear) foremost among them. But an impalpable traditionalism also underlay the actions of many well-to-do investors in Philadelphia. At least until the mid-nineteenth century, caution emphasized long-term predictable returns over preoccupation with short-term leases and raised rent. Portfolios of Philadelphians included risky high-interest investments, but as a safe instrument, the 6 percent yield of a ground rent had more advantages than disadvantages. Furthermore, one wonders how buyers and sellers would have calculated graduated payments for *perpetual* rents. What purchaser would have submitted to a clause doubling the sum even every fifty years? Consumers were unlikely to buy lots on an open-ended basis. Given the availability of land in Philadelphia, they could have negotiated more satisfactory terms with other ground lords.

As a further contrast to their midAtlantic neighbors, consider the approach Philadelphia ground lords took toward rent redemption. Redemption enabled the grantee to tender the original purchase price of the lot (i.e., the initial value from which the ground rent derived) and be released from the annual rent. Such was the transaction William Tilghman noted in 1824: "Charles Johnson paid me $666.67 in full for the purchase of a ground rent of $40. a year issuing out of a lot in Bonsall Street, which I conveyed to him by deed dated 16 May 1817 in consideration whereof, I released the said Ground rent by my deed dated this day." Johnson had held the property on ground rent since 1817 when the value of the lot was set; but, as noted, he redeemed or "extinguished" the rent in 1824.[31]

First and foremost, Philadelphia ground lords focused on maintaining long-term income from their investments. Purchase prices, such as the one Charles Johnson paid, could be sharply out of line with appreciated real estate. To protect against this possibility, ground lords restricted the window for redemption. Once the ground rent existed for (usually) seven years, the grantee or his assignee had only the next seven years to redeem it. Still other agreements stipulated that the rent could never be redeemed (i.e., it was "irredeemable"). The will of Edward S. Burd further illustrates the emphasis on the long run, specifically to guard the financial security of heirs. To guarantee yearly income, Burd instructed the executors of his estate not to allow the cashing in of irredeemable ground rents. Potential purchasers sought to preserve their right to buy their rent charges, but ground lords called for limitations. When the Pennsylvania legislature attempted to make all ground rents redeemable, the state's Supreme Court found the statute unconstitutional. Even as late as a legal challenge in 1869, ground lords resisted turning annuities into ready cash. They preferred secure investments at 6 percent interest, even when inflation chopped away at that income. In addition to the importance placed on sound investments, ground lords expressed reluctance that the court interfere with a clear contract. They also argued that the law would create havoc in the real estate market.[32]

In spite of earnings, ground rents raised problems for investors and their agents, who had to work at estate management. Collecting rents proved the main annoyance. Late payment occurred often enough to be unremarkable, even to ground lords. "I have not called upon [the grantee]," explained one agent, "as tis only 20 days since [the rent] fell due — & he has commonly not paid in less one. two & three Months after due." Another explained that "I rec'd [November 25, 1814] . . . after hard cunning the balance of Com[mander] Hubs's Ground Rent," accruing since January 1810.[33]

Through legal action, title to the property could be reconveyed. "James Haviland is dead, & Insolvent," one lawyer noted; "I demanded the arrears of Rent [$374.] on the premises, & made Entry [of the premises] for default of payment." At times, however, collectors avoided suit, admitted defeat, and wiped the slate clean. "I this day [in 1825] discharged John Wilson from the [balance] of the above account, in consideration whereof he executed a release of the lot . . . to Thomas Woods to whom I had conveyed the same on a ground Rent." Similarly, this individual "gave up the Arrears of Rent [on another lot] & took a reconveyance." He then sold it on ground rent to a second prospect. Within three years, that party, too, had failed to pay the rent, and the sheriff sold the lot to yet another buyer.[34]

Failure to improve the lot also provoked action from ground lords. The requirement of the timely construction of a house to secure the principal of the ground rent represented an important guarantee. The ground lord could seize or "distrain" valuable property if rent fell into arrears.[35] Elizabeth Shippen, widow of Philadelphia's eminent Doctor Edward Shippen, allowed carpenter George McKay the unusually generous period of four years to erect a brick building. McKay reneged, however, so Shippen conveyed the lot to another (who in turn neglected to pay the rent).[36] Type, not lack, of a structure incurred the rancor of one estate administrator. The lot in question "was taken under the promise . . . of building *houses* not churches, upon it," he protested, "and if this had been done it would not now . . . be surrounded by negro huts — and which is the real ca[u]se of its depreciation." This agent knew that rent was overdue; on the instigation of a suit and the search for another buyer, the property (by his reckoning) had lost value.[37]

Joined with abundant acreage and a diverse economy, ground rent influenced the physical contours of the Quaker City. The number of houses artisans undertook was likely augmented by the chance to make money that ground rent accorded. Mechanics undertook a greater number of structures than they might have in other places, moreover, because the constraints on raising starting capital were minimal. As a result, the stock of housing proportionate to the population was higher and available at prices lower than real estate in similar cities. While New Yorkers, for example, witnessed perennial crises in inexpensive housing, Philadelphians across a range of incomes fared better.[38]

By affecting quantity and price of houses, ground rent facilitated the distribution of ownership and helped perpetuate the row house. Though small and typically densely packed, contemporaries viewed row housing as preferable to the tenement slums of other major urban areas, in particular New York and Boston.[39] In his 1857 survey of Philadelphia manufactures, Edwin Freedley made the link between the ground-rent system and the row house: "The custom . . . that prevails of selling lots on *ground-rent*, gives to the man of small means facilities that he cannot ordinarily obtain in other cities. . . . By this means, it is quite common for mechanics, small tradesmen, and even laborers, to become owners of homesteads."[40] A quarter of a century later, another Philadelphian agreed with Freedley that "Philadelphia was a city of homes, made so primarily by the ground-rent system."[41]

Although the commentator credited "the force of local custom" for continued use of ground rents and row housing, unconstrained barriers to growth better explain the behavior of ground lords and grantees. An 1877 discussion on the evolution of Philadelphia housing conceded the difficulty of transplanting ground rents and row houses to other cities. In New York, the writer averred, "the difficulties of distance, and the water surroundings, become more nearly insuperable." Moreover, "it is generally believed that land is too valuable near New York and Boston" for building to be capitalized through a ground-rent system.[42]

Owing to the lower immediate costs of obtaining land on ground rent, property prices reflected the value of the house exclusive of the cost of the lot. In New York, a respectable brick house required from $2,000 to $3,500 to erect (in the decade 1825–35); to that sum $500 to $1,000 would have been added for the lot. In Boston, too, builders found land prices a major hurdle. Ground rent in Philadelphia, however, shifted the cost of the land away from builders and onto the eventual purchasers of the completed house (and even they could prolong redemption of ground rent indefinitely). The initial purchasing price of a house was, therefore, lower.[43]

Housing acquisition came within the reach of Philadelphians as well because small dwellings predominated. More than 80 percent of new dwelling construction for which information was recorded in the 1840s consisted of three-story brick structures.[44] Quaker City builders continued to offer a relative abundance of single family structures selling from $1,200 to

$2,000—sums within the range of many artisans, laborers, and middling households. Men in construction enjoyed better incomes than most artisanal groups, but their gains suggest the fortunes of Philadelphia's master mechanic households. Master carpenter Joshua Sharples, who gained $1,450 on one development of two houses, enjoyed a yearly sum of $580 for the duration of this work alone. Another master claimed that in all the years of his independence, beginning in 1826 and continuing past midcentury, his yearly remuneration was never less than $700—a startling achievement in light of periodic recessions in the economy. The many masters who enjoyed the advantages of building work could accumulate the purchase price or obtain a mortgage loan for a Philadelphia row house. Real property could also enable a family to raise funds in times of stress or business expansion. Raising capital or financing to build a multistoried tenement of the sort developing in New York and Boston, however, remained more difficult.[45]

Lower rental rates helped the mechanic family save for the purchase of a house. Rental housing in Philadelphia was 50 to 75 percent cheaper than in New York (while wages were closely matched). From approximately 1800 to 1820, a family could rent a small brick dwelling in Spring Garden or Southwark for $40 to $80 per annum. In 1810 the wife of one artisan described their house in Spring Garden as "a very nice Brick House" probably containing upward of five rooms. They paid $80 per annum rent.[46] In New York, however, landlords demanded the same sum for one or two rooms, or for a one-story wooden rear house of comparable distance from the city center. Even a small wooden house in New York cost $250 per annum; the same amount in Philadelphia guaranteed a genteel family a large brick dwelling not far removed from the commercial heart of the city.[47]

At times from necessity, and sometimes to get ahead of their bills, families in the Quaker City employed their cheaper and larger spaces as financial assets. Middling as well as poorer families converted space into cash by taking in boarders.[48] One source counseled mechanics to find comfortable board and meals for three dollars per week, an amount that allowed a modest supplement to the host household after expenses.[49] If the family netted even half the charge each week, the labor a woman contributed by taking in lodgers could augment the income of a young master carpenter's household upwards of 10 or 15 percent. Providing lodging for apprentices, moreover, enabled masters to increase their work force and enlarge production with little expense.

Female family members also conducted commercial activities in the home, and some residences functioned as veritable workshops. One woman,

for example, ran a small shop out of the family house in Northern Liberties. She sold "such things as she could make with her needle," supplemented by the dry goods her husband traded from "his pack."[50] The well-
educated wife of one mechanic kept school in the upper story of their rented
house. Another woman in the heart of the city made straw bonnets at her
residence, and a neighbor whitened and cleaned the same wares.[51] Boarding, shopkeeping, teaching, and manufacturing contributed to the long-
run economic viability of Philadelphia's laboring families. These strategies
also enabled them to exercise choices as consumers in its housing market,
stimulate the demand for single row houses, and keep building mechanics
independent.

*   *   *

"I commenced the Carpenter and House building business about the
spring of . . . 1830," attested Philadelphia artisan Daniel Glenn, "being then
about 23 Years of age." Initially in partnership with another inexperienced
carpenter, the pair "commenced building two . . . Houses," wagering that
they would later find a buyer. This project inaugurated Glenn's career as a
master house carpenter. The partners next built several more dwellings. In
exchange for a "bond and mortgage on all said Eight Houses," the ground
lord advanced the builders $4,500 for materials and labor. The pair then
undertook a row of nine houses, for which they gave a mortgage to the
ground lord of that parcel for $4,000.[52]

A powerful mixture of motivations—accumulation, mobility, and survival—fueled speculative construction. Recall that John Munday had "resolved no longer to continue in the capacity of a journeyman, but to try his
fortune in the way of building." Glenn's contemporary John Miskey also
marked his advance as a master by "tak[ing] up lots and build[ing] on them
for the purpose of selling again."[53] Integrating advance building with contract work and small jobs, a mechanic could look forward to modest success
or even dream of great fortune. He might realistically expect to profit by
$800 on a house marketed for around $2,500—circumstances favoring the
enterprise. Erecting a row of dwellings at once, a builder could garner a tidy
sum toward his next project.[54] He could point to several house carpenters—
John M. Ogden, James McCloskey, and Robert O'Neill among them—who
had amassed big estates through buying and improving property. Contemporaries estimated that the worth of each of these men surpassed $50,000 in

1846. In the same year, brickmaker Peter Grim and bricklayer Isaac Harbert boasted property worth $75,000 and $50,000 respectively.[55]

Ground-rent building, observed critics, encouraged rapid buying and selling. Detractors did not criticize craftsmen. Rather, they targeted men who usurped the social and economic prerogatives of Philadelphia's elite property owners. Small capital requirements encouraged building by both underfunded and dishonest individuals, observed one commentator—who happened to have extensive real estate interests of his own. In 1815 he portrayed artisans as unwitting victims of the avarice of these capitalist pretenders—hardly the image one forms from John Munday's and Moses Lancaster's machinations. Another (a disgruntled ground lord) noted that purchasers must be compelled to erect substantial dwellings, lest leniency encourage excessive trading.[56]

Notwithstanding the self-interest of these voices, the criticisms hit the mark. Dangers of advance building were chronic, catching artisans in reversals of fortune when real estate prices plunged. Many marginal concerns drowned in downturns, or faltered even in more stable climates; their ruin heightened market instability. Overall business failures evinced the vulnerability of construction craftsmen, who resorted to legal protection as insolvents in greater proportion than their representation in the population (Figure 10). In a bad year, they accounted for a quarter of all insolvent mechanics, though they comprised no more than a fifth of Philadelphia's mechanic population.[57] Despite the community's close experience with failed enterprise, the urge to build on one's own account continued to drive artisans into the market. Stories were legion, but most emphasized the unpredictability of building in anticipation of a sale. "[B]uilding Houses on Ground Rent wherby [he] sustained many & heavy Losses" ruined one house carpenter in 1822. Influenced by a tenuous upswing, a painter and glazier "took up ground on high prices and built houses," but "lost large sums of money in consequence of the great depreciation in the value of Real Estate" in 1819. A brickmaker joined his colleagues in 1820 to find that, having taken lots at high ground rents, "[t]he depreciation in the value of his real Estate has occasioned him to . . . a heavy loss."[58]

Few artisans amassed adequate personal savings to start construction without borrowing. Michael Barron "had not even the tools of his own to work with" when he began journeywork in 1830. Within five years, "by . . . Industry and œconomy," Barron had saved $850 (and this with the expense of—or contribution of—a wife and two children).[59] The $300 with which

Printed and sold at No. 24 Arch Street—A. Walker, Agt.

To the Honourable the Judges of the Court of Common Pleas of Philadelphia County.

The Petition of *Daniel T Glenn*

Respectfully Showeth,

THAT your Petitioner, by reason of sundry losses and misfortunes, is now unable to pay and satisfy his just debts, and therefore is compelled to apply to your Honourable Court for the relief provided for Insolvent Debtors, by the existing Insolvent Laws of this Commonwealth; that your Petitioner has resided within the County of Philadelphia six months immediately preceding this his application, and is now willing and offers to deliver up to the use of his creditors, all his property, real, personal and mixed, to which he is in any manner entitled, a schedule whereof, on *oath* ——— together with a list of his creditors, and the nature and amount of their debts, as far as he can ascertain the same, with a statement of his losses, and the means whereby he became insolvent, are exhibited with and annexed to this petition.

Your Petitioner therefore applies to your Honourable Court, and prays that your Honours will grant him such relief as is prescribed by the existing insolvent laws of this Commonwealth.

Daniel T Glenn

Daniel T Glenn ——— the above named petitioner being duly *sworn* ——— according to law, saith, that the annexed schedule contains a just and true account of all the property, real, personal and mixed, to which he is in any manner entitled; and that the list of his creditors, and the nature and amount of their debts, as far as he can ascertain the same, and the statement of his losses, and the means whereby he became insolvent, exhibited with and annexed to this petition, are likewise true, just and correct, to the best of his knowledge and belief.

Sworn ——— and subscribed before me, this *fifth* ——— day of *September* A. D. 1835 *Daniel T Glenn* another mechanic commenced his building probably also resulted from earnings as a journeyman.[60] But for every mechanic who saved, another could not. When Daniel Glenn embarked on the business, he was only "about 'even with the World.'"[61] One journeyman carpenter who labored two and a half years even acquired a debt of $45 during his stint.[62]

Short-term notes, likewise, were an unsatisfactory and inadequate means to finance material and labor costs. Builders used them at best as emergency funds and repaid them as quickly as possible. Notes were an expensive way to borrow (especially in inflationary periods); few such loans appear to have observed a maximum legal interest rate of 6 percent. John Munday, for example, struggled to pay 2½ percent interest per month (34 percent per annum) on a note. Yet other craftsmen complained of rates amounting to as much as 88 percent per annum.[63] Discounting, or immediately taking a fee off the top of the loan, also made cash expensive. The practice led carpenter Philip Justus to object that "[h]e has been compelled to procure his notes to be discounted at large Usurious interest."[64]

Mortgages presented a much more attractive alternative to personal savings or high-interest notes. Mortgage borrowing complemented ground-rent purchasing, and by joining the two instruments mechanics embarked on building. John Munday found mortgagees whose advances, "notwithstanding his [own] want of funds," enabled the carpenter to engage in speculative construction.[65] Having "no Capital with which to build," Glenn and his partner procured money on mortgage to finance projects and persisted by "Credit & Industry." Throughout his mid- and late twenties Glenn continued to rely on ground-rent purchases and mortgage loans as major components of his strategy to accumulate wealth.[66]

In an era predating thrift institutions, private capitalists offered the principal proportion of mortgage financing.[67] The big money came from merchants like Isaac Loyd, lawyers like Edward Shippen (who lent to John Munday), or successful brokers like Horatio Pennock (who accommodated Warnet Myers). Builders also relied on sisters, aunts, and other female relatives, particularly for small start-up capital. Though Isaac Loyd extended

10 Building craftsmen resorted to protection under Pennsylvania's insolvency laws to stay out of debtors' prison and to restructure debts from failed endeavors. Courtesy of City of Philadelphia, Department of Records, City Archives, RG20, Prothonotary of the Court of Common Pleas, Insolvent Petitions, Daniel T. Glenn, September 5, 1835.

William Green money to develop property on ground rent, Green concurrently executed mortgages for a few thousand dollars to a female creditor who was probably his mother-in-law.[68] Savings funds and insurance companies advanced money on mortgage in the antebellum era, but most credit was surely secured by existing housing. Only a fraction of all mortgage loans from these conservative sources would have underwritten new building. Many savings funds were organized to serve mechanics and laborers, but staid investment decisions likely limited availability for most master builders.[69] Until at least the 1840s, private lenders, and not institutions, continued to make the largest number of mortgages and lend the most money to construction tradesmen.[70] Building societies appeared in Philadelphia as early as 1831, but did not have any considerable effect for at least two decades.[71]

Intermediaries of another sort, however, recognized a chance to develop critical roles in the real estate world of the nineteenth-century metropolis. A burgeoning group of specialists—conveyancers and brokers—linked creditors to borrowers. Conveyancers claimed familiarity with the intricacies of property law and practice. In 1802 John Harrington marketed his capabilities, assuring the public that "deeds, wills, leases, bonds, mortgages, & other instruments of writing, are drawn on the most moderate terms." Conveyancers touted an expertise in the morass of legal documentation that was unsurpassed by real estate lawyers until the second half of the nineteenth century.[72]

New professionals used the era's expanded print communication to hawk services. Through newspapers, conveyancers made it known that they had "MONEY TO LOAN ON MORTGAGE OF REAL ESTATE. Several Small Sums of 300 to $1000 at Six Per Cent." They also undertook the "negotiation of Loans on Mortgage and the purchase and sale of Real Estate."[73] Established business contacts turned up potential lenders since many conveyancers knew ground lords through service as rent collectors. Conveyancer John Bonsall conducted a gainful practice as agent for merchants and landowners, selling ground rents and drawing the requisite deeds. Builders ranked among conveyancers' principal clients. Bonsall, for example, assisted carpenter (and self-proclaimed architect) Thomas Carstairs to procure a mortgage of $1,000. Carstairs paid the broker 1 percent of the loan and the expense of drawing up the documents—nearly $17, or the equivalent of two weeks pay of any journeyman Carstairs might hire.[74]

At the close of the Revolution, conveyancers acted mostly as scriveners, adapting new deeds and mortgages from prototypes, and drafting by hand copies of documents. Simple transcription could also be done by non-specialists, including parties to a deal. By 1850, however, conveyancers had come to be regarded as skilled professionals. Many delegated copying jobs to subordinates and focused instead on reviewing title, arbitrating sales and purchases, researching legal complications, and mediating loans. By mid-century, "Real Estate Brokers" competed with conveyancers as negotiators and property listing agents. Brokers did not immediately catch the public's trust, however—perhaps owing to the number of unsuccessful builders and speculators filling the ranks. (Warnet Myers marketed himself as a real estate broker after his debacle.)[75] Their advent, however, pushed conveyancers to concentrate on steering buyers and sellers through the technical and juridical issues of property and credit transactions.

By the early decades of the nineteenth century, mechanics discovered that it was hazardous to ignore the services of conveyancers in buying and selling property and borrowing large sums of money. The costs of mistakes—invalid titles and mortgage debts that bumped builder's claims to property—could be high. While building artisans tried, few could keep abreast of the complicated procedures for filing documents, the errors to be avoided, and the growing body of legal decisions refining the dos and don'ts of ground rents and mortgages. Artisans did not lose skills that they had once had, but rather harnessed existing skills to interact with experts in a more specialized economy.

Two examples illustrate the shift in artisan focus and the emergence of professional conveyancers. Sometime in the 1780s, carpenter Robert McKnight agreed to assist Philip Flick, for whom he was repairing several houses in Southwark. Flick appealed to the craftsman as "more conversant in such Business to look out for Purchasers for the Houses." Much as a broker would do, McKnight "conversed with several Persons on the Subject," was present at negotiations between prospective buyers and Flick, and arbitrated mortgages on the properties. Six decades later, the actions of John Bosler, a sixty-five-year-old brickmaker, contrasted with those McKnight had undertaken with confidence. Although Bosler negotiated the purchase of a brickyard lease himself, he "submitted the papers to Mr. Cavendar [conveyancer] to see if they were correct as I would a deed or any other papers." Bosler asserted that it was "customary" to have a professional review documents and "to give advice as to the title." Despite decades of building experience, Bosler "kn[e]w nothing of the law" and resorted to conveyancers to avoid its quagmires. Specialized professional expertise had became part of the cost of business in the building trade.[76]

*   *   *

Commonly, a builder procured an advance money mortgage, or an agreement on the part of the lender to supply the borrower with capital or credit in anticipation of a completed dwelling.[77] The mortgagee (the lender) turned over sums as the house took shape, while the structure in its progressive stages secured the loan. William and Ealy Green contracted an advance money mortgage with Isaac Loyd, who was also the ground lord for the carpenters' lots. Michael Barron claimed also to have arranged an advance money mortgage with Loyd, also ground lord for his lots. Daniel Glenn mortgaged his buildings in progress to the ground lords in some instances, and to other mortgage lenders in other cases.[78]

Most mortgages in the early nineteenth-century stipulated repayment of the principal within one, two, or three years, but in practice borrowers and creditors rolled the loan over indefinitely. As long as the borrower paid interest, usually at 6 percent per annum in twice yearly installments, the principal could remain outstanding. If the mortgagee (the lender) owed money, he could assign the debt to placate his creditors, or sell the mortgage to another party.[79] Consequently, like the right to collect ground rent, the title to mortgage installments was a good investment; a thriving secondary market for mortgage paper developed. If the mortgagor (the borrower) sold the property that was security for the debt, he generally applied the purchase money to satisfy the mortgage. Alternatively, he sold the house subject to the debt. William Green chose the latter option when he conveyed a dwelling to Thomas Bunting, who purchased the property subject to three mortgages amounting to $1,700 and interest. Bunting could satisfy the mortgages, continue interest payments on them, or execute new ones in his name.[80]

Landowners and financiers would have looked in vain for builders to develop properties—or for buyers of finished houses—if they required loan principals returned in steady installments. Flexibility of repayment grew out of several conditions in the early republic. Abundance of undeveloped property, persistence of economic fluctuations, and difficulty of maintaining personal savings demanded it. Extending the life of the mortgage and the accompanying mortgage bond served both lender and borrower. The creditor benefited from continued interest on the original loan. For a long-term owner, the absence of a repayment schedule enabled him to amass the principal as circumstances allowed. Requiring interest alone, mortgages attracted particularly those who would not long hold the property. A builder who intended to sell immediately upon completion of a structure, for instance, continued interest payments but tied up no funds in reducing the principal. He depended on repaying the original loan from the profits of the structure, although setbacks and shifting values often fell short of expectations. Delaying satisfaction of the mortgage, nonetheless, stimulated speculative construction, much as ground rent diminished the builder's need for initial funds, and encouraged rapid resale.

Ground lords commonly invested in mortgage lending; they often had to do so to convince builders to buy their lots. In 1834 Doctor Josiah Stewart held undeveloped land near the Schuylkill River wharves, but missed his chance to sell the property on ground rent. He could only make sales "provided he could advance $1000 a lot, to aid in building." Stewart, however, could not muster the capital. (A lawsuit also complicated the situation.) Fifteen years later, a long depression having intervened, the lots remained unsold and undeveloped.[81]

Mortgage lending also was attractive to ground lords as an interest-earning outlet for capital. Creditors could monitor improvements on lots they sold on ground rent (though on many lots, the ground lord and mortgage creditor were different parties). When wealthy William Samsom publicized his lots "For Sale [on ground rent], Upon Building improvement," he added that purchasers would "be accommodated with the means of building"—that is, they would be provided with advance money mortgages.[82] For loans, builders sought out men with whom they already had a business connection, such as those from whom they had purchased land (or they returned to the same brokers). Having the same person as a ground lord and creditor did not reduce master artisans to employees. It might have encumbered builders with additional pressure and oversight, but interaction often ended with the signing of the deed and mortgage. Indebted builders might have worried about attentive creditors, but so did other borrowers.

Debt priority under the law made selling property on ground rent and lending money for its development attractive choices. In property disputes, proceeds from public sales cleared outstanding mortgages after ground rent arrearages.[83] A careful mortgage creditor advanced only as much capital as the progress of construction warranted, hedging his loan against the value of the structure in case the builder defaulted. If legal suit forced the sale of a property—the proceeds satisfying first the ground rent and second the mortgage (or mortgages)—little might remain to compensate subcontractors and journeymen. Penalties for default on mortgage bonds (and most other bonds) doubled the original sum, further protecting the mortgage

creditor above material suppliers and craftsmen. In such cases, artisan creditors who had advanced materials and labor scarcely received more than 25
to 50 percent of the value of their claims.[84] If construction finished on schedule, however, the ground lord/mortgagee might buy the house—as Loyd
bought at least two of Green's finished properties.[85]

By encouraging another party—William Green, for instance—to undertake building, financiers such as Isaac Loyd avoided contracting debts to
develop property. Green bore the risks of building, that is, the liability for
obligations to material suppliers, craftsmen, and laborers. The house carpenter also suffered the management headaches of coordinating supplies,
subcontractors, and the cheapest possible labor force. For ground lords and
mortgage creditors, the arrangement was a virtual win-win situation. What
risk they could not push onto builders, they managed to temper through
legal provisions. Certainly losses occurred, particularly when forced sales
took place during real estate depressions, although a creditor might then
buy the house himself and resell it in a better climate. But assiduous oversight of one's portfolio guarded against many difficulties. Ground lords and
mortgagees needed to collect rents and interest promptly, record mortgages
immediately, monitor the state of construction (to assure sufficient collateral), and take legal action when all else failed. Or, investors could employ
conveyancers to conduct affairs on their behalf.

Risk offered an excellent reason for capitalists to leave development to
artisans, but class and gender ideology that shaped the appropriate behavior of wealthy men and women also contributed. Elites succeeded during
the eighteenth century in distancing themselves from mechanical or manual
laborers, and the emerging middle class of the nineteenth century strived to
do so as well. Labor—even craft labor—fought against political, social, and
ideological currents that discredited its contribution to the republic.[86] Tasks
required in managing building may well have been too closely associated
with common labor for elite men to undertake (except in the case of public
buildings, when prominent individuals from the community assumed control). Lack of access to the business world and to capital disqualified most
women, elite and middling, from negotiating even ground-rent sales and
mortgages independently.[87]

At the same time builders used ground rent and loans obtained from
mercantile and financial investors, they exploited resources within the artisanal community. Running unsettled accounts featuring debits and credits
of labor and material for months or even years continued as a common practice among Philadelphia's builders at least as late as the 1830s. Exchange

based on cash prices (but not on cash itself) likely persisted longer within craft communities than in the more anonymous urban economy as a whole. Because the custom was ubiquitous, judges expressed no surprise when builders and suppliers presented accounts in court as "unsettled."[88] These exchanges—the basis of trade and book networks—depended upon first-hand acquaintance, recommendations, or reputation. Knowing one another, each other's whereabouts and financial viability, reduced the risk that debtors would elude payment. Lumber merchant Josiah Bunting revealed in his ledger the importance of referrals in exchange networks. Customers, for example, came "recommended by J. C. Emary."[89] Moses Lancaster's affiliation with the Society of Friends, as his career has shown, immediately tied many of his borrowers to a vast repository of reputations.

Generally, tradesmen drew upon the value owed them in book accounts by paying other parties with orders on the obliged craftsman or material supplier. Where building artisans labored at many of the same houses, debts often cancelled each other out or were balanced by the transfer of debits and credits to third and fourth parties. For example, when stonemason John Wilson accepted payment by an order from Lancaster & Company, the order drew on their lumber merchant. Wilson could call at the lumberyard and demand the amount of the order in boards, or pass it on as payment in another transaction. When the order arrived in the hands of the lumber merchant, he would debit Lancaster & Company's account accordingly.[90]

If stonemason John Wilson knew little of Lancaster & Company or had not trusted the firm's solvency, he would have demanded cash. Their order would have been worthless if malignant rumors circulated in the artisan community. Horatio Gates discovered this problem when he attempted to use an order on distressed carpenter Daniel Glenn. The intended recipient rebuffed Gates by the assertion that Glenn "was not getting on."[91] Reports echoed beyond Philadelphia to other cities where artisans and material suppliers carried work and contracts. A friend based in New York insisted that brickmaker Samuel Fox explain tales injurious to Fox's reputation and trade credit. Could it be, as he heard in New York, that "you [are] not worth any thing, that [your creditors] had your Books, and that you had stopt business[?]" Understanding the consequences of slander, Fox's defender proposed immediate action. "If it is a Damd lie," he promised, "I will whip the Damd rascal [responsible] before he is 24 Hours Older."[92]

Orders and exchanges could also extend to labor. For example, when a carpenter and a plasterer planned to work on each others' buildings, they stipulated that "when the whole was done, a settlement of their accounts" was to be made.[93] In a similar arrangement, mechanics and material men cooperated to construct several houses, agreeing to work on each others' dwellings according to expertise.[94] Such an accord, argued one proponent as late as 1844, enabled mechanics to "build without paying more than half as much cash, perhaps not more than one fourth as much" as under subcontract arrangements.[95] Exchange of labor was critical in estimating building costs. John Henson undertook roofing on James Stonehill's house, agreeing that "he would take plastering for the zinc roof." As Stonehill explained, "I would not have had a zinc roof put on [instead of a shingle one], unless I had expected some part was to be paid in plastering." Similarly, a bricklayer revealed the distinction between exchange and cash price, noting among his debts "trade work $300 equiv[alent] to $150 Cash."[96]

The expense of cash was particularly pronounced in an industry characterized by long periods between outlay for materials and labor, and sale of the product. Even after the sale, a builder might find himself cash poor—having agreed to take a buyer's mortgage or goods in partial payment, in order to get the property off his hands. (Recall, for instance, that John Munday accepted dry goods in payment for a property, thus initiating his wife's trade in shopkeeping.)[97] To ease cash-flow problems, labor and material exchange in the artisanal community flourished. On the one hand, the phenomenon strengthened craft cooperation and networks in construction by encouraging lasting business relationships. Familiar and trusted tradesmen presented better prospects for credit than those with whom one had few transactions. Furthermore, if, for instance, a bricklayer already owed a plasterer for roughcasting, the plasterer would want to offset the outstanding amount by turning to his debtor when in need of his skill. One did not want to make his circle of trade too narrow; vesting too much credit or debt in any one craftsman could be dangerous if a peer went broke or demanded immediate payment.

On the other hand, rather than encouraging cooperation, labor and material trade could, at the same time, encourage competition. Parties took advantage of market conditions to gain an upper hand in a bargain. In particular, artisans tried to get payment in cash, but give back in kind (i.e., trade); those with more leverage were more able to get cash. Terms of trade could reflect a hierarchy attributable to the career stage of masters or to their degree of desperation. Eager men recently out of journeywork acceded to unequal contracts with senior colleagues in order to get a foot up the craft ladder.

To illustrate these power relations, consider a contract between an established bricklayer and a young master carpenter. Terms stipulated compensation for bricklayer's work "one third Cash one third in Lumber at Cash Price & one third Part in Carpenters work at Thirty Per Centum Deduction."[98] The first ingredient, cash, had a clear value. The second component, "Lumber at Cash Price," encompassed the two-tiered notion of rates: a higher price if the buyer paid in exchange, a lower price (usually by half) for cash tendered. Other artisans agreeable to both parties determined the value, in each case, of the bricklayer's work and the carpenter's work—the third and fourth ingredients of the contract. This disinterested "measurer," a well-regarded and experienced member of the respective trade, consulted standards such as those of the Carpenters' Company or the Bricklayers' Company to arrive at a bill. Still, the deal was subject to inequities. In this instance, the bargain favored the older bricklayer, who not only received payment for lumber and his own work at the cash price, but also obtained carpentry work at a discount.

Intricate trade credit networks assured reverberations throughout the community when a builder failed. The demise of other seemingly sound tradesmen followed. More than one builder, attesting to his dependence on exchange, attributed failure to the "[i]nsolvency of many of his debtors."[99] In an economy erected on credit, the interests of fellow building artisans demanded that each try to keep his peers solvent. The hope that a struggling debtor would recover and make good on his obligations compounded the urgency. The alternative—that the tally of work or materials owed would soon become a bad debt—reduced the trading "currency" of the artisan creditor. Pressure from craft and kin, consequently, enticed men to sign notes on behalf of supplicants. "Indorsement," nonetheless, led many to personal financial ruin.[100]

Because of mounting insecurity, and despite relations within the artisanal community entangled in exchange, craftsmen frequently acted to secure their own survival. Their motives did not necessarily entail enmity against tradesmen, but rather the assurance that, among ground-rent, mortgage, and note creditors, they could vie for distribution of assets. When a long-due imbalance on book accounts between two parties existed, creditors took measures to secure outstanding sums. Book debts did not regularly accrue interest, but promissory notes that creditors exacted did. Tradesmen beyond the building community, moreover, readily accepted notes. Creditors could pass them more freely, and some did so quickly when they believed the original debtor's stability in danger. Debtors tendered notes of thirty days or greater, which were discounted or interest-bearing instruments. Builders who traded regularly also extended small cash loans in exchange for a borrower's short-term notes.[101] To judge from bankruptcy accounts of the 1840s, various builders increasingly favored written instruments over book methods (i.e., debts more likely to be settled for cash than for kind) in the competitive and complex economy of a mushrooming city. Nonetheless, exchange enjoyed surprising persistence in construction.[102]

Other trends indicative of more complex market relations and the growing importance of credit from outside the artisan community are more sharply discernable in mortgage borrowing. Demand for funds to build, accompanied by periods of flush capital supply, altered the relative importance of exchange networks for building artisans. In the boom of the War of 1812, bricklayer Francis Douglass procured approximately 40 percent of $50,000 by mortgage. In a later upswing, Warnet Myers also borrowed $50,000 (almost exclusively in institutional mortgages) which he used to start sixty houses in the space of two years. Smaller builders were also prone to pursue mortgage credit. Moses Lancaster's mortgage debts amounted to $19,000. Of the $16,000 Daniel Glenn owed in 1830, nearly 60 percent stemmed from mortgages (from only three mortgage lenders). By the late 1830s, builders increasingly borrowed major portions of credit on mortgage. For some artisan builders, mortgage bonds were rapidly superseding the primacy of trade credit.[103]

The institutional structure and conditions that emerged in early Philadelphia laid the foundation for independence among building mechanics and were key to their mobility. Ground-rent tenure assured easy entry into speculative construction. Space, unmarked by major geographic obstacles, diffused competition for parcels throughout the county, moderated housing prices, and fueled the popularity of the single house. Mortgage credit and the ability of men in construction to tap it provided yet another element that sustained a trade of small producers. Credit networks based on craft exchange persisted alongside more impersonal sources of financing mediated by the urban market. This constellation of legal and financial factors caused the experiences of artisans in the City of Homes to contrast with those of their peers in New York and Boston. Whereas their northeastern contemporaries slipped increasingly into wage labor, building artisans in mid-nineteenth-century Philadelphia continued to aspire to and achieve craft autonomy.

Speculative opportunity, however, was a mixed blessing for artisan builders. It held out a promise of independence but bound mechanics to financial capital whose availability fluctuated. Easy entry into the industry did not translate into ready success. Large loans compelled mechanics to build aggressively. Aggressive building in turn pulled many deeply into debt, subjecting all to the incessant drive for credit to meet ever increasing commitments, crises of capital shortage and business failures.

Private investment capital continued to fund mechanics' ventures, although institutional loans were gaining in importance. Reliance on mortgage credit, and less on artisan trade credit, rose particularly among ambitious builders. Yet cyclical trends over the sixty years under consideration confound a linear conception of change; investment capital (backed by mortgages) fueled building expansion in the era's early decades.

At midcentury, the route to craft autonomy still lay in advance building of brick row houses, a product that builders, financiers, and consumers continued to endorse. Although a number of recognizable operators flourished in Philadelphia, between 1790 and 1850 they never held a monopoly on residential construction. Reputation, track record, and property to secure mortgages gave some mechanics an edge, but others could still push into the business. An erratic economy leading to high turnover guaranteed a fluid cast of characters and continued audacity of penniless novice craftsmen. Thanks to the panic of 1837 and ensuing depression, which bankrupted numerous seasoned masters, newer upstarts found openings as the half-century closed. Mechanics in the 1850s rose from origins that builders in 1790 would have recognized to undertake, like Irish immigrant and carpenter by trade Joseph Montgomery, thirty-two houses on ground rent. Montgomery's initial means were not much different from John Munday's. New to Philadelphia's building community in 1792, Munday was quickly able to construct a half dozen houses.[104]

Origins aside, the difference in scale between Munday's and Montgomery's operations is important. The increasing complexity involved in financing and building houses at midcentury came at a cost. Informed legal counsel, conscientious estate agents, expert conveyancers, pricey recorders of deeds, aggressive brokers, and accommodating mortgage lenders all raised the price of developing real estate. Putting up more row houses in one place and at one time enabled a builder to spread costs over more houses, decreasing expenses per dwelling. Conversely, smaller projects would carry proportionally higher "transaction costs" (to use the economist's phrase). As the optimum size of projects grew, the smaller builder was at a competitive disadvantage. The likelihood that he would fail rose. Survival as well as profit were powerful incentives to become aggressive, ambitious, big builders.

Growth in the size of projects sped the reorganization of building. It heightened the significance of the managerial and business skills of the master builder over his manual skills and reversed the equation for crafts-men who did not undertake advance construction. Artisans struggled to find ways to complete multiple houses. The method building craftsmen settled upon, extensive subcontracting, would have profound ramifications throughout the industry.

THREE

Dimensions of the Master Builder

O N S E P T E M B E R 7, 1827, lumber merchant George D. Croskey contracted with Robert S. English, house carpenter, for the construction of a two-story brick house on the western edge of the city. Croskey wanted the house to measure seventeen feet four inches in front and thirty feet in depth. (The odd frontage length reflected the dimensions of the lot.) A brick piazza, or covered walkway and stairs, would extend back an additional seven feet. The parties decided to add a brick kitchen thirteen feet wide and seventeen feet deep at the rear of the piazza.

Specifics of the work to be completed by English comprised the bulk of the agreement. English would build a sturdy dwelling, with walls nine inches thick that met the standard for a structure of this size. Croskey demanded oak for the lower joists, the framing members that supported flooring. Durable and close-grained, oak resisted dampness better than other hardwoods. In the selection of the remaining hemlock joists Croskey deferred to English's craft know-how to ensure grade and dimensions "sufficient . . . for a good building." Lower floors called for rough, sapped heart boards, presumably of white pine. Compactness, absence of sap, and the evenness of grain found in "heart"—wood cut from the center of the tree—provided strength for frequently tread surfaces. Window sashes, door frames, and shutters also needed good heart pine, but cheaper "clean sap or first common white pine boards" sufficed for the upper floors. Moved by the architectural tastes of the day, Croskey stipulated shutters outside the first and second story windows, "folding doors between the parlours in the lower Story," and garrets plastered in the "best manner." Additional features suggest the high quality of the house Croskey retained English to build. Marble mantels, parlor paperhangings, three coats of paint on the woodwork, a paved footway to the privy, and planed (not the cheaper rough) fence boards targeted an occupant of means. Schuylkill River water, pumped into a hydrant in the yard, was also a mark of a better property. In exchange for Croskey's demands, English secured payment terms and obligations to supply materials. The carpenter also bound himself to complete the house within fewer than three months.[1]

The agreement executed between George Croskey and Robert English typifies written arrangements for construction extant from the period. Implicit in the document is an expansive set of undertakings by English, the master builder. He would design the structure and formulate construction plans, and calculate the type and quantity of materials and arrange for their purchase and delivery. He would estimate costs and meet his estimates by driving bargains with bricklayers, stonemasons, glaziers and painters, plumbers, plasterers, and ironmongers. English's shop had to stand ready to produce—or to contract to other carpenters—the manufacture of window sashes, doors, moldings, and all remaining carpentry work. He needed to hire day laborers and carters to dig a cellar and haul trash, and he engaged journeymen house carpenters whom he needed to keep steadily at work. As the master builder, any engineering questions regarding the soundness of a brick wall or depth of the foundation were his alone to resolve. Not least among his concerns, English juggled the payment of subcontractors and journeymen carpenters against the sums Croskey advanced at each stage of building.

Complexity of coordination and diversity of tasks and skills characterize the house building trade in the antebellum era. To attain success, artisan builders had to wear many hats. As Chapter 2 has shown, access to capital through mortgages, trade credit networks, rapid land turnover, and savings influenced the financial viability of the artisan builder. Managing an enterprise fueled by such capital presented yet another challenge. Whether in a speculative undertaking or in work for a client, effective construction oversight by the master builder was crucial. Technical skill and familiarity with craft garnered over long apprenticeship proved essential. Knowledge of a wide range of materials complemented managerial expertise. Interactions with laborers and subcontractors required yet other talents of networking, superintendence, conciliation, toughness, and decisiveness.

This chapter is the first of four to focus on the organization of production in the building trades; it describes the preliminary stages of housing construction and illustrates the demands of being a self-employed businessman in construction. Integral to the artisan's life as a master were soliciting work, designing a house, drawing plans, and making estimates. Contract terms between master builders and clients comprise another episode in this tale. Speculative building has been the focus of Chapters 1 and 2; this chapter elucidates aspects common to both mechanic-initiated advance building and customer-initiated construction.

The building enterprise was characterized by diverse independent processes integrated at critical junctures, all focused on the completion of a structure. House building, to a great extent, confounds a linear description. This chapter focuses on the complicated, even chaotic task of coordinating materials, subcontractors, and laborers. Chapter 4 examines at length the materials used by builders. Chapter 5 attends to carpentry—the principal element of home construction—and examines its production within the shop and at the building site. The final chapter of this study considers difficulties and pitfalls in the trade, but ultimately brings the story to a close with the completion and marketing of housing.

George Croskey must have deliberated over his selection of a master builder. As a lumber merchant, Croskey had sold material to English for the house carpenter's other projects. But Croskey traded with many similar customers in his business, and the qualities that distinguished English remain obscure. Perhaps Croskey admired dwellings that the carpenter had recently erected. Or, perhaps English owed Croskey a debt for lumber, and the material supplier took the opportunity to strike a good bargain. While the origins of the agreement between Croskey and English cannot be known, other sources offer a glimpse into practices and relationships common in the construction industry in the early decades of the nineteenth century.

It may have been the house carpenter who approached Croskey with the proposal to build. As self-employed tradesmen, English and his peers spent many hours chasing business. The experience of carpenter William Eyre illustrates the pressures of administration and marketing in independent building businesses. Eyre spent many an evening, sometimes until 10 o'clock, away from home making calls on business or at home receiving clients and subcontractors. He offered his services to individuals contemplating buying property, visiting the sites with them to help visualize their prospective houses. He also attended to requests by potential customers for estimates, working at his desk at home during the day and late into weekday evenings to meet clients' impatient demands. While Eyre secured most of the projects that he went after, many jobs did not materialize because property titles proved faulty, customers decided not to renovate, or competing craftsmen tendered lower bids. In one particularly exasperating instance, Eyre "ascertained that [the client] had employed other persons to do his work. which is quite a disappointment in as much as several days have been spent, in calculating & summing after the Job." Eyre lamented that there were few times "when my mind can feel free from the cares & anxieties of attending a large business" and he could be "employed in the manner which pleases me best (to wit, working with tools at the bench[)]."[2]

Among those builders who came forward with estimates and proposals, the client's choice was steered by recommendation, reputation, and family and community associations. (Price, we will see, was also a factor.) The adverse experience of client Eliza Barnes exemplifies the importance of referrals. Barnes advanced several hundred dollars on a written contract with carpenter William Page, whom she engaged to put up a house. The bricklayer asked Barnes "what kind of pay Page was" (that is, would Page pay his bills), but Barnes could not verify the carpenter's reputation. Page disappeared, exposing Barnes to the harangue of uncompensated workers and subcontractors.[3]

Selection based on recommendation and association aimed to separate those with dubious intentions and fleeting ties to the community—such as Page—from those with both integrity and skill. A gentleman informed his correspondent that "I have met with a Man that I think would undertake this Building for George and probably he cannot get one more worthy of the trust from what I hear of him." David Evans likewise emphasized trustworthiness in his referrals. "[I]f thou should incline to employ a Carpenter," he wrote his cousin, "I can recommend one who for industry and honest Integrity I believe can not be exceeded . . . he is a *distant Relation* of mine *lives next door* to me." Evans, a member of the Carpenters' Company and of the Society of Friends, drew heavily on craft and religious affiliations to advance the chances of fellow artisans. His position as a director and surveyor of the Insurance Company of North America enabled him to dispense jobs, among them several to his "distant Relation." To his misfortune, carpenter John Thompson had no such associate to recommend him. Because he was "absen[t] from the City a long time" while building in nearby Bristol, Thompson "lost his Customers."[4]

Thompson deduced correctly that propinquity in a predominantly face-to-face business remained an important edge in winning customers. Even in the sprawling metropolis of the mid-nineteenth century, builders presented their portfolios to clients in person. They entertained inquiries from artisans who dropped by their shops, and they called on craftsmen whose services they required. Whenever news of a job circulated, for example, tradesmen approached house carpenter William Eyre in his shop or, after hours, in his home. "Braddock the Painter calling in," Eyre noted in one case, "we concluded a bargain for him to Paint & Glaze" the dwelling that the builder had commenced recently.[5]

A builder needed to assess the desires of a potential customer and be ready to revise estimates, drawings, and plans repeatedly in response to changes that the customer proposed. The back-and-forth of custom work had long characterized construction, though the emergence of professional designers in the early 1800s may have subtly encouraged house carpenters to be increasingly accommodating. A number of men who proclaimed themselves architects by virtue of European training—John Haviland and Benjamin Latrobe, for example—now waged battle for prominence in Philadelphia.[6] This cadre gradually assumed the design and superintendence of public and religious buildings, and expensive residences. Few architects, however, worked on common housing, though styles that they promoted influenced residential architecture. Craft, business, and design skills enabled master builders to exercise principal authority over home building in Philadelphia throughout the first half of the nineteenth century.[7]

Incorporating ideas and tastes of clients into designs was a prime task when building a custom residence. When his client requested a modification of the original house plans, carpenter David Evans responded that "I perceive no difficulty in having the fireplaces in the middle of the Chamber." He then enumerated changes to framing supports that the redesign and shift in weight entailed. In the repair of John Dickinson's house, Evans queried whether Dickinson "would Chuse the stairs with Quarter or half paces or Winders" and "[w]hether or not the Kitchen is to be below the principal Story."[8] He continued his inquiries as he played with the design, asking Dickinson for preferences and proposing ideas as an experienced house carpenter. He asked, for example, if Dickinson intended "any Dormer windows in the Roof and how many[?] I thought one on the north side over the upper flight of the Garret stairs would be useful for air and light with one 16 light window in the East Gable end may be sufficient."[9] Dickinson made suggestions as well, sending Evans "the dimentions of every particular part." He also sought the house carpenter's approbation for alterations to the scheme of the roof.[10]

The exchange between Evans and Dickinson took place in the first decade of the nineteenth century, but fifty years later, the successful builder continued to be responsive to the client's contributions. Carpenter William Eyre spent close to an entire "day in drawing plans" to build for one James McDonough, "exhibited the plans" to the client, and subsequently returned to his drawing board to integrate McDonough's criticisms. The client accepted the next incarnation of the plan, but only after "a slight suggestion of alteration." McDonough then put construction on hold, returning ten months later to press Eyre to draw "an Elevation of the house." Eyre complied immediately, rising the next morning at 2:30 to finish the graphics and "make out an Estimate." Shortly thereafter, the parties signed a contract.[11]

Eyre's negotiation with McDonough alludes to the practical as well as persuasive power of plans and elevations. Skills necessary for crafting ideas on paper that could be transformed into a tangible structure developed through instruction and experience. Surviving documents generated by building artisans show a wide distribution of literacy and numeracy, particularly among carpenters, the overwhelming majority of master builders. Apprentices to the building trades spent days in the shop developing mechanical abilities, but some also attended school at night or for a quarter of the year to acquire basic reading, writing, and arithmetic skills. One master promised his apprentice "Two years day Schooling . . . and Five Winters Night Schooling," after which "the residue of Night Schooling say Five Winters [till the apprentice turned twenty-one] to be at the expence of the Boy." Another consented that his apprentice "have as much time of winter nights to go to School as the Father wishes, he paying for the same." Only five years old, apprentice Francis Reed looked ahead to "16 quarters half days schooling," presumably three months during each winter, until his majority at age twenty-one.[12] Builders employed arithmetic beyond mere numeracy when they calculated materials and approximated their cost, and when they assessed finished work. Geometry and trigonometry aided those builders who supplemented construction with surveying land and regulating lots, that is, marking out the building lines, privy locations, and rights-of-way.[13]

A number of builders attained true proficiency at drawing. At the master's expense, carpenter Moses Lancaster sent his apprentice Charles Noble to drafting school in 1820. His apprentice Charles Conard may have also attended, affording Conard conversance with architectural drawing useful to him later as superintendent of construction for Philadelphia's Academy of Music.[14] The young men would have learned a range of " 'linear' " and mechanical drawing, perspective, and " 'practical architecture.' "[15] In 1820, however, drafting school did not so much signify a formal instructional institution as occasional classes offered by master craftsmen or by men who promoted themselves as design professionals. In the winters of 1821 to 1823, William Eyre attended "Evening Draughting School" conducted by his master, but open as well to other apprentices. Meanwhile, architect John Haviland also taught drawing in Philadelphia during this time and could well have enrolled Charles Noble in his class. Attempts to encourage training in architecture and drafting, notably by the Franklin Institute beginning in 1824 and the Carpenters' Company in 1833, got off to hesitant and sporadic starts. Often troubled by financial difficulties and staff turnover, such efforts nonetheless endured several decades.[16]

Cost determined, in part, the question of who could acquire expertise in architectural drafting. Instructors stipulated five dollars each quarter as the going rate for drawing lessons. Classes at the Franklin Institute met two quarters each year, amounting to ten dollars per annum for each student. Moses Lancaster paid Charles Noble thirty-two dollars for one year's service as apprentice; but an additional ten dollars and expenses for supplies could easily exceed the generosity or means of other masters.[17] Expense was likely a factor leading advocates of the "workingman" to fault masters for undereducating apprentices by denying them "geometry, architecture, [and] drawing."[18] Yet the training proposed was not a traditional part of an apprenticeship, and had only recently been deemed crucial to the operation of a building business.

While masters might balk at sending apprentices to classes, established mechanics themselves frequented the architectural lectures at the Franklin Institute. Publicity surrounding architects was growing in the early decades of the nineteenth century, and the conventions of drawing and design were emerging quickly. Together with an explosion of visual vocabulary, developments convinced some craftsmen that drawing skills and a knowledge of Grecian forms could enable them to compete for grand projects.[19] Discourses over architectural orders and training in drawing, however, had little relevance to the construction of row houses. When building craftsmen integrated novel styles in façades and interiors, albeit drawn from neoclassical conceits, they did not need theory to do so.

Trade manuals, pattern books, and treatises offered tutelage in drawing and architectural detail for the multitude who did not attend drafting courses. Handbooks served as references for new styles. Aimed frequently at amateur practitioners, publications legitimated the claims to status that Haviland, Latrobe, and colleagues made.[20] Comprehensive treatises found an eager audience among aspiring craftsmen as well. Specifications, material estimates, structural calculations, and design templates abounded. For the autodidact, manuals included lessons and problems in geometry. For easy reference, tables listed the stress properties of various types and dimensions of timbers. Geometric schemes for staircases of all styles, measurements for ornate moldings, and details of the "five architectural orders" filled volumes.

To prepare the master builder to supervise other tradesmen, handbooks provided recipes for mortar and plaster, methods of firing bricks, and proportions for mixing and tinting paints.[21] Guidebooks did not merely raise the status of architects or the chances of builder-architects; treatises worked as well to educate architects who lacked artisanal origins (hence lengthy dissertations on mixing mortars and erecting scaffolding). An observation that architect Samuel Sloan made in 1870 may have been more germane to the later decades of the century, but the problem he noted underlay many of the guidebooks of the early decades as well. Sloan (who spent his early adulthood as an artisan in Philadelphia) emphasized the primacy of practical construction knowledge, "without which [the architect] cannot possibly indite an ordinary specification, or give directions he will undoubtedly be called on to give to those working under him at some time or other."[22]

Access to architectural and builders' guidebooks varied. Few could rival the collection that the Carpenters' Company maintained exclusively for its membership.[23] By 1805, the Company's library held several precious treatises, among them Palladio's *Architecture* and Gregory's *Mathematics*.[24] Other handbooks, for example Pain's *Practical House Carpenter*, Haviland's *Builders' Assistant*, and Nicholson's *Carpenter's New Guide*, had fewer pretensions.[25] Builders who were not members of the Company could not borrow from its collection, but they could afford manuals such as the "Carpenters Assistant."[26] Picked up used, a carpenter could procure the *vade mecum* for one dollar. At a cost slightly less than a day's wage, trade books were not widely owned, but probably shared informally among artisans.[27] While learning the craft, a young man might borrow an instructive volume from the Apprentices Library. House carpenters on its board of managers would have seen to it that the collection contained several building books.[28]

As long as design varied little and the vernacular was widely understood, drawings — that is, elevation or exterior views — of prospective dwellings were superfluous. Few drafts of houses survive, in all likelihood because they never existed, or were so rough as to be ephemeral. Master builders had little reason to document widely known conventions. In contrast, plans — representations of the layout and dimensions of a structure, viewed from above — were important practical aids to mechanics. William Eyre drew plans for stairs, but mostly, he made "plans for framing joist . . . to ascertain the number & size of joist." (Eyre did so much work at a desk, in fact, that he decided to make himself "a new, large T square & prepar[e] a drafting board.")[29] Failing the availability of a two-dimensional graphic, a mental image outlining measurements, structural supports, room sizes, and location of doors, windows and stairs, even for repetitive undertakings, was imperative. Existence of such schemes, in the mind if not on paper, satisfied the court considering one dispute. Judges ventured that "[t]he vault, it appears, was a part of the original plan." The tentativeness of the court implied that no one submitted fully executed depictions. Rather, all parties had a general composition *in mind*.[30]

When master builders did execute drawings, they represented ideas and clients' preferences informally in the course of negotiations or construction, or in correspondence. One can imagine the extemporaneous exchange at the building site suggested by the faint and imperfect pencil lines, later covered by writing, contained in one carpenter's receipt book.[31] Similarly, carpenter Peter Crouding offered his client rough illustrations from which to select the brickwork for the façade of his house: "I send 2 patern of window heads . . . Chuse wich you pleas and pleas to Let me know as soon as you can." Distance (Crouding was in Philadelphia and his client in Delaware) compelled the artisan to put pen to paper, and to append his recommendation that "the all stone head Looks very well in a Strecher frunt."[32]

Mechanical skills embodied in training fostered an ease with visual representation among builders. When David Evans assisted John Dickinson in the construction of his house, the carpenter described the design to the client in words. Evans added that "in order to explain I have drawn a rough Scetch of the Rooms and Stack of Chimneys *which I think the mason will understand*" (see Figure 11). The sketch was not meant to benefit Dickinson (just as the text was not intended to enlighten the mason), but to serve as a means of communication between craftsmen hindered from direct conversation.[33]

Similarly, while a client might provide a verbal description, the builder would translate ideas into nonverbal representation. In 1843, landowner James Pollock drew up a "specification" on his two proposed houses. The description included the number of stories and rooms on each floor, placement and number of windows, and details of interior work. Using the specifications and measurements of the lot, house carpenter George Haas drew up a plan—that is, a sketch of the perimeter of the houses and their position within the lot. Haas's estimate then competed against those of two other builders to win Pollock's business.[34]

In Haas's case, initial exchange between carpenter and client to conform design to price considerations led to the composition of a plan. Neither Haas's outline nor subsequent competitive bidding necessitated an elevation or a rendering (a shaded or colored drawing) of the façade. Sales-

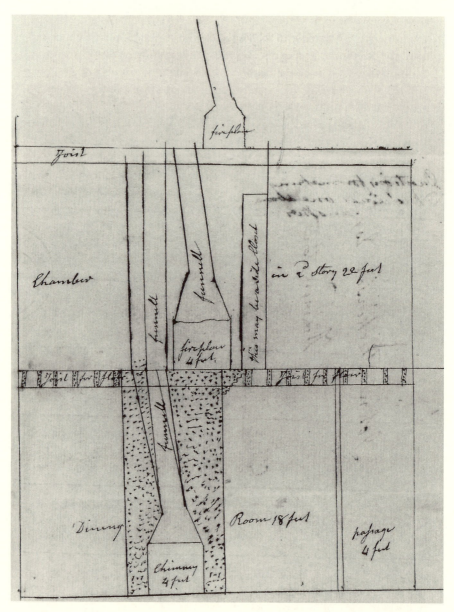

11 Mechanics communicated easily among themselves with sketches. David Evans to John Dickinson, Aug. 14, 1798. Courtesy of The Historical Society of Pennsylvania, Logan Collection.

manship, however, occasionally sparked master builders to produce impressive graphics. Thomas Carstairs, house carpenter and self-proclaimed architect, produced a plan and elevation of twenty-two row houses for merchant William Sansom. These graphics showcased the the carpenter's design skills successfully; Sansom chose Carstairs's scheme to develop his properties.[35] Self-conscious artistry, as well as competitive bidding, could have provoked carpenter Michael Pepper. His watercolor and ink drawing was attached to an agreement to build a row of dwellings, an unnecessarily elaborate inclusion for mere contractual documentation (Figure 12). Pepper sketched floor plans, indicating placement of the doors, windows, chimneys, and stairs. Above the plans, he drew a view of the façades to the same scale and included decorative elements on the exterior of the houses (the number of panels on the doors, for example). He shaded the sketch to evoke three dimensions and also washed the drawing in color.[36]

Perhaps Pepper's compliance with conceits of design was encouraged by the practices and presence of Haviland and other reigning architects. Thoughts about autonomy and craft pride also motivated artisans to execute complex images. When carpenter John M. Ogden received a building contract, for instance, he commemorated the accomplishment with a detailed plan and an elevation (Figure 13). The structures, Ogden noted proudly, were " 'the First Buildings Erected by J M Ogden In Buisness on His own acount He being 21 Years old.' "[37] William Eyre spent two days and two long evenings drawing plans and elevations, finally "colouring & shading" his work to impress his brother, the client for the house.[38]

Builders and clients borrowed extensively on the houses around them for room plans, decorative elements, and material choices. When house carpenter Samuel Copeland and his partner agreed to develop land owned by a wealthy brewer, details of the houses fell to the discretion of the builders. The partners simply promised that " 'all the houses which shall front on Tenth and Eleventh streets shall be at least three stories in height, to have marble water tables and ashlers.' "[39] Relying more on tangible models than delineated contractual particulars, the brewer stipulated only that the buildings " 'not . . . be inferior in size and quality to the houses built [nearby] by Haas and Myers.' " Caroline Mason demanded that her new building "correspond in character and appearance with the house now in process of erection on the lot adjoining." Its front was to be "in all particulars . . . the model or pattern for the erection and finish" of the second structure. David Evans referred to an extant city landmark as a negative model when he rejected slate roofing for John Dickinson's house. "[Slate tiles] cannot be made to

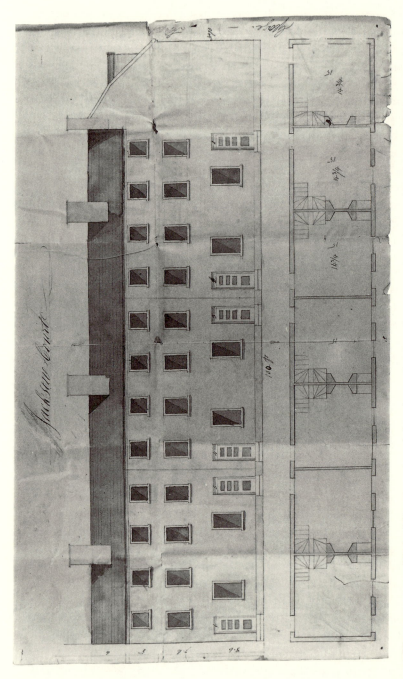

12 House carpenter Michael Pepper executed this plan and elevation in pen, ink, and watercolor to document a contract signed May 18, 1829. Client George Ewing retained Pepper to complete rental houses for "Jackson Court" in Southwark. Courtesy of The Historical Society of Pennsylvania, Society Collection.

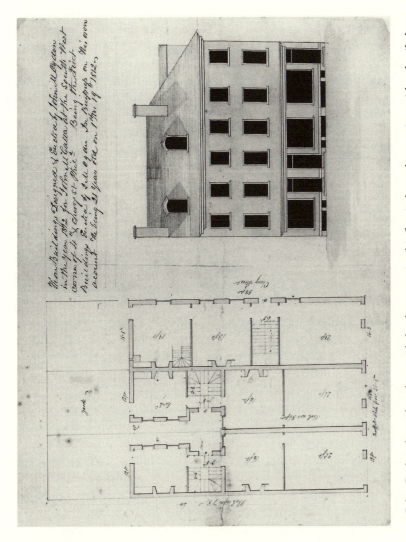

13 John Ogden showed evident pride by documenting his first independent project with a detailed set of drawings. Prints & Drawings Collection, The Octagon, The Museum of the American Architectural Foundation, Washington, D.C.

lay so close as to prevent the snow from drifting through between them and are much more expensive than [cedar] shingles. . . . Remember [the] Slate House in Second Street," the house carpenter warned.[40]

Existing structures served as standards of design and quality among artisans as well as between builder and client. In his subcontract with a master builder in 1817, Robert Flinn agreed to do all plastering of a house "in a work manlike manner Equal to the house adjoining." In so subscribing, Flinn also invoked commonly understood craft standards that only after many decades deferred to legal contractual language. Both parties to this agreement knew, for example, the number of coats of plaster Flinn's work entailed (two or three). They understood implicitly whether Flinn intended "coarse stuff" of lime and hair, or "fine stuff" of slaked and sifted lime, fine sand, and a "due quantity" of hair. The expectation of a "workmanlike" product and example of the contiguous house was sufficiently precise. Similarly, plasterers Allen and Hollowbrush consented to plaster "Five rooms and Entry Corniced" in the same fashion as the other rooms they examined.[41]

Numerous contemporaries also relied on physical models. When bricklayer Benjamin Harker engaged a carpenter to put shelves in his cellar, he told the man, " 'I want you to finish the vault, as Ware's house [next door] is.' " The artisans then "went into Ware's house, and saw the vault." [42] Painter and glazier William Haydock likewise insisted that his house be finished "with good Materials as [the carpenter] has Put in the Houses he is building on the Old York Road." So, too, did John Croman agree to paint ten houses "to be finished in the same way that those 4 houses were finished in Julian Street." Implicitly, master builder and subcontractor agreed on the number of coats and kind of tints that Croman would apply.[43]

Clarification—in writing or verbally—of the terms and schedule of payment were also critical points in building. George Croskey and Robert English spelled out the terms of compensation: the lumber merchant was to pay the builder $250 cash and $1,350 in boards and scantling. Croskey, moreover, accepted responsibility for providing materials, stipulating "the Lumber to be delivered as the work . . . progresses." Another client agreed to pay his house carpenters a total of $2,000 cash for a three-story house. The client promised installments of approximately $200 at each stage of construction, from the time the carpenters laid each floor of joists, until "[e]verything [is] ready for a tenant." Plasterers Allen and Hollowbrush negotiated that they be paid "one fourth . . . as the work is going on and the Remainder the first of the Sixth Month Next." And Robert Flinn agreed to take $100 cash "as the work is going on" and the remaining $225 upon the sale of the house, or, lest it linger on the market, "within one year after the same is finished."[44]

Artisans who neglected to insist upon schedules for payment, or those unable to extract money from a client, could lose the value of their work. Michael Barron articulated a lament common enough among building mechanics and material suppliers. The house carpenter trusted Isaac Loyd to compensate him for labor, material, and subcontracting debts he had assumed in building and in "doing sundry work." Barron complained, however, that "in consequence of [Loyd] not paying him according to his contract [Barron] was obliged to quit work and did not receive money enough" to pay his creditors.[45]

In addition to setting terms for compensation, the contract or subcontract delineated who "found" materials. Procuring one's own materials distinguished a master craftsman from a day laborer or journeyman. But agreements had to designate which party would pay for the items. Where the house carpenter engaged in custom work, he frequently advanced money for materials and labor of subcontractors, adding the expenses to his own bill. The plan was logical, since generally private parties knew little about suppliers and materials—though the plan did enmesh builders in legal responsibility for payment. (It also allowed artisans to charge a markup on materials for the trouble of arranging for them.) In 1821-22 Robert Adams charged John Beck "for materials found & for work and labour done and performed" on his house in Northern Liberties. Similarly, Eliza Barnes and her untrustworthy carpenter William Page explicitly addressed material supply in their contract. Page agreed to build at a prearranged price, "finding all the materials, and doing all the work of every kind."[46]

By the mid-nineteenth century, verbal and implicit agreements for physical models, workmanlike expectations, and payment details seemed increasingly unsatisfactory to builders, subcontractors, and clients. Hence the tendency toward contractual documentation gave drawings a meaning removed from structural and design questions. Attached to an estimate and specification, and signed by both client and successful bidder, a plan served as a legal contract—more easily scrutinized in court than oral transactions. Paper contracts clinched a precise moment that building (in the legal sense) began; groundbreaking may have occurred months later, but to establish debt priority for mortgages, as well as supplies and labor, the date of the written transaction reigned supreme. When carpenter William Eyre and his client "made & signed our contract for building" in March 1850, they did so in the presence of a witness, a real estate conveyancer. Cognisant of the law arbitrating debts, Eyre recorded that the contract was "conditioned for the execution of the mortgage before 1st proxima [April], before which we do not intend to operate." Indicative of Eyre's increasing reliance on written proposals and accords, he subsequently distinguished a bid for work on the client's house by emphasizing that the subcontractor "gave in [his] estimate verbally."[47]

The method of arriving at compensation for work varied. Client and builder locked into a specific price in a "stipulated" or "lump sum" agreement, or the parties had the finished work "measured" or assessed by an appropriate craftsman upon completion. A third alternative called for payment of the builder at daily rates. This final scheme prevailed when the craftsman was doing a variety of tasks, repairs, or alterations, or when he was superintending a large structure (e.g., a church or school). Each payment method—lump sum, measurement, and day rate—ruled the bargains between the master builder and those subcontractors he engaged.

Numerous examples of lump-sum arrangements in a variety of building crafts exist. For instance, in 1829, plasterers fixed on a total price of $550 to plaster ten houses and privies. When house carpenter Michael Pepper undertook to build eight brick dwellings for merchant George Ewing, the parties also settled on a stipulated price. At $600 per house, Pepper would not have made a huge profit, though Ewing wanted small and simple (rental) houses.[48] Stipulated sum contracts required a clear understanding of the work encompassed in the agreement. If details remained elusive under the rubric "workmanlike manner," the contract spelled them out. When one painter quoted $32.50 per house for work on four structures, for example, parties elaborated. Paint the houses "as follows," the master house carpenter likely dictated (and the contract recorded): "all the outside work including the fence Steps to Back doors and Privys to have 3 Coats of Paint the Kitchen 2 Coats inside the first Story 3 coats inside the 2nd Story & garret 2 coats in side."[49]

Stipulated sum bargains relied upon the ability of the contractor or subcontractor to predict accurately the cost of a job. The one who was engaged to perform the work carried the risk of increases in labor and material costs and the uncertainty of delays. Slow material deliveries or procurement problems, labor shortages or strikes, and structural complications added to a myriad of potential quagmires. Carpenter Abraham Strickler tallied his losses by stipulated price contracts at $900 spread over six houses.[50] Already a loser in construction "on his own account," Martin Beck agreed to "Lump Jobs" at "two other houses on which he lost about $300." Like his peers, Joseph Hughes lost money in taking on a fixed price accord. The estimate plasterer Hughes quoted amounted to only half the actual cost "on settlement with his workmen." Carpenter Charles Middleton concluded a contract for a stipulated price but discovered his miscalculation. Middleton proposed to no avail that the contract be set aside, and the final price for the house determined by measurement.[51]

Parties differentiated emphatically between stipulated price agreements and measurement. Measurement allowed artisans to charge customers (or, in the case of subcontractors, master builders) for work that turned out to be more costly or complicated than originally estimated. Craftsmen and the public alike considered this mode of assessment a means of assuring both purchaser and seller of work a just price and quality workmanship. To perpetuate disinterest, both parties to the agreement shared evenly the assessor's fee of 3 percent on the total measurement bill.

Measurement literally applied a rule to the finished work. For example, an 1817 agreement between bricklayers Pettit & Smith and a master builder attested that the partners would lay stone at one dollar each perch (a cubic foot measure) and brick at $3.12½ each thousand.[52] Upon completion, a measurer applied his rule to the foundation, arrived at the dimensions of the wall, and multiplied by the unit price (one dollar) to get the portion of the bill for stonework. Similarly, he measured the dimensions of the brick wall and deduced the number of bricks used. He then calculated a total charge at $3.12½ each thousand bricks.

Although Pettit & Smith's agreement fixed a unit price, many measurement agreements did not. For example, in 1795 Jacob Vodges undertook carpentry work in the house of Isaac Ashton. Ashton agreed to pay "fifty dollars in Cash when the Work is judged to be half done and the remainder When the Work is Measured." Relying likewise on a craft standard, painter and glazier William Haydock committed to performing $1,700 worth of work "at the Rate by Measurement."[53]

Master associations established and upheld craft standards on which Pettit & Smith, Vodges, Haydock, and others relied. The Carpenters' Company, and the Bricklayers' Company of the City and County of Philadelphia (composed also of stonemasons), had price books that designated the men (measurers) to be consulted within their associations (Figure 14).[54] Craft members zealously guarded information in a strategy to retain control over prices and, hence, income. Notably, the 1786 book of the Carpenters' Com-

	£.	s.	d.

Ditto, framed with ftuff 1¾ inch thick, finifhed with a three quarter moulding, bead and flufh on the back fide, four pannels in each fhutter, and a moulding on the raifing, per fuperficial foot, - - -   2 | -

    Thofe laft mentioned fhutters are fuppofed to meafure about 20 fuperficial feet.

    If the ftiles are rabbeted, and the back pannels nailed, as is fhewn in the plate, charge per foot, - - - - - -   2 | 8

SHUTTERS framed in two parts, and fcrewed together, making about two inches thick, bead and flufh, or pannels raifed with a moulding on both fides, per foot, - - - - -   2 | 6

if four Pannells add ¼ foot   - | 3

INSIDE fhutters, the back laps framed fquare, to fall behind the wainfcot or architrave, for windows of 18 or 24 lights, glafs 8½ by 12 inches, per fuperficial foot, - - - - -   2 | -

    If the back laps are plain, and only clamped, charge them per foot, - - -   1 | 3

    If divided in four pannels, per foot, - -   2 | 6

Ditto, with mouldings both fides of all the laps, per foot, - - - - -   3 | 3

SASHES, as common for glafs 10 by 8 inches, per light, - - - - -   0 | 7

The arch'd part of fuch fafhes, per light, - -   3 | —

Safh-lights in doors, glafs 10 by 8 inches, per light, —   1 | -

Ditto, in doors hung in two parts, per light, - -   1 | 2

The arch'd lights, at - - - - -   3 | -

    The wainfcot part of fafh-doors at the fame price as other doors of the fame fort of wainfcot.

Safhes

pany and the moderately revised 1805 version were issued without the actual prices filled in. Measurers, moreover, were enjoined from appraising work done by mechanics who did not belong to the Company.[55]

Unwillingness of the Carpenters' Company to reveal the mysteries of its trade or, more precisely, the means of arriving at assessments, went to extremes. Member David Evans captured the seriousness with which the Company took its rule of nondisclosure. Evans loaned his "book of dimentions with the price affixed" to a nonmember for consultation. Knowing he risked expulsion, he sent the book under seal. The carpenter admonished his associate that "this book I intend for thy inspection only and wish it not to be known out of thy family that thou hast it."[56] Exclusivity occasioned one rival organization, the Practical House Carpenters' Society (PHCS), to slap the more established Carpenters' Company in the face. The upstart society announced its formation in 1811 with a book of dimensions published complete with prices.[57]

Measurement standards also failed to keep pace with changing economic conditions and new architectural styles. Measurers and craftsmen had no associational guidance on the price to demand for novel work. In the case of the Carpenters' Company, no official new price book appeared between 1805 and 1831. Imagine, too, the awkwardness in assessing new construction when the Company restricted all twelve copies of the 1831 volume to use at Carpenters' Hall. So tightly held was this later edition, that years afterward carpenters continued to use "old price" when they measured work.[58] Claimants filed suit in Philadelphia's local court in 1835, for example, using a preprinted form with "old price" appearing in the printed text—further evidence of the lingering influence of the Carpenters' Company's early schedule.[59] The Company recognized the threat that the lack of uniformity in pricing caused to its reputation, cohesion, and power. In 1827 it noted that "great inconvenience has arisen . . . in consequence of the great diversity of opinion existing in the minds of many Members . . . who undertake to measure . . . Carpenters Works & . . . serious evils have arisen, & the character & high standing of this Co^y brought into discredit."[60]

14 Price books guided measurers in assessing carpentry work. In their *1786 Rule Book*, the Carpenters' Company published specifications for framing and joinery work, but omitted prices. Company members subsequently added rates and additional categories of carpentry work. Courtesy of The Carpenters' Company of the City and County of Philadelphia.

Carpenters did not readily resolve the problem of valuing new styles and housing features. Unable to wait for updated price manuals, artisans dealt with fluctuations in labor and material costs by adopting percentage adjustments. During the building boom of the 1790s, for instance, house carpenters made agreements to work at "old price," referring to the Carpenters' Company's price book. But measurers were to "advance 25" or even 37½ percent on the 1786 prices to arrive at the final bill.[61] Rapidly rising labor and material costs of the late eighteenth century yielded predictably confusing results. Craftsmen found themselves uncertain of the going rate (and some may have intentionally taken advantage of price turmoil). House carpenter Robert Jordan agreed in 1795 to work "at one price and a quarter with a fifth deduction." (The "fifth deduction" was a discount for work between mechanics, in contrast to full price between mechanics and the public.) Although Amos Yarnall and Jacob Cousler agreed to the same terms, Jordan reprimanded the partners for having "bitched it . . . because you have taken it at a price & a quarter, which with the deduction will render it to you at old price."[62] Shortly thereafter, one customer insisted that he had negotiated for work at "old price," while the house carpenters contended that their bargain included a 25 percent increase.[63]

Laggard price manuals, moreover, did not hinder mechanics from building to suit client tastes or from keeping a keen eye on designs and amenities that would make their own speculative development appealing to buyers. William Eyre, for example, scrutinized the latest innovations in residential housing. Eyre visited retailers and construction sites to evaluate various "new style[s]" of kitchen ranges, furnaces, and bath features. Immediate needs for his own building projects sometimes motivated the house carpenter, but usually he acted out of general occupational curiosity. He also spent great energy evaluating new techniques of cast iron construction for commercial buildings and traveling to New York City to look at examples there.[64]

Neither the secrecy of the Carpenters' Company nor the disclosure of the Practical House Carpenters' Society could assure the long-term survival of the measurement system. Though still healthy in the 1840s, this method for valuing craft labor was declining; it remained useful in William Eyre's time for pricing alterations and unique construction, but less practical for evaluating more standardized products.[65] (The practice today of pricing houses per square foot suggests links to an antiquated measure and value system.) Several factors account for the waning of appraisals by measure. One difficulty with the system was the lack of craft associations that represented any large proportion of tradesmen. Together, the Carpenters' Company and the PHCS represented only a fraction of house carpenters active in the nineteenth century. Other trades—plasterers, painters, stonemasons—had even fewer and less enduring associations. To whom could mechanics turn to supply a measurer that held the confidence of tradesman and client, if he carried no organizational imprimatur?

Parties might consult published sources, including pirated (and outdated) editions of the Carpenters' Company guidebook—prices included.[66] Ultimately, however, it was the stipulated price agreement that made sense when comparing bids and facilitating transactions between the master builder and subcontractor. Tradesmen shared an implicit mental computation of the work involved and negotiated knowledgeably before its commencement. That common understanding led to remarkably close bids for jobs—so close, in fact, that one project with a final price of $83,263 elicited three sealed proposals that differed by only $400. Lump-sum arrangements also served big speculative development and cookie-cutter housing. Post-construction measurement of diverse craftmanship became superfluous, and houses could move to market more quickly.[67] Similar projects by artisan builders, moreover, could draw from understandings (or misunderstandings) of previous construction. Consequently, craftsmen cast measurement aside on routinized building.

Heightened competition in the building business also contributed to the increase of stipulated sum contracting. Similar trends were at work in the nineteenth-century industrial economy as production of consumer goods rose dramatically. Merchant-manufacturers sought predictability in their price bargains with subcontracting shops as they undertook to turn out ready-to-wear clothing and showroom furniture, and then stimulate customers to purchase their wares. The lump-sum bargain—so much per piece, with the subcontracting shop assuming the uncertainty of labor management and costs—shifted risk away from the capitalist. Contractors and subcontractors, meanwhile, undercut each other in their push to win jobs and to meet price demands of manufacturers.[68]

Depending on the business climate, building mechanics bidding for jobs to produce their quickly assembled consumer wares could be pressured by clients or master builders to reduce their price. As contractors have testified, they sometimes failed to break even on stipulated sum jobs. But because masters (and journeymen) often distrusted organized efforts to set prices, they were ambivalent about retaining measurement methods. Alone, then, competitive contracting does not explain the apparent rise of lump-sum pricing; work by measurement, after all, was also undertaken at discounted rates (see Chapter 5). Rather, the practical complications and mixed interests in maintaining a measurement system, exacerbated by the fast pace of real estate development, suggest that set price contracts streamlined the process for getting houses to market. They also made houses cheaper to build, since neither the craftsman who executed the work, nor the person who commissioned it, needed to pay an appraiser. In light of the hefty amount of capital tied up until the sale of a house, speed and lower costs were powerful incentives to shift craft practices to favor stipulated sum methods.

To build a house—to visualize it, and to modify it in thought, on paper, and as it took shape—was no minor feat. When house carpenter Robert English embarked on his bargain with George Croskey, he applied years of mechanical training and experience. English called to mind Philadelphia houses encountered in his daily routines and combined features from several to meld with his client's demands. He might have consulted a trade book— John Haviland's volume of neoclassical forms, for example—to build in a style that would please his well-to-do patron.

Business and managerial responsibilities added to English's concerns with design. Croskey might have been one of the clients that English drummed up through his own time-consuming and continuous efforts to keep his operation working. Then, as master builder, English would have visited men he had worked with before and put out the word that he needed their skills in bricklaying, painting, plastering, and allied trades. Having determined what Croskey would pay for the dwelling, English probably pressed his subcontractors for their lowest price, or set them to competing against fellow tradesmen. Only if he managed costs carefully, and supervised the progress of subcontracting masters, could he complete the house within the promised three months. Starting each venture anew, the master builder combined his talents and took his chances in a complex, competitive, and multitiered building economy.

As well as master designer, manager, and labor bargainer, English and his peers were purchasers of large amounts of materials. Once he directed attention to procuring lumber, bricks, lime, stone, and the like, the master builder entered a wider regional economy. Again the master builder would test his skill at judging quality, negotiating bargains, and coordinating delivery. He would do so as a player in an industry that offered its own set of challenges and potential pitfalls.

Enterprising Nature

Materials

PICTURE A MODEST three-story brick house, seventeen feet in front, and twice that in depth. It stands among eight nearly identical dwellings that master builder James McCarter erected in 1835. The house sits in the district of Moyamensing, a fast-developing section of southwestern Philadelphia. Many sorts of people might have resided within its walls. The household of a clerk, a carter, a gentlewoman, a stonecutter, or a cabinetmaker could have inhabited its rooms, but not impoverished Philadelphians. A house like this one, in a neighborhood like Moyamensing, would have brought its seller $2,000, or even $2,500 in 1835 when the real estate market looked promising.[1]

Of the materials required to build this row house, perhaps a bit surprisingly, lumber was the major requirement. Typically, its expense contributed 20 percent to the total cost of a brick dwelling. Brick was the second major expense. Even excluding transport and laying, it accounted for 10 to 15 percent of the cost of the house. Lime for brickwork and plaster, and stone for foundation and decoration, added roughly another 10 percent to expenses. These four principal materials—lumber, brick, lime, and marble—are the focus of this chapter.[2]

McCarter and his associates faced several obstacles in getting materials. The brute muscle applied in transforming resources into housing would impress a home purchaser today. In 1835, harvesting, transporting, and converting bulky and heavy items for building materials were monumental ventures in labor and in capital. A dependence on seasons that stemmed from the innate properties of the materials and from the limitations of transportation further distinguishes this important branch of the economy of the early nineteenth century. Meteorological and climatological phenomena affected supplies in compounded ways and at a speed that producers and consumers could not anticipate.

A variety of persons supplied materials to the Philadelphia construction market. The very essence of the trade—the unpredictable variety of factors radiating from diffuse directions—did not recommend the business to the fainthearted. In addition to weather, idiosyncracies of local geology challenged the men who supplied materials. Would the clay of a site's deposit make consistently sound bricks, and how did the earth need to be tempered to suit its mineral composition? Would coal-firing destroy the market value of lime from Plymouth, Montgomery County, but serve for lime from deposits in Upper Dublin, a nearby township? Could blue marble be worked profitably, or would a white lode, even if the quarrier had to blast, yield better returns? Not only suppliers but also master builders raised these concerns with an eye toward timely delivery of materials in the most cost-effective manner. Builders selected certain suppliers over others, often for the reputations that particular lime deposits or brickyards gained.

Close local knowledge of materials developed slowly. Simultaneously, however, tradesmen had to keep pace with dynamic transformations. They introduced novel processing methods and weighed them against traditional technologies and particular attributes of local material. Mechanization varied widely across trades, as well as within specialties. Waterpowered sawmills coexisted with steam-generated establishments, and farmer-millers matched commercial lumber suppliers into the postbellum period. By midcentury, Philadelphia brickyards had adopted little new technology, relying mainly on hand and horse power. Low entry costs continued to facilitate artisan ownership of brickyards. In lime manufacture, coal-firing led to more intensive and bigger operations, but yielded stuff ill suited to mortar and plaster. Small operators competed with more capitalized concerns by gearing production for builders who continued to demand lime burned with wood. Marble was the most highly capitalized of the four building supply trades. A small number of owners established control over limited deposits, and at midcentury combined quarrying with milling the stone for market. Cost and extended family proprietorship reduced opportunities to enter the trade.

In the face of such challenges, however, new categories of businessmen experimented with alternative ways to organize industries and circumvent barriers of entry. Middlemen increased their roles in some trades, especially lumber, and derived lucrative commissions from brokering. Men tried leasing land and equipment in intensely capitalized trades; capitalists rented resources to them or subcontracted production in ways analogous to manufacturing. Hindrances, ironically, proved advantageous to a number of risk-takers. Looking for better stone further afield, for instance, they left the increasingly costly extraction of the region's depleted marble supply to older concerns.

Entrepreneurs in the material trades also lobbied authorities to develop new transportation networks. They took quick advantage of the euphoria over canals and railroads to secure contracts to build them; they then exploited them to get commodities to urban consumers. In lumber and marble, water networks improved by canals remained the foremost means to send products to Philadelphia into the second half of the nineteenth century. Lime regions inconvenient to rivers, however, found the key to competitiveness in constructing railroads. But the transportation revolution also linked urban customers to a wider market. Suppliers found themselves in competition with distant regions and diverse products. To remain successful, material men had to open new sources, continuously innovate manufacture, and adapt product lines. Despite the cumbersome character of building materials, suppliers even sought to extend markets beyond Philadelphia.

Like commercial agriculture, urban housing construction integrated the economy of the Quaker City with nearby counties. In 1835 surrounded by lumber, clay, stone, and minerals, James McCarter and fellow builders enjoyed rich raw sources for their trade. Timber used in McCarter's Moyamensing house might have originated in the Pennsylvania, New Jersey, or New York counties touching the Susquehanna, Schuylkill, and Delaware rivers and their tributaries. Of principal importance to the Quaker City was lumber from the northwestern section of New Jersey. Already by the mideighteenth century, oak, walnut, maple, ash, tulip, hemlock, birch, and pine traveled through the streams and sawmills of this vicinity to southern markets on the Delaware River (Figure 15).[3]

Choice timber disappeared quickly, and scarcity and regional competition shifted the search for it into other areas. As accessible forests declined, transportation projects opened more remote growth to exploitation. In the late 1820s, canals linked Susquehanna traffic, initially routed toward Baltimore, to Philadelphia. An Upper Delaware River tradesman worried then that his stock offered "no pine of a Quality equal Susquehanna," a wood easy to work and straight of grain. Concurrent development by the Lehigh Coal and Navigation Company facilitated shipments down the Schuylkill River.[4] Imports of mahogany from South America and the West Indies, and the coastwise trade of pine, cedar, and oak from Delaware, Maryland, Virginia and North Carolina also widened James McCarter's choices.[5]

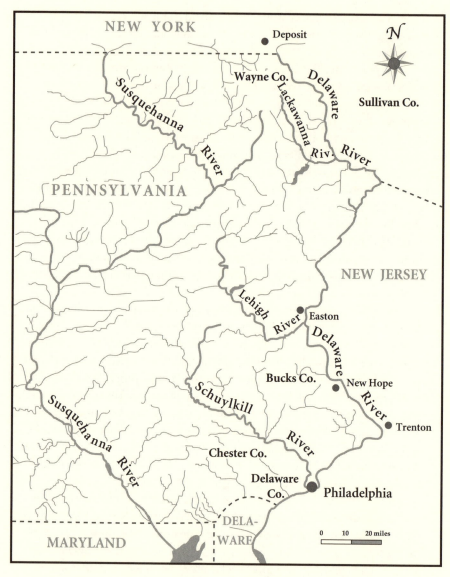

NEW YORK

Deposit

Wayne Co.

Delaware

Lackawanna Riv.

River

Sullivan Co.

Susquehanna

River

PENNSYLVANIA

NEW JERSEY

Lehigh

River

Easton

Delaware

Bucks Co.

New Hope

Schuylkill

River

Trenton

Susquehanna

River

Chester Co.

Delaware
Co.

Philadelphia

DELA-
WARE

MARYLAND

0   10   20 miles

15 Until the early nineteenth century, the Delaware River remained Philadelphia's most vital link to lumber supplies. By the late 1820s, however, canal construction and navigation improvements on the Schuylkill and Susquehanna river networks opened new timber sources to the Philadelphia construction industry.

Substantial intervals between harvest and retail sale tied up massive funds; few concerns could stretch capital and credit over the entire process. Managerial constraints (given that activities were distanced by hundreds of miles) also limited integration under single firms. Consequently, owners of timber sources, sawmill operators, transporters, urban lumberyard proprietors, and major consumers (e.g., house carpenters) functioned generally as distinct entities throughout the early decades of the nineteenth century. Sawmillers might own a portion of the timber they sawed; they also cut substantial amounts on shares or commission for other individuals. Millers arranged transport with independent raftsmen who bargained for short stints. Upriver sawmill owners depended on raftsmen or designated agents to sell their merchandise to lumber dealers in Philadelphia. Merchants, in turn, transported lumber to boardyards for storage, seasoning, and sale. A few family enterprises or mercantile partnerships sometimes supported a principal in Philadelphia to manage orders and sales. On the whole, however, the different facets of lumbering remained independent.[6]

Proprietors of sawmills before midcentury fell mainly into two groups. They were either agricultural producers or merchants with diverse commercial interests. In the Upper Delaware region, for instance, in 1835 farmers owned about 60 percent of extant sawmills. Both small and large landowners combined lumber production and other commercial milling with crop cultivation. Henry Sampson of Wayne County, near the northern border of Pennsylvania, farmed a tract covering one hundred and eleven acres. The "lumberman" also owned a quarter interest in a sawmill. Sawmilling was a lucrative business that Samuel Preston, a gentleman farmer from the same region, combined with raising crops. Lawyers, merchants, businessmen, and the like, both absentee and local, accounted for the remaining investors. From his riverside seat of New Hope, Bucks County, Lewis Coryell captured the trade of northern Pennsylvania and New Jersey. He operated or held part interest in several sawmills on the Delaware River. Trade in cotton, iron manufacturing, anthracite coal investments, canal and railroad contract building, and state banking added to Coryell's diversified portfolio.[7]

Coryell was one of three partners interested in the "Lackawaxen Establishment," a commercial operation several times more costly than that of a farm mill. In its initial phase between 1821 and 1823, building the dam, digging the raceway, equipping the saws, and outfitting the laborers with tools, rustic housing, and "spirits" amassed a debit of $2,300. During start-up, the mill sawed little lumber but drained capital reserves. Such circumstances prohibited farmers and other small capitalists from entering the business. Men of manifold assets who were partners in the concern, however, could abide the expensive wait.[8]

Ongoing repairs and replacement of equipment and sawmill dams inevitably followed initial building of the mill. For "accidents and charges arising from delays," one proprietor recommended budgeting 25 percent of operating costs.[9] After construction, operators turned their attention to keeping the supply of timber trees coming to the mill. Harvest from his own forest provided one source of raw material for the miller. Samuel Preston, for instance, had "traversed the Mountains abundance & viewed the Quantities & Situation of *my* Timber." In designating the trees "timber," historian William Cronon has observed, a miller had already abstracted nature's cornucopia into a commodity for far-reaching markets. To this end, Preston proceeded to make a running account of the profit in sending his "good Chestnut enough to make one or two Rafts," red oak, poplar, sugar (maple), and hemlock trees to market.[10]

Timber purchases were a second source vital to mills, especially to those organized principally as commercial ventures. A well-managed operation relied on continuous supply during peak season. Coryell tapped diverse channels, including outright purchase of woodlots and "cropping the timber on shares." To secure trees, he frequently trekked "up the river" or "journey[ed] to the *Poles*"—the latter a comical reference to trips to Jersey swamps for cedar trees.[11] Coryell also sawed logs that other men consigned to him, and then used his established networks to market the seasonal production of area farmers.[12]

A timber property "ritely taken care of . . . will last many years," averred Benjamin Stickney, overseer of an Upper Delaware River mill. Stickney derided his employers for leasing out timber land in return for a portion of the sale of the crop. Men without "an intrust" in the property, Stickney warned, would fell immature trees, undermining the long-term yield of the forest. "[T]heir is Pine Enough to last 12 or 15 years and do a good business and their is also a good quant[it]y of Hemlock and Oak"—but only, of course, if the owners abandoned shortsighted governance.[13]

Seasons and weather dictated the rhythms of lumbering into the second half of the nineteenth century. Producers upriver contested nature's capriciousness, while downriver in Philadelphia James McCarter contended with reverberations in prices, deliveries, and production. Climate touched each segment of the trade: chopping trees, hauling logs to a waterway or directly to the mill, sawing timber, and transporting lumber to market. Loggers felled trees in the winter, before the sap ran.[14] Crews needed "[s]now before much can be done at halling" the logs by ox- or horse-drawn chains and sleds. Mild weather could also be a problem. "[T]he Ground none froze but wet & muddy under [a foot of snow] so far it indicates an unfavourable Winter for any kind of halling Lumber," Samuel Preston lamented one December. On the other hand, freezing temperatures and abundant snow could also prove exasperating, even a quarter century later. "[T]he Snow is verry deep," explained a sawmill manager in March 1843, "and their was never known to be more ice in the River and Streemes."[15]

As late as the 1850s, Pennsylvania mills operated predominantly on waterpower. An appropriate level of rainfall, enough to release a continuous moderate flow in the race, was necessary to power a waterwheel. Along with the seasonal trends that influenced log supply, sparse precipitation shut down mills four to eight months in each year.[16] "[N]o Mills doing any Thing in these parts," Preston observed one October, and consequently "there will be but little Lumber sent down next Spring."[17]

River transportation also depended on water levels that changed with season, and snowfall and rainfall. Traders needed high water in the spring to float logs to the mill and boards to market.[18] Freshets signaled both the spring rush of water for transport and potential disaster to riverfront property (including mills) and lumber rafts. "[I]f we wait until late to Raft," a foreman warned his employer, "we may miss a Freshet and if Rafted and lay in the Water over Summer you know is a damage." While one mill-owner tallied losses from "the raft which was stuck fast . . . in the Spring Freshet," another warned "that if there comes a Fresh the People had rather run" to avoid rafts "stuck last Spring."[19] By summer, however, low water often plagued dealers and builders with long and costly delays. Waiting impatiently in Philadelphia in early May, a customer demanded that if his order "cannot be brought down by *water* it must be by *land*." The close of navigation also fluctuated (and reflected origination points). One favorable season, a Delaware County miller forecast as late as the first of December that "an open faull" would get the customer's shipment to him in Philadelphia "before Christmas."[20]

Gauged to the condition of the stream and density of the wood, the raft a miller sent to market contained generally from 15,000 to 50,000 feet of lumber. (McCarter might want roughly 7,000 to 10,000 feet of diverse woods and cuts for his Moyamensing house.) The number of feet that could be milled from one tree varied widely depending on its type, maturity, and quality. A raft this size might contain the product of 50 to 200 logs (trees).[21]

16 Lumber rafts required skilled pilots to steer merchandise from northern locations to markets in Philadelphia. © Bettmann/CORBIS.

Raftsmen stacked lumber 12 or 16 feet in length in crosswise layers, piling it to one foot or more in thickness. They lashed links together to form a raft measuring from 100 to 200 feet long, and 16 to 36 feet wide (Figure 16). In normal transport, the cut lumber that comprised the raft remained wet for a period of weeks, but nonetheless arrived merchantable in New Hope, Trenton, or Philadelphia.[22]

A crew of three to six pilots could handle a raft. Distance and raft size, and the skill necessary for the undertaking, made this phase account for approximately half the cost of bringing timber to market. For the venture in 1819, Preston complained, steersmen "talk of 40 dols for a single Raft & 60 for a double besides their Expences say 30 dols more."[23] At the piers in Philadelphia, retailers negotiated on the spot with raftsmen for the purchase of shipments. A dull market could compel crews to idle for weeks in the city. The distant miller, in the meantime, was vulnerable to the ability and integrity of rivermen to anticipate market swings, scout out buyers for his valuable commodity, and inform him of prices and opportunities. Rather than vest his trust in raftsmen, a sawmill owner might subscribe to prior arrangements with urban lumberyard proprietors who personally visited his mill, or who corresponded with him before the opening of the rafting season.[24]

By the mid-eighteenth century, producers and builders had arrived at conventions for lumber dimensions and, with less exactitude, grades of quality.[25] By conforming length, width, thickness, and quality to standards, rural sawmillers and urban lumber merchants were able to conduct business effectively over great distances. Personal networks and public avenues of market information further facilitated trade. Upriver men, such as Preston and Coryell, monitored prices and supplies through trusted raftsmen, active correspondence with associates, and print communication. Millers shared a current awareness of the state of the urban markets. A modest mill owner on the Lackawaxen in 1842, for example, subscribed to the Philadelphia *Saturday Bulletin*, as well as the *New York Observer* and the *Easton Centinel*.[26] A miller from nearby Sullivan County, New York, watched prices in New Hope (and presumably Philadelphia), declaring that "he woul[d] not raft until he know[s] w[h]at the price of Lumber was and if it was low he woul[d] not Raft at all."[27] The seasonal character of the business was both boon and bane to millers, who could predict market shortages or gluts from previous steps in production. Lumber, however, was not perishable in the same way that other agricultural commodities were. If the miller could afford to hold his boards and managed to store them properly, he could raft drier, more valuable merchandise the subsequent year.

Urban lumberyards connected sawmillers with James McCarter and other urban consumers. Lumber mercantile enterprises within Philadelphia were frequently partnerships that drew heavily on family networks and capital. Artisanal training was not requisite to advancement, and women occasionally headed yards, bridging gaps in male succession.[28] Their stewardship was of particular importance in a trade whose stock and fixtures made entering it expensive. Several thousand dollars were required for boards, lot rental, investment in "[l]umber yard Strips Horse and Carts Good will," a stable, and counting house. Turnaround was slow, as lumber needed to be seasoned for upward of one year between arrival and sale—though the onus rested on consumers, not sellers, to avoid merchandise that was "green." Because "yard Room" for storage, as one observer noted, "[c]omes high hear," lumber merchants had incentives to sell it quickly.[29] At any given time, proprietors had a great deal of capital invested in stock. Well in keeping with the typical operation was Robert McMullin's boardyard valued at more than $15,000 in 1828.[30]

At the turn of the nineteenth century, a sizable minority of former house carpenters headed lumberyards. The transition can generally be linked to career stage—for example, nearing retirement, when a man might seek respite from physical labor—and to at least modest prior success in the building trades. Many artisans in related trades saw "lumber merchant" as the occupational step above master status, or as a pursuit compatible with building. Annual income sufficient to ensure middle-class gentility—a minimum of $1,000 according to one lumberyard proprietor in 1842—also attracted venturers.[31]

For men with little capital, however, entry and persistence in the trade increasingly meant creating intermediary roles in the lumber commission business. The "Commission Merc[h]ant," a broker explained in 1843, found buyers, reported sales to the owner, delivered the goods and collected bills. The name partner in David B. Taylor & Company demonstrated the potential of commission sales. Taylor had once amassed wealth through lumber trading and milling, but lost it all and filed bankruptcy under the federal law of 1841. A few years later, he "com[mence]^d the Sale of Lumber in a sm[all] way on Comm^n." In 1856, an R. G. Dun agent estimated the firm's worth at about $40,000.[32]

Henry Croskey (a young man who inherited his father's lumber business after his mother safeguarded it) reputedly introduced consignment operations to the Philadelphia market in 1842. Croskey systematized sales of Lehigh and Susquehanna shipments, and thereby altered distribution and wholesale organization of the trade. The merchant "made it known throughout the lumber region that he was prepared to receive consignments of lumber on commission and attend to all the details of sale as agent for the owners." He offered to exchange the personal relationship and product-specific knowledge raftsmen had with millers, for his own expertise in urban commercial markets. Over the next two decades, the method succeeded in placing wholesale dealers at the forefront of the commission lumber business. Traders charged a cumulative 7 to 10 percent for handling, insuring, and selling lumber. In addition, they advanced credit to milling operations to finance new machinery, further guaranteeing them the production of associated mills.[33]

Enough mills conformed quickly to Croskey's system to make him and many of his followers enormously wealthy. By 1875, Croskey was thought to be worth in excess of $250,000. Thereafter he no longer based his success on sales of actual lumber, but on "Lumber paper." Croskey captured the quintessence of a capitalist: he moved from retail lumber sales, where he made his profit directly from the product, to commission trading, where he extracted his gain from his activities as intermediary. Finally, Croskey severed connections to the product itself and enjoyed his profit from the speculative opportunities of a commodities market.[34]

Croskey's innovation in the commission business took advantage of increased lumber production and new regional supplies. After 1835, millers markedly advanced output. Successive modifications to the milldam and log carriage throughout the nineteenth century reduced leakage, harnessed more power, and augmented the speed and number of saws a mill could run. Improvements in waterwheels and sawing technology lengthened the milling season and increased cutting efficiency. By 1850, the average water-powered sawmill had nearly doubled its production.[35]

Erratic waterflows owing to seasonal and weather variations long restricted locations of mill sites. Developments in steampower transformed that dependence. Where streams could be harnessed, and as long as timber was available near water, incentive to install costly fuel-consuming machinery was minimal. The expense of steampower worked against the comparative cheapness of water mills and the ability to integrate seasonal milling with agriculture. Even gradual adoption, however, accelerated deforestation. A water mill sawed about two to four acres of trees per annum, or one hundred acres over twenty-five years. A steampowered mill processed logs at more than three times that rate. Slow consumption and the costs associated with hauling, moreover, led water-mill owners to bypass small trees in favor of mature growth. Whereas the older practice encouraged the natural regeneration of forests, the expense and singular focus of steam-powered mills drove investors to clearcut entire tracts before abandoning a location.[36]

Steampower also caused a shift in the personnel engaged in milling, diminishing the role of farmers and extending the sphere of commercial investors. To install machinery run on steam and to move it every eight years (the point at which surrounding forest would be consumed) added great expense to an enterprise. Because a steam engine could run year round, moreover, an establishment employed two crews of men working simultaneously—one in the field getting the materials to the mill, and the other sawing logs.[37] Continuous ventures required constant attention to labor management, operating capital, repairs and technological upgrades, sales, and transportation. Steampowered mills called for full-time professional oversight.

To guarantee a steady supply of logs to an undertaking with high equipment costs and full-time labor force, investors sought to eliminate seasonal transport problems. They lobbied aggressively and successfully for river projects and contracted for railroad construction.[38] Railroads had minor immediate impact on the lumber trade as a means of conveying product to market. In depleting raw materials, however, rail construction during the 1830s and 1840s, and contemporary plank road building, drove local demand. Improvements in sawing efficiency, and the lure of markets for railroad and plank materials, eventually yielded outputs beyond the ability of millers to raft the commodity to market. By 1872, an estimated 40 percent of Upper Delaware lumber found its outlet by railroad. Nevertheless, the bulk of material continued to be carried by river even in that late period.[39]

The retail end of the lumber trade in Philadelphia also became more capital intensive. By the mid 1830s, planing mills competed with lumberyards by subsuming both features—stocking and processing—into one enterprise. In 1835, house carpenter James McCarter could choose wood from a yard and cart it to a planing mill to be tongued and grooved. He could also buy directly from Mark Richard's planing establishment, which incorporated both functions. Richards bought "boards in the rough—sawing, stripping, planing, ploughing, and grooving them." Commercial experience unrelated to the lumber industry characterized the experience of many planing millers. Richards began as a novice to the trade shortly before 1834, already "extensively engaged in cotton manufacturing in Philadelphia . . . also in the making of iron." A $70,000 loan he procured to finance iron manufacturing speaks to the capital Richards and like investors in planing could marshall.[40]

The cost of such a venture—the machinery for planing, patent assignments to use it, and litigation to defend exclusivity—surpassed that of a traditionally organized lumberyard. In 1837, rights to a planing machine with tonguing-and-grooving capability sold for $10,500—a sum excluding the expense of building the apparatus (upward of $3,000). In 1850, the steampowered planing mill of George B. Sloat in Kensington reported $50,000 invested in the business. Purchasing white pine lumber, Sloat was able to produce flooring valued at $200,000. Long-established yards, even if they chose to innovate, labored under high entry costs and restricted access to new technology.[41] Proprietors guarded rights to Woodworth's Patent Planing Machine in particular, an act which apparently enabled one holder to amass a fortune of $300,000 in a few short years. His son benefited from technological oligopoly as well and was able to "plane boards cheaper than others." [42]

Capital consolidation in sawmilling and retail lumberyards took shape gradually and was by no means complete by the time of the Civil War. Indeed, the stalwart survival of farm sawmilling throughout nearby counties and of small lumber concerns within Philadelphia testifies to the staggered pace of industrialization. The direction of the change, however, is evident. In forest cutting and milling, as well as retail lumberyards, the capital threshold of entry rose severalfold in the antebellum years. Capital demands precipitated mainly by technological innovations squeezed out or barred most small entrepreneurs. Standardization of quality and dimensions worked in concert with the rise of commission traders and wholesalers. By midcentury, the efforts of these parties facilitated further integration of production and distribution in the trade. Fewer farmers diversified agricultural production by milling, and fewer house carpenters translated craft experience into lumber retailing. Rarely did either farmer or building mechanic run a planing mill. When builders did venture into the lumber business, they did so as middlemen.

*   *   *

Second to lumber, brick was the principal material in row houses like that of carpenter McCarter's. Bricks could be manufactured locally, minimizing transportation difficulties and costs. Clay, water, and sand composed bricks; quality varied with mineral content, characteristics of additives, and proportion of ingredients. Throughout much of Philadelphia, a bed of clay lay dispersed within twelve feet of the surface, and (more so in some areas than others) made strong bricks of limited porosity that were durable and incombustible. [43] Even after two centuries of exploitation, a geologist observed in 1898 that the county's bed of clay made more bricks than "any deposit of equal size in the United States, and it is still producing at the rate of more than two hundred million bricks per year." [44]

Brickyards and their clay pits were located on the periphery of Philadelphia's more populous streets and were relocated outward as they exhausted superficial deposits on rented lots and as the city expanded. (By 1850, Philadelphia brickmakers had spread as far as the New Jersey side of the Delaware River to mine clay.) Holes from clay extraction readily served as the beginnings of house cellars, and proximity of the yards to areas of development saved effort and money in carting bricks. [45]

Mechanics raised to the trade predominated as owners of brickmaking establishments. Peter Grim, in business by 1814, was patriarch or near relation to generations of brickmakers. J. & N. Grim, H. & J. Grim, S. & G. Grim, and B. & J. Grim each owned yards in Philadelphia county in 1849. Similarly, the Lybrant family—George, Michael, Christian, and others— operated yards from 1800 to 1850. Though by dint of trade and training they were craftsmen, brickyard owners were, like their lumberyard counterparts, capitalists. After generations of family proprietorship, successful brickmakers commanded wealth comparable to accomplished merchants.[46]

Bricks took seven steps to produce: digging, weathering, and tempering the clay; then molding, drying, burning, and sorting the bricks.[47] The season usually lasted seven or eight months in the year, from early April to early November. Beyond this period, the "ground is [too] damp and the weather unsettled" for making brick. In tribute to the determining influence of daily weather, accounts juxtaposed meteorological information with summaries of yard production.[48]

The yard of Nathan Sharples located in West Chester, a growing town in nearby Chester County, illustrates the processes and personnel of brickmaking in 1828. Sharples employed two "gangs," each composed of four men: a molder, a temperer, a wheeler, and an offbearer (the latter probably a boy in his teens). In molder Henry Gill, Sharples got an experienced foreman to take "charge of the yard," and he paid him accordingly.[49]

Although labor customs demarcated work, all members of the gang contributed to the first stage of production, digging clay. A man in Sharples's employ might dig 2,000 to 3,000 feet in a day, depending upon his strength and the condition of the ground. A crew of four would need approximately three days simply to dig the earth contained in one of James McCarter's houses.[50]

According to a process believed to make quality bricks, gangs dug earth in the early winter and left it exposed to weather before use in the spring. Describing a widely endorsed practice, one brickmaker counseled that clay "will be easier to work, make better brick, and burn smoother by having been frosted and exposed for two or three months." Periodically, laborers turned the material and relieved it of rocks and other impurities. Frosts and rains worked to break up the clay and wash away salts. Winter and early spring digging also eased some of the seasonal unemployment typical of construction work.[51]

After at least one winter's exposure, the clay was tempered. The yard's temperer directed the mixing of clay with a balance of sand and water to make it pliable, give it the desired color, and enable it to burn properly. (Philadelphia clay required little or no additional sand.) With the intention of easing the mixing, the temperer put the clay in a vat or "soak heap" overnight. Sharples's men, for example, were engaged in "throwing up a Soak heap for tomorrow," to be churned with the aid of a shovel. As late as 1898, while other regions used steampowered apparatus, Philadelphia yards favored turning the heap with a horse- or ox-drawn wheel pulled around a central pole (a ring pit).[52]

Positioned near the tempering vat, a wheeler transported the clay to the molding table, where the molder threw it into rectangular forms.[53] The molder, the most skilled member of the group, set the pace for the entire crew and determined daily production. Minus the temperer, the offbearer, or the wheeler (or "working three handed") manufacture was handicapped —though Sharples's gangs still reached 60 percent of the daily target of 2,500 bricks. Absence of the molder, however, paralyzed production. "Henry sick and all hands Idle" or "Henry had a sore thumb & the men did not work," Sharples lamented on some fine brickmaking days.[54]

The offbearer conveyed the filled molds to open space in the yard, where he emptied them carefully onto the ground. Bricks remained there about a day until dry enough to be turned on edge. Each worker then participated in moving the bricks to open-sided sheds and stacking them for further drying. If the weather turned wet before the bricks could be thus protected, the product of two or three days lay ruined. For example, whereas one day Henry Gill's gang made twenty-four rows of stretcher bricks (totaling 2,500 bricks), they "did not get them in" before a downpour. An estimated 15 percent of bricks drying in yards succumbed to damage from rain.[55]

Depending on weather and clay, bricks dried in two or more days. For burning, the gang piled them systematically in temporary or permanent kilns (the former built with the bricks themselves). The men took care to place each brick so that air circulated and created an even burn. Sharples's kilns typically numbered over 80,000 bricks—enough for two of James McCarter's Moyamensing dwellings. A single house would use all the bricks that one gang produced in an entire month.[56]

The kiln was then partially closed and fired at a "slow burn" (250 to 350 degrees), which steamed water off slowly to avoid excessive shrinkage. Once the foreman judged that adequate evaporation had taken place, the men sealed the kiln and raised it to a red heat (about 1800 degrees Fahrenheit), where they kept it for several days. Supervising the operation at

Sharples's yard, Henry Gill and two assistants passed the greater part of five days and nights at the kiln. Laborers not employed in watching and feeding the fire, meanwhile, engaged in "digging kelly [clay]," doing odd jobs, or "keeping holiday."[57]

Skill and experience told in the firing. Attendants learned to recognize temperature and water content, for instance, from the nature of emissions in the initial "water-smoking" and subsequent "blue-smoking" stages. Witnesses reconstructed the degree to which firing bricks entailed a mixture of experience, judgment, and guesswork. A laborer at one burning recounted differing interpretations: "Thos Cook said the brick was too much burned and Ja^s Hayes said they were not burned enough." Hayes prevailed, feeding the fire for another few hours, at which point participants volunteered additional contrary views. "Jacob Hillman said they were not burned Jn° Hillman said they were burned." At Sharples's yard, Gill's management occasionally failed, a kiln "bad attended and [bricks] badly burnt."[58]

Once the kiln had cooled for several days, the crew sorted the bricks by firmness and color. Grades depended on intensity and uniformity of the burn, and, thereby, on placement of the brick within the kiln. One customer complained to a yard owner that "a great part of the bricks [I have been] receiving from you now are much too soft and will not answer." The brickmaker's partner linked color, a result of the intensity of the burn and the mineral content of the clay, with the inferiority of their product: "[D]one [don't] send any Light . . . Brick nothing But dark [red] ones. . . . [I]f you send light ones we are dammed."[59]

Though law did not regulate size and quality, artisanal practices developed a basic classification system. Lowest quality bricks were "chuff" and "place" bricks, underburned and unfit for building construction. "Salmon" bricks burned too soft to withstand exposure, but could be used in interior walls. Common stock emerged sturdy though slightly imperfect, whereas face (or facing) and stretchers appeared more homogenous in hue and form, and answered for the façade of a building. "Paviours," yet a harder, better contoured, and more uniformly colored facing brick, usually commanded a few dollars per thousand more than common stock. Typical of the grades produced in one burn were the four kinds (stretcher, paving, "hard," and "Salmon") that Michael Fox sold direct from a single kiln.[60]

A product subject to so many variants, however, did not conform to precise grading. In 1800 a carpenter apprised his client that "Mr Fox Mr Liburn [Lybrant] and Maney others" sold bricks at "6½ Dollars," but Mr. Crips demanded a higher price for wares of a "superer quality." The carpenter confirmed that "[b]rick Leyars & oners that have had brickes from Mr Crips saise that his Bricke is worth ½ Dollar Pr Thousand More then the Comon Run." What made Crips's bricks "Ginarely sound" and able to "go More then that much farther in a building"?[61] Before buying or leasing a lot, a brickmaker bored into the ground to examine the earth. Crips likely found particularly "strong clay," well suited for brickmaking, on his premises.[62]

Prices for bricks, quoted by the thousand, fluctuated each building season. Between 1790 and 1850, common grade ranged from $5.50 to $10 per thousand. Collusion may have accounted for somewhat consonant pricing. Before the start of the 1798 season, carpenter Peter Crouding observed that "the Price of bricks is Not yet fixed upon by the brick makers." A few weeks later, his tour of several yards established that brickmakers stood firm at $6.50 per thousand. In 1800, the carpenter again watched the market. "[M]oney is very scarce and wood plenty Proveble bricks may be Cheaper afew weekes will Determen."[63] Within the building season, prices also fluctuated. Another brickmaker explained that "it is allways understood that Bricks increases in price in September and October and November in every year and so continues untill New Bricks are made & Burnt the Next Spring." Scarcity was particularly acute in 1828, he suggested, "[f]irst By Reason of the General prevailing sickness amongst the Labouring men Last summer and fall [cholera?] and [second] by the increased demand for Bricks" owing to a strong building market. "[T]he master Brickmakers" consequently fell "Short of their Calculations of the quantities they were prepaired to have made."[64]

Three principal factors affected brick prices: demand, supply, and production costs. Usually production costs are subsumed in models of supply and demand. Under the volatile conditions of the industry, however, and with decisions made early in the production process, these three elements functioned somewhat independently. Brickmakers could often do little more than wager a calculated bet to match supply with demand. They attempted—and Peter Crouding's remarks would indicate some successes—to keep market forces alone from controlling prices. Like other material suppliers, brickmakers took their cues from the local building cycles. Manufacture of bricks, unfortunately, did not respond immediately to fluctuations in construction, but lagged behind demand by nearly a year. If the yard owner allocated insufficient labor to dig earth the previous fall, he might miss a lively market in the next building season. Conversely, if the brickmaker excavated more clay than he used the subsequent year, he would have spent scarce resources on labor needlessly. From the perspective of Moyamensing builder James McCarter, then, abundance of rain, shortage of fuel, pessimistic market expectations of brickmakers, and shortage of labor could solely or in combination escalate prices the builder anticipated.

Could brickmakers predict production costs? Relative to lumber enterprises, entry costs for land rents and equipment were low. In Philadelphia County in 1820, most yards invested between $500 and $1,000 in rent, tools, kilns, shedding, carts, molds, and the like. In the late 1840s, manufacturers could outfit a yard for a similar amount.[65] In contrast to fixed costs, however, operating expenses in this highly labor- and fuel-intensive trade were enormous. Novice brickmakers—and their creditors and laborers—had to endure several months before income from sales could catch up to the need for circulating capital.

Labor amounted to roughly 60 percent of the cost to produce bricks. For instance, Peter Benner employed six men and two boys in his yard in 1820, and paid upward of $1,300 in annual wages—more than 60 percent of his "contingent expenses." Thirty years later, wages continued to account for between 50 and 70 percent of production costs.[66]

The sheer muscle involved in the industry can also be gleaned from the number of workers in the trade. A minimum of 600 men and boys in 1810 toiled at brickmaking in the county. Representing approximately 3 percent of the white male population ranging in age from sixteen to forty-five, this force composed about 5 percent of the mechanic population of Philadelphia County. In 1810, yards were concentrated within or near the boundaries of the city; brickmaking thus provided employment for an even larger proportion of laborers in the built-up sections of Philadelphia. By 1849, nearly 2,000 laborers worked in the trade—a number augmented by 300 teamsters who hauled for the brickmakers. A striking feature of brickyards continued to be the number of workers in one enterprise. While most male producers still labored in small shops, high concentrations of workers characterized brick industry sites. Many yards in the later years employed about twenty-six men and boys; a half dozen ran on more than 50 laborers each.[67]

Next to labor, cord wood was the second principal expense of brick manufacture. As late as 1850 wood accounted for approximately 30 percent of the cost of production.[68] Sharples carefully noted the amount necessary to burn each kiln, usually 25 to 27 cords, or nearly an acre of forest. (Bricks for McCarter's eight houses would destroy four acres of woods.) Fuel consumption was fairly regular in comparable climates. One tradesman spoke from experience and grasped the concept of marginal costs, however, when he averred that "the more brick that are burned, the less will be the expense per thousand."[69]

As late as 1850, wood remained the overwhelming choice as fuel for brickburning. To compensate for extensive forest depletion near Philadelphia, the commodity was shipped from northern New Jersey and the Chesapeake region. One source estimated in 1849 that production of the year's bricks used over 38,100 cords of wood (equivalent to 1,360 acres of forest depleted in one year alone). Supplying fuel added laborers to the already sizable force busy in the yards. The 1849 account asserted that "[t]his will give employment, at 10 days to a trip, for a fleet of say 43 vessels, from the 1st of March to the 20th of November, the time they are usually employed by the trade."[70]

Brickmakers reported a range of achievement at their enterprises. In 1820 George Lybrant estimated his annual expenses at $3,950, and the value of annual production at $4,620. Lybrant was disappointed, despite a profit of $670 (nearly 15 percent above costs and more than twice the yearly income of a journeyman bricklayer). He complained that bricks had "declined in price and demand within the last 4 years at least 30 percent"—a statement echoed by other brickmakers following the panic of 1819. William Stinemetz conducted his trade on a scale slightly smaller than Lybrant. He held an acute sense of his unit costs, indicating that he made twenty-five cents per thousand bricks—which accrued him only $175 profit in 1820.[71] A better building economy improved profits considerably. A brickmaker expected to "clear on two kilns, if they can be sold each season, at least $1.75 pr thousand, and perhaps as much as $2.25" at 1844 prices.[72] A few years later, a number of proprietors reported gains of close to 40 percent on their endeavors.[73]

By the time of the Civil War several machines for brickmaking had been patented across the nation. To address outlay for fuel, innovators in regions other than Philadelphia experimented with a mix of anthracite coal and wood. (They found that alone, coal did not properly burn bricks.) Others continued to use wood fuel, but tried to reduce the overall amount consumed in the burn. By midcentury, some brickmaking machines took stiffer clay, thereby reducing the moisture to be evaporated in the firing process and decreasing time spent at this stage. In the 1860s and 1870s, kilns distributing heat more evenly claimed to increase efficiency of the burn.[74]

Far less innovation occurred in the Philadelphia trade than in brickmaking elsewhere in the country. The most popular innovations in Philadelphia yards were brick presses. The "Press Brick" Samuel Fox manufactured in his yard in 1838 was hand molded, but squeezed a second time to make a denser, more regular product with cleaner corners. Such presses cost only one or two hundred dollars.[75] Given the relative simplicity of the apparatus, it did not create the technological monopolies of planing mills; Fox's brother James indicated widespread use of recent machinery. James instructed Samuel that "[t]he Press that G. Read had was made by Bisell the man who built ours you can learn from him. If its the same that Bobb has the [patent] right of get that one of Saml Winnakers and have it done up [and sent to me in Natchez, Mississippi]."[76] Brickmakers thought of presses, operated by hand, as simple instruments, easily replicated, imitated, and modified. This perspective explains why, while omitting mention of the machinery in the census of 1850, several yards nevertheless listed "pressed brick" among their merchandise.[77]

While innovators elsewhere contrived diverse steampowered molding machines by midcentury, most Philadelphia yards molded by hand as late as 1898. The nature of clay deposits goes a long way to explain developments in the trade in Philadelphia compared to other regions (for example, New York's Hudson River Valley). While Philadelphia's deposits were widespread throughout the county, Hudson Valley clay beds were concentrated to depths of a hundred feet or more. Philadelphia's high-quality clay also contrasted with the Hudson Valley substance suited only to low-cost common bricks.

Geological factors in the Hudson Valley encouraged investment in stationary equipment and production in mass quantity. As early as the 1820s, several brickmakers experimented with mechanized processes; throughout the postbellum Hudson Valley, tempering, molding, and pressing were done with the aid of steampowered equipment. In Philadelphia, however, the comparatively rapid exhaustion of a clay bed induced brickmakers neither to purchase land nor to invest in expensive technology. Nonetheless, owing to the composition of the city's clay, Philadelphia yards turned out superior bricks in many grades. They even shipped large quantities to builders in Brooklyn and New York City who could not procure satisfactory wares from the Hudson Valley. As architectural fashion by midcentury embraced uniform façades that Philadelphia bricks could provide, the city's establishments took the lead in the national market for pressed brick.[78]

Expensive machinery and exclusive patent rights, thus, were insignificant to Philadelphia brickmaking in the nineteenth century. So were economies of scale. In 1850, yards that employed as many as seventy or one hundred men made no more bricks per hand than yards of twenty men. Indeed, a worker in either of Philadelphia's biggest establishments actually made fewer bricks than his peer in a yard with twenty men, suggesting that there may have been *disadvantages* (managerial?) to large concerns. Even when 1850 enterprises are compared with those of 1820, a worker's productivity did not improve; the number of bricks a yard hand made in 1850 matched his output in 1820.[79] Managerial concerns (and a firm's circulating capital), however, may not alone account for why some yards remained modest in size. Nature of clay deposits—depth, purity, and consistency—influenced the number of men an establishment would engage.[80]

Owing to localized manufacture and the widespread availability of superficial clay, the nature of brickyard ownership in Philadelphia at mid-century had not changed radically from earlier decades. Small yards competed with large ones. Mechanic brickmakers, however, did not enjoy exclusive dominance of the trade. Low entry costs and the limited number of mechanical innovations that kept the door to proprietorship open to mechanics also tempted a range of other artisans and noncraft entrepreneurs, particularly in strong building climates. In 1848 alone, for example, one south Philadelphia brickyard passed through the hands of a tailor, a carpenter, an entrepreneur in the anthracite coal trade, and a prominent "brickmaker by trade." Another party in this concern had various experience, including a decade spent in the iron business, in tax collecting, and in an agency "for a Western firm to collect moneys of an Estate" in Philadelphia.[81]

Nonmechanic enterprises did not match the longevity of artisan establishments. When operations floundered (as the experience in 1848 south Philadelphia suggests), men without roots in the crafts tended to seek other prospects. The resilience of once-failed brickyard owners, on the other hand, captures the continued path to leadership in the trade that mechanics enjoyed. Of the seven Philadelphia brickmakers who filed for bankruptcy in 1842 and 1843, four again headed their own yards by 1849.[82] In nineteenth-century Philadelphia, brickmaking remained the province of family proprietorships and family dynasties, and of entrepreneurs with roots in a mechanic's trade.

* * *

Bricks would have been of little use in James McCarter's houses without mortar to bind them together. A geological belt that stretched through eastern Lancaster County to the western half of Montgomery County held rich deposits of limestone. Burning caused the stone to calcinate and crum-

ble into a powder, or "quicklime." As early as the 1690s, the abundance of
lime, more so than that of clay, contributed to the pervasiveness of the Philadelphia brick house.[83]

Lime was primarily a fertilizer, and kilns dotted farms in the region.
Along with meadow land, a watercourse, a mill, and timber, a Chester
County seat typically advertised "a good conveniency of burning lime" and
a "good kiln thereon built."[84] Important as a flux in iron production, lime
complemented the valuable lodes of ore in the valley. But lime was also basic
to mortar for brick and stonework, as well as plaster. Building consumed
lime in huge quantities. At least 4 to 5 percent of the cost of a brick house
was spent on the substance, though the statistic masks the sheer volume applied. The exemplary house of James McCarter needed about eight wagon
loads (280 bushels) of lime and twenty loads of sand for brickwork alone
(that is, not including either mortar for foundation stone or interior plaster). McCarter's entire row of houses consumed about one eighth of the
annual production of a typical small limeburner.[85]

In preparation for burning lime, stone had to be procured. Limeburners either purchased quarried rock or employed laborers to extract it
from their own tracts. Laborers quarried throughout the year in operations
that did not burn lime. Concerns that quarried and burned dedicated the
winter months to digging stone to feed the kilns as soon as the weather
warmed (spreading out demands on labor). Cold temperatures must have
made quarrying an unpleasant livelihood; snow and ice made it an unreli-
able one.[86]

Winter also caused difficulties for regulating kiln temperatures and assuring proper burns, and low temperatures required additional fuel. Burning, therefore, began around the middle of March and continued until early
December. A "*good* man," suggested one quarry owner, "can burn at least
once a month or 12 Kilns a yr. or more." Most one-kiln operators of his acquaintance, however, burned closer to eight kilns—placing their own considerations and knowledge of conditions above those of the landlord.[87]

In addition to stone, kiln operators contracted for, or cut their own
wood for fuel. Expense of cordwood was about fourfold that of stone.[88]
Contemplating rapacious consumption, lessee Jacob Smith extracted from
his kiln's owners their promises to supply him with fuel. Limeburners also
bought wood leaves (rights to cut trees) or timber tracts on an ongoing
basis. Upper Dublin (Montgomery County) limeburners in the Fitzwater
family bought more than one hundred parcels, including numerous woodlots, during the first two decades of the nineteenth century.[89] A lime pro-

ducer who owned timber stands could be confident that he would have abundance of fuel. But woodlots also served as speculative commodities that could rise in value and be sold or traded.

Like brick burning, loading and firing the limekiln required skill gained from experience. Sizes and arrangement of stone, and the interspersal of fuel, influenced distribution of heat and burning time. Monitoring the appearance of smoke, the attendant guarded against overburning, a result that rendered the substance unfit for mortar. Qualities of the limestone and fuel, and drafts in the kiln, provided a narrow temperature range for well-burned stuff, and relied on the competence of the burner. A burner would come to know the peculiarities of deposits over time, but even moving from one enterprise to another within a township required adjusting for differences. Not surprisingly, then, the vast majority of producers had longstanding local roots, and frequently continued an enterprise in which family networks passed along proprietary knowledge.[90]

Intense heating of lime resulted in quicklime. Quicklime dried rapidly, and used in a brick or plaster mortar, had to be applied shortly after the heating process. If not spread immediately, it was transported in a powdered form and later "slaked" or hydrated with water and mixed with sand, creating a cement. Prepared lime lost plasticity within a few hours; thus the bricklayer or plasterer generally slaked quicklime at the building site.[91]

Organization of lime manufacture derived principally from the nature of the deposit. In Abington and Upper Dublin townships (Montgomery County), rock excellent in quality lay close to the surface (Figure 17). The two-man force typical of an Upper Dublin producer in 1820 managed quarrying, hauling, breaking stone, and loading and attending the kiln. As late as 1850, a small operator retained three hands, ran one kiln, and in one year produced lime for thirty to forty houses. Although known as lime merchants, many of these producers integrated quarrying and burning with farming (for their families, but also to provide food for hands). Kiln proprietors assigned agricultural tasks to laborers when such needs took precedence over lime operations (and vice versa).[92]

In Upper Merion and Plymouth (Montgomery County), quarriers extracted blocks for building alongside rock for burning. One Plymouth quarry owner described the ideal undertaking in his search for a tenant. "[P]erhaps I can Lease the Quar[r]y to some responsible Person who may see his way to engage in the Stone Trade & burning Lime in the Kiln too," he mused. His tenant could then "put a new sett of hands to work in [the] Quarry to dig Stone by the 'hundred' [perch?] & the filling of the

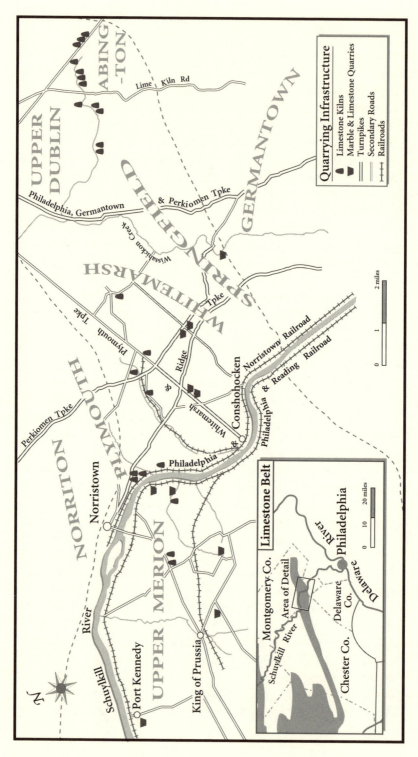

17 Southeastern Pennsylvania lime and marble industry, circa 1850. After Smith & Wistar, 1849.

Kiln would not be much to him having teams enough on hand or at Command."[93] In Upper Merion and Plymouth, in contrast to Abington and Upper Dublin, abundance of lime and its marketability as building stone warranted a large "sett of hands." The quarrying and burning establishment of Nathan Rambo, for example, engaged forty men who extracted 32,000 tons of stone in 1850. Rambo sold 20,000 tons of blocks for building, as well as 200,000 bushels of lime. John Kennedy's operation employed forty-five laborers and quarried 33,850 tons of stone. Though he concentrated on limeburning, manufacturing more than twice the yield of Rambo's kilns, he still sent 1,600 tons of blocks to market.[94]

In Whitemarsh, where the rock was of the best quality for building stone, limeburning remained a minor activity to capture the value of quarry waste. For example, Robert Potts ran a marble quarry and steam sawmill in the township in 1850, between which he employed eleven men. A limeburning operation with one kiln and two hands burned stone rejected from Pott's other concerns. Potts used the lime in his iron manufactory.[95]

By virtue of early good luck or shrewd purchases, a few dozen families dominated the premier limestone deposits in the region. The Fitzwaters and Tysons, for example, produced major quantities of the substance for colonial and early national markets. The Corsons entered the field late, but combined land and financial resources with newly built railroad systems in the 1820s. The result—a major lime operation—continued as a family business until 1972.[96]

These families did not, however, continuously undertake limeburning themselves. Rather, owners frequently leased some or all of their quarry tracts and kilns, and stipulated a monthly rent and a royalty on each bushel (and frequently an annual production quota). Consider Benjamin Albertson, who owned land in Plymouth, but lived in Philadelphia. "I transcribed the *Lime advertisement*," Albertson reported to his brother Josiah, and "took it to the U States Gazette." In the city, Albertson kept a general store that proved instrumental in transacting lime sales that the publicity generated. The Philadelphia shopkeeper instructed Josiah to "make arrangement for Somebody"—he suggested lime carters in the employ of various Plymouth kilns—"to call daily at the Store for orders." For his trouble, Benjamin expected a percentage of sales made on behalf of Josiah, neighboring lime merchants, and "my Kiln & tenents." Josiah Albertson, meanwhile, collected debts owed his brother, recounted problems at the quarry, swore out warrants against delinquent tenants, and recommended new ones who would keep the "Quar[r]y *well* cleaned."[97]

Ownership of lime quarries and kilns placed Benjamin and his brother in an advantageous economic, commercial, and political position. Benjamin Albertson's interests required some attention, and he anticipated substantial return. "Isaac Jones . . . offers to Lease my Quarry," he informed Josiah. Jones agreed to pay "½ ct a Bushell & will Burn not less than 100,000 Bus per yr. = this will be $500. per Annum to me," Benjamin calculated. The quarry (and kilns) Jones leased comprised only one of Albertson's properties. Moreover, Benjamin, Josiah, and associates lobbied actively for railroad construction to eliminate "the slow and expensive mode of get[t]ing [Plymouth lime] to Market by waggons." They helped secure a charter for the railroad and turned that political coup into economic opportunity by contracting to build a main section of track.[98]

Many limeburners, then, produced on rented land and in rented kilns. Some scraped by, burning the minimum number of kilns the landlord allowed. They fit limemaking into the demands of agricultural production, and bartered field labor with the landlord to pay the kiln rent.[99] But leasing could also gain tenants a profitable trade. Consider Plymouth limeburner Abraham Marple, who in 1836 already rented at least three kilns from Josiah Albertson. When a property of Benjamin Albertson's became vacant, Marple eagerly applied to rent it as well. Benjamin informed Josiah that when "asked if [Marple] intended to give up any of thy kilns—[Marple] said no—that he intended to Carry them all on." Josiah was shocked by Marple's aggressive confidence and protested that the tenant "would have his hands too full." Marple countered that he would hire more laborers. He argued that he could disperse his fixed costs, such as the horses and wagons already employed, over a greater number of kilns.[100] Thus Marple's rental of quarries and kilns, generating capital gains for landlords through his care and sweat, proved a thriving concern for him as well.

With leasing, an entrepreneur did not require capital to buy all means of production. Landlords or previous tenants might already have constructed kilns on the property (though kilns needed regular replacement), and quarrying and burning on shares could return enough to purchase and operate one's own property. Thus, starting out as a renter might eventually make an operator a man of wealth.[101] The partnership of Swartzengrover & McInnis exemplifies the lucrative possibilities for entrepreneurs beginning with little capital. Initially, the firm leased a quarry. In spite of its location on the Norristown Railroad, it was "not con[sidere]^d a profitable investment though the working fully pays its way." That any improvements to the site "cannot be taken away" seems to have inspired Swartzengrover & McInnis to purchase its own property. Savings of $2,000 and credit of more than $8,000 enabled the concern to buy a second but "Valuable Quarry," situated advantageously on the Chester Valley Railroad. The firm owed its capital and credit to the success and connections cultivated as a leaseholding lime manufacturer.[102]

Technological developments in lime production failed to exclude small operators, though changes did restructure the trade. Similar to brickmaking, innovations focused on reducing costs for fuel. As early as 1815, limemakers in the Delaware Valley region began burning anthracite to benefit from its greater efficiency. In Upper Merion by 1850, a kiln using coal could be burned at nearly half the cost of one consuming wood fuel. Although coal led more easily to overburning, and consequently increased the skill demanded of the attendant, savings in raw materials enticed producers to switch. Savings in labor resulted as well; a coal fire maintained its temperature longer and rendered night watches extraneous. Since coal burned at a higher temperature, a kiln also finished jobs more quickly, enabling the producer to get more quicklime to market in reduced time.[103]

Availability of canal and railroad connections influenced adoption of the fuel. By 1850, limeburners in Upper Merion used coal exclusively; their quarries lay conveniently along the Philadelphia and Reading Railroad. Higher coal prices and limited supply in Abington and Upper Dublin led producers to alternate the fuel with wood.[104] Chester County limeburners similarly paid higher rates for coal. In 1835, wealthy quarry owner John R. Thomas voiced support for a Downington-Reading rail line. He argued that the railroad "will enable us to get the fine Coal suitable for Lime burning at so low a rate as to be able to furnish that valuable article at about 8 cents a Bus[hel]." Reduced production costs, Thomas wrote his state representative, would allow Chester County burners to "send [lime] to the Phila Market as cheap as the people about Plymouth &c [Montgomery County]."[105]

Transportation alone did not determine the choice between coal and wood fuel. Limeburners also burned with both because each fuel yielded lime of different attributes. Builders and their customers continued to insist as late as 1849 that "for the Brick work they want *wood burned* Lime."[106] They did not object to lime for all elements of construction but, rather, for mortar. Thus tangible distinctions, as in plasticity or strength, and not conservatism, ruled their decisions. Farmers seem to have advanced no objections to coal-burned lime fertilizer; its lower price—it was about four cents per bushel cheaper—recommended it. Regions with reputations for lime of outstanding quality (from excellent deposits) weighed consumer demand in their choice of fuels. Most lime merchants in Plymouth township, for example, continued to send both wood- and coal-burned lime to market as late as 1850.[107] They differentiated their products according to the diverse requirements of the builders and farmers who bought them. Others, such as producers in Upper Merion, did not compete with Plymouth suppliers to the construction trades. Instead, Upper Merion specialized in cheaper lime for agricultural and allied uses.

Coal fuel encouraged a shift toward consolidation of kilns under one operator and toward the maintenance of full-time labor for ongoing manufacture. Burners in major limestone areas in reach of coal supplies shifted production to reap the benefits of continuous kilns. They built several draw or coal kilns on the same site; as they filled and fired one, another completed its burn and was emptied. Robinson Kennedy, who operated a quarrying and limeburning business in Upper Merion, ran nine coal-fueled kilns with a labor force of sixteen men. William Kennedy, probably a kinsman, managed six kilns and twenty-five men. In 1850 with yet another Kennedy quarrier (John), these producers averaged $11,000 in capital invested and over $26,000 in sales.[108] Nevertheless, owing to the nature of deposits, differentiated products, transportation routes, and the frequency of leasing arrangements, the lime trade at midcentury featured small and large producers exploiting both old and new technologies.

*   *   *

Within a small area of Upper Merion, Plymouth, Whitemarsh, and Springfield townships in Montgomery County, limestone had crystallized to form white and blue marble deposits.[109] The earliest opening of a marble quarry in the region occurred sometime around the American Revolution. Reading the architectural evidence, local marble production had its heyday from the 1810s to the 1840s. Major buildings were constructed in the city of Philadelphia with Montgomery County stone. Girard Bank, completed in 1798, is an early instance. The Merchant Exchange (1832) is also a prominent example. Besides building blocks, the stone was also hewed into fireplaces, mantels, exterior ornamental work, and gravemarkers. In the eighteenth and nineteenth centuries, this rock supplied the material for the signature doorstep of the Philadelphia row house. In 1835 when McCarter was building, the marble doorstep was a familiar feature on even modest accommodations.[110]

The Hitner and Lentz deposits illustrate the personnel and processes of the marble trade in the early republic.[111] Like many holders of quarries, Daniel Hitner's fortune rested on a serendipitous land purchase by an ancestor, from whom he inherited property in the late eighteenth century.[112] Over the next few decades, Hitner made his fortune by leasing out the quarry. While tenants assumed the financial risks of extraction, Hitner reaped enormous benefit.

Sometime before 1814, Hitner leased part of his land to his son-in-law Abraham Weaver. The quarry had already been extensively excavated, as shortly thereafter its depth was estimated at 160 feet. Abraham Weaver died in March 1817, leaving unexpired time on his lease. He named brother William his executor. William Weaver had diverse experience by the time he assumed the trust, but none of it was in quarrying. He had ventured into shipping, cotton manufacture, and was then extensively engaged in iron production in Virginia. Executorship served him well. He earned management commissions and invested his brother's estate in his cash-poor iron business.[113]

William Weaver also turned to a nearby quarry which had been operated by John Lentz until his death in 1812. Abraham held a lease on the Lentz property, but he had not yet worked it. The year following Abraham's death, William ran both the Lentz and the Hitner quarries. But the Lentz site, owing to the quality and bedding of the stone, returned little profit. Weaver had the good luck of selling the lease, machinery, and tools for $1,250, though an experienced quarrier had first refused to pay even $500 for them.[114]

The buyer, John White, was a blacksmith who had worked at both sites. Upon acquiring the lease, White immediately brought a partner, Andrew Trollinger, into the venture. Trollinger contributed critical assets. Both Abraham Weaver, and later William Weaver, had employed Trollinger to cart stones to market in Philadelphia, and Trollinger's teams did the same for the partnership. By the following spring, White abandoned the business, which Trollinger conducted on his own until his insolvency in 1822.[115] For the next few years, the quarry lay idle. It reverted to the owners, and a Lentz son then operated it until 1841. Subsequently Catherine, the wife of the deceased John Lentz, opened the quarry intermittently according to demand for building materials. Each time the market quickened, Catherine "again commenced to work the [quarry]." She "continued the direction thereof until her death" in 1844.[116]

None of these individuals sought these opportunities, but rather stumbled into quarrying through a series of events. Once a quarry property presented itself, however, each readily invested energy in the exploit. William Weaver's role as executor and his wide business experience inclined him to continue the Hitner lease. John White's employment as a blacksmith enabled him to cultivate some knowledge of the trade (though it was inadequate to judge the stone well). Catherine Lentz gained a chance the way most women in the early republic could—by marriage. Like women in the lumber business, Lentz's role administering her late husband's estate compelled her to maintain its value by working the quarry.

Others sought quarry tracts more aggressively. Artisans trained in stonecutting, for example, saw ownership or rental of a quarry as a means of furthering craft independence. Firms founded on shared management, locating one principal in Philadelphia and another at the quarry, commonly arose among stonecutters.[117] Christopher Hocker and Peter Fritz—a halfbrother and former apprentice of Hocker—divided the responsibilities of their business. Hocker superintended the marble quarry, while Fritz managed sales at the yard. Hocker asserted that the arrangement " 'was to be the means of affording . . . a vent for his marble without imposing on him the necessity for seeking it, and a place of deposit in Philadelphia, under a party interested, in whose fidelity reliance might be placed.' " Fritz, for his part, secured lucrative contracts to supply and lay the stone for the Arch Street Theater and the U.S. Mint.[118]

Beyond imperatives of management, capital needs also played a vital role, regardless of the background of the entrepreneur. In the cases of both the Hitner and Lentz properties (and recalling arrangements in the lime industry), rental agreements minimized capital requirements of undertakers. Hitner's tenants paid him a third of proceeds, and Lentz's tenants paid a flat fee on each cubic foot of marketable stone.[119] Although extraction on shares could cut radically into profits, outright purchase was expensive. In 1817, for example, a one-third interest in an eight-and-a-half acre quarry, improved for extraction, sold for $4,050. Christopher Hocker paid $15,400 when he bought an improved twenty-acre tract in 1826.[120]

Fixed capital also figured into costs in both rented and purchased properties. In working the Lentz tract, William Weaver had a machine constructed to hoist blocks and rubble. At a cost of approximately $500, it consisted of a timber frame supported by more than a ton of wrought and cast iron.[121] To position the apparatus securely atop the quarry, Weaver ordered "Blowing [blasting] & filling up to place the Machine on." Hoisting boxes, pulleys, blocks, ropes, and chains were also required. Moreover, "[t]here were crow bars, augers, picks, hammers, Sledges, Shovels with all the tools necessary for working a quarry." "Sheer[s] for Loading," or a simple system for lifting the marble blocks onto wagons, and a horse and cart for use on the site, added to the investment.[122] Tallying these expenses, the minimum equipment cost for opening a quarry amounted to about $1,100.

Once machinery and tools stood in place and overburden had been cleared to expose valuable rock, extraction could begin. "After the picking and boring [of channels] was done," according to John White, the quarry superintendent "would direct the manner of cross-boring, and lay out the size of the blocks." Laborers could dislodge soft marble with crowbars. For hard stone, the men drove iron wedges, or wooden wedges wet to expand in place, into the bored holes between the base of the outlined block and its bed. Pressure from the wedges would split the marble and detach it from the base.[123]

Quarrying demanded skill at the level of assessing the potential of a lode and in superintending extraction. Joints and rifts, which caused the rock to break more cleanly and pliantly in certain directions, influenced the methods and cost of production. The foreman had to recognize the bedding plane and the grain (and their continuation below the visible surface) to bring about easy splitting.[124] Whereas stonecutters could apply craft training to oversee the process, novices had to overcome their ignorance. Abraham Weaver (and William Weaver after him) relied on foreman Charles Faust, who "understood the beds of the marble and Shewed it to the quarrymen."[125] Faust undoubtedly knew the local deposits and had worked with the veins in nearby quarries. He exhibited critical technique in blasting, so as to avoid damage to the "high price Marble" and reap the most from the expenditure. Blasting in the Lentz deposit particularly, owing to the bedding, "uncommon hardness and strength of the stone," drove costs high.[126] John White suggested that an expansion of the quarry by blasting ran at least twice that of a similar procedure on the Hitner property. An effective superintendent, however, "blowed [a quarry] deeper, and got out more marble, with the same picking and labor."[127]

Under William Weaver, "the Quary was pushed as hard as it could be in order to get as Much Marble as possible and as many hand[s] put into it as could work with advantage." Weaver's optimal labor force numbered more than twenty men who, under William Weaver's oversight, must have had little rest. In the Hitner quarry, Weaver "[went] down with his blowing" so quickly that he "threw a part of his Spawls [waste fragments] down on one side . . . because the Hoisting machine could not hoist them out as fast as the blowing was done." Weaver's management raised additional challenges. "[T]here was a great deal of water in the [Lentz] quarry, which had to be hoisted up," John White recalled, and a culvert made "the whole front of the quarry" so that teams could cross over the break.[128]

For whom was quarrying profitable? John White asserted that the Lentz quarry "could not alone have been profitable to the estate" of Abraham Weaver—"At least we did not find it profitable ourselves." The problem lay in the stone, which proved "hard, close grained and Strong" and only "about middling" in quality.[129] White and Trollinger, moreover, chose unfortunate timing in entering the trade. By 1818, building construction had already slackened, and in 1819 depression began.

The Hitner quarry, which produced a more valued white marble, was clearly a lucrative affair. William Weaver estimated expenses at forty cents per foot, which presumably included labor (but excluded rent). Much of its stone sold for a dollar or more per foot. Proceeds for one period (whether one year or four years is not clear) amounted to nearly $30,000. As per the terms of the lease, William Weaver paid Hitner $9,500 for a third of the profits of the quarry.[130] As in lime manufacture, both tenant and owner could make large sums in the industry.

The Hitner and Lentz properties, like the area's other quarries, sat conveniently near the Germantown-Perkiomen and Ridge Turnpikes. Roads for which limestone quarriers lobbied successfully in the late seventeenth century served marble producers as well.[131] Horses carted marble some fourteen miles into Philadelphia. Each stone weighed approximately 150 pounds per cubic foot, and hauling entailed formidable animal muscle. Teamster Thomas Morgan, for example, owned five heavy wagons "used for hawling Marble, with the Blocks and chains used with the same, and Fifteen team horses with all the Gears collars &c." Andrew Trollinger, who hauled for two quarries, had upwards of twelve horses.[132] After improvements made the Schuylkill River navigable between Norristown and Philadelphia, tradesmen also sent marble downriver by special flatboats.[133]

Because stone risked damage in transport, laborers only roughly shaped blocks at the quarry site. After initial "ripping" and "slabbing," hand dressing would be completed at the stoneyard or at the building site in Philadelphia.[134] Milling represented another option for readying marble for its markets. In 1796 James Traquair and John Gullen, stonecutters, purchased a paper mill near the Falls of Schuylkill in Philadelphia County. The partners converted the establishment to a "Marble Saw Mill" with "Sawing Utensils." As late as 1814, James Traquair's sons operated the concern. The Traquair family also worked quarries in Montgomery County and sent blocks by the Ridge Turnpike to be sawn by waterpower and sent to the Traquair yards in Philadelphia.[135]

By the 1820s, mills for sawing marble had greater capacity, flexibility, and speed. In 1826, Samuel Wood established a mill "for sawing marble . . . calculated to drive upwards of 100 saws" by wheels and shafts, and reputedly capable of cutting slabs of any thickness.[136] By 1830, Wood's mill enjoyed the advantage of 174 saws to handle "the rough and shapeless mass" of blocks taken directly from the quarries. The Schuylkill River at Norristown powered the machinery. From the riverfront location Wood transported slabs by canal to Philadelphia, and "without the [expensive] addition of the refuse parts." Moreover, the machinery allegedly cut "fifty slabs with only the attendance of boys and one man, while an individual with the hand machine [saw] would complete one." Marble slabs used as veneers on buildings, one commentator predicted, would even revolutionize Philadelphia's housing market: "[I]n a few years, we anticipate it will confer no particular gentility to live in a marble house."[137]

At least initially, quarry operators used hand labor alongside the new mills for marble processing. Hocker & Fritz, for example, continued to employ manual labor to saw stones but simultaneously sent materials to Wood as a merchant miller. He processed the stone and sent it on to Fritz in Philadelphia. Hocker & Fritz also patronized the mill of Nathaniel Linnard, a venture probably akin to Wood's.[138]

Just as marble quarriers included practitioners from outside the stonecutting ranks, in processing stone (cutting, dressing, polishing), entrepreneurs from outside the crafts entered the trade. Prior to his marble mill venture, for example, Samuel Wood ran a white lead factory in Norristown and was in partnership with a cotton mill owner. Years later, the census identified him as an iron manufacturer.[139] Like William Weaver, Wood had no direct experience in quarrying or stonecutting before his milling interest.

Over time, artisan stonecutters such as Traquair and Hocker & Fritz lost ground to entrepreneurs like Samuel Wood. Craftsmen had difficulty securing quarry properties, and at the simpler tasks, their marble yards had to compete with stone mills. Four factors account for their near disappearance. First, marked appreciation of quarry lands threw the expense out of the reach of craftsmen. Consider the quarries, later known as "Cedar Grove," that Christopher Hocker bought for $15,400 in 1826. In 1854, a corporate entity—the Pennsylvania Land and Marble Company—purchased them for $100,000.[140]

A second reason for the failure of artisan entrepreneurs to compete reflected the nature of marble deposits. Whereas lumber stores grew through-out the region and could be replenished over time, quarry tracts were finite and concentrated resources which remained under narrow control. At any point in time, only two dozen or so enterprises existed in the marble trade. The business, moreover, was lucrative into the 1840s, and leases stayed within families. For example, Robert Potts, who ran Cedar Grove, was the son-in-law of Daniel Hitner.[141]

Third, artisans could rarely raise capital sufficient to finance steam hoisting machines, milling equipment and, by the time of Civil War, chan-neling machines. Extraction costs became increasingly capital intensive as concerns exploited quarries more deeply. Robert Potts, among others, ap-plied steam to hoisting blocks from his quarry—accounting for part of the $10,000 capital invested in the business. Many quarry owners had additional income to fund improvements. Potts had managed a lucrative dry goods wholesale business in Philadelphia before acquiring marble tracts. As his father-in-law had done, he also pursued iron manufacture.[142] Costs and as-sets could be shared among interests. Consider Cedar Grove, owned by the Pennsylvania Land & Marble Company and operated by Potts. While "un-covering [the] Marble Quarry," the company found iron ore "of a g^d quality in sufficient quantity to about pay the expence."[143]

Fourth and finally, similar to the consolidation of lumberyards with planing mills, quarry operators began to integrate extracting with process-ing at their sites. Potts ran a steam sawmill, capitalized at $7,000, which produced $13,000 worth of sawed marble (nearly three times its value if left as blocks.)[144] His thirty-five-year-old brother-in-law Daniel O. Hitner in-vested $18,000 in a marble quarry and steam sawmill. (Hitner's real estate, meanwhile, was assessed at nearly $80,000.) By integrating mining and mill-ing, Potts and Hitner captured the profits of processing for their quarries. But of course this step required even greater resources, and small entrepre-neurs had slim hope of entering the marble trade. Nor could artisans easily back into the business from the processing end; the sum required to do so in Philadelphia in 1850 was prohibitive. Edwin Greble, for example, laid out $68,000 for a steam marble works, while another entrepreneur claimed his sawing and manufacturing operation to be worth $45,000.[145]

Unfortunately for some Montgomery County quarry owners, how-ever, investment in immobile property locked them into a shrinking ven-ture. As better marble from New England arrived in Philadelphia, Mont-gomery marble failed to compete for higher end uses. By midcentury, those who retained Montgomery marble sites increasingly retooled their "quarr[ies] of Inferior Marble" to manufacture lime.[146]

By the early 1830s, artisan entrepreneurs unable to gain a foothold regionally turned their energies to investing in Massachusetts quarries. Marble mason Findley Highlands, for example, was partner in a Philadelphia yard and also held an interest in a leased quarry in western Massachusetts. Similarly, several firms that were committed heavily to marble manufacture moved to assure supplies of raw materials. They formed companies to quarry in the Berkshire Mountains of Massachusetts. Some also imported Italian stone.[147]

Three scenes in a lithograph made for S. F. Jacoby & Company capture the consolidation necessary for marble manufacturing at midcentury. In one frame, the artist depicts Key Stone Marble Works at Conshohocken (Montgomery County). A hoisting crane lifts stone slabs, sawn at the site, into a canal boat. A second frame details the Bay State Marble Works of West Stockbridge, Massachusetts. Here, marble is loaded onto railroad cars. The "Marble Depot, Chestnut Street Wharf" wraps the two frames together. At the Schuylkill River dock, slabs and blocks are stacked on the wharf, ready for additional finishing, or for wholesale and retail sale out of S. F. Jacoby's Philadelphia operation (Figure 18).[148]

Thus the story of marble quarrying resembles that of other material supply trades that fueled Philadelphia construction. Early in the nineteenth century, a mixed group of entrepreneurs characterized the industry. As operations became more capital intensive, older businesses (many initially family-based) able to marshall diverse assets predominated. Firms that exercised tight control over an exhaustible geologic resource particularly remained strong—so long as raw goods were mostly local. New entrants from artisanal backgrounds rarely pushed into the field. When they succeeded, craftsmen did so mainly by introducing new supplies to the Philadelphia market.

*   *   *

The pace of mechanization and consolidation differed from one material business to another. Distinctions offer an important reminder of both the diversity and the gradual nature of industrialization in nineteenth-century America. Of the four trades discussed, marble illustrates the most pronounced mechanization. Brickmaking, on the other end of the spec-

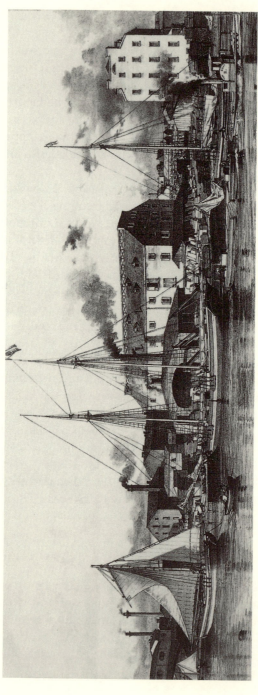

18 Marble businesses such as that of S. F. Jacoby & Company built formidable enterprises that looked beyond the region for raw materials and engaged in both quarrying and processing operations. In this scene depicting its Philadelphia location, special boats transport stone to the city to be sawed and prepared in the steampowered mills lining the wharf. *Marble Depot, Chestnut Street Wharf, S. F. Jacoby & Co., Importers & Dealers in Foreign and Domestic Marble / J. K. & M. Freedley.* W. H. Rease, artist, printed by P. S. Duval, ca. 1850. Courtesy of The Library Company of Philadelphia.

trum, retained nonmechanized production methods and, owing to relatively low entry costs, artisan ownership. The intrinsic nature of raw materials, moreover, greatly shaped the trades as well as the pace and direction of technological change. Brick, lime, and marble production also depended on particular knowledge that was passed through generations of family enterprise or gained through years of experimenting and contending with local resources.

New ways of organizing capital—or, perhaps, older ways employed more widely—emerged in some sectors. Commission brokers became central to lumber merchandising in the space of one or two decades. As middlemen, they gained their livelihoods by forging networks of lumber producers and wholesale consumers. In time, they influenced mill production and developed markets to trade on lumber futures. Producing materials on rented premises also emerged as critical in trades where high capital costs and finite availability of raw resources restricted artisan or entrepreneurial mobility. In the lime and marble business, venturers typically paid rent and a charge for each kiln burned or block extracted. Tenants in building supply trades engaged their own laborers, managed operations, and struggled to meet production quotas dictated by agreements with landlords. Landlords gained a return on capital through the exertions of tenants and laborers their tenants engaged. Working on leases yielded success stories in the lime and marble business. Generally, however, consolidation of marble extraction and processing, and coal-burning of lime, minimized the viability of small producers.

Building material suppliers also sought to shape transportation developments to tap remote resources, overcome seasonal and geographic obstacles, and compete with producers in other regions. Watercourses, however, remained the premier means of sending raw and partly processed materials to mills and thence to Philadelphia markets. Tradesmen often placed canals and navigation improvements, therefore, at the top of their priorities. Only in lime production—and in a different manner in marble—did railroads make an appreciable difference before 1860. Kilns in regions too remote from track continued to send lime by horsedrawn wagon until this period, but found the cost of hauling prohibitive. Big concerns located adjacent to railroads could get fuel inputs and lime to market more cheaply. In the case of marble, regional sources continued to rely on river transport. By the 1830s, rail links with the northeast enabled entrepreneurs to bring superior marble from Massachusetts and vie with local production.

Entrepreneurs in the supply trades discovered innumerable challenges in nature's variety and nature's capriciousness, and in labor management, processing, and transportation. Constructing his Philadelphia houses, James McCarter dealt with material availability. Within a few months of conceiving building plans, freshets, lack of snow, or little rain could make lumber scarce and expensive. A wet spring, labor shortage, sickness in the city, or conservative predictions of brickmakers could bring few bricks (at high prices) to market. Scarce cordwood and coal fuel could plague lime-burners, leading to disruption in quantities. Any number of these characteristics could derange supplies of marble as well. Together, unpredictable and swiftly changing factors affected the price, abundance, and quality of building materials as McCarter and his peers went about their work. While dynamic conditions in construction opened opportunities, they could as easily precipitate the failure of a builder's project—and his career.

FIVE

"Windows Sashes & Sundry Other Light Things"

The Production of Carpentry Work

ON NOVEMBER 5, 1803, house carpenter Joshua Sharples left Philadelphia to spend the winter in his native Chester County. He took up residence with his brother Benjamin, and—as the mechanic confided in his account book—on November 8 he "began to fit up a bench to work on and other necessary preparations." Two days later, having readied the makeshift shop, Joshua Sharples "began to Work."[1]

Sharples was familiar with work, so why note the day that he commenced to labor at this craft bench? His care suggests that the sojourn marked a transition in his life. In 1796, an apprenticeship to an urban house carpenter attracted Sharples to Philadelphia. In January 1801, just a few months after his twenty-first birthday and the formal end of his training, the young artisan began a rough accounting of jobs, earnings, and purchases. In the city he worked for daily wages and assembled doors and windows for payment by the item. Though a journeyman, he snapped up small subcontracts or "jobs"—work arranged by task rather than time. Wider in scope than piece work (which was also a form of task labor), jobs might be rewarded in the "lump" (for a stipulated sum) or as measured carpentry.[2]

"Jobbing" enabled Sharples to make tentative inroads into master's status. Early in 1802 or late in 1801, for example, he earned £60 ($160) for "finishing the inside of a house in Wood St 15 by 16 three St^y with a Kitchen 12 by 14 two St^y." During the next spring, he earned £37 working ninety-two days at daily wages for master carpenter John Smith. For a house Smith was erecting, Sharples shaped "sundry window frames Shutters and Sashes" (joinery he likely completed between January and March). Piece work netted Sharples £25. He turned up additional subcontracts in the spring and summer, for instance, one to "[finish] a lower St^y at Keyser & Gorgas house in second St," undertaken jointly with a fellow carpenter, and another for "work done at Joshua Smiths new house in Wood Street in Co with W Bunting." Spanning less than two years (and possibly as little as one), wage work, piece work, and small subcontracts provided Sharples a minimum income of £220 ($290) for each year.[3]

Gains whetted the appetite of the young mechanic, especially for remunerative subcontracts and buildings he could construct for his sole profit. Sharples's stay in Chester County spared expenses during the slowest season of construction; while there, he renewed contact with two sisters and a female cousin, each of whom lent him money. Bent over the workspace he equipped at Benjamin's, the carpenter might also have made joinery at piece rates for various builders, or for his own upcoming projects. Finished carpentry—doors, window sashes, shutters, paneling, trim, molding, baseboards, and chair rails—required clean cuts. Tight fits with mortise and tenon joints, gluing, smoothing, and decorative treatments made joinery a time-consuming and frequently repetitive task, ideally suited for months when winter weather impeded outdoor construction.[4]

Sharples returned to Philadelphia in 1804, prepared to take aggressive steps to secure craft mobility. He saved from the proceeds of "jobs," piece work, and day labor, and he added rapidly to his stock of tools. In 1803 and 1804, he spent $55 to buy joinery planes (ogee, ovolo, bead and bench planes, and one "Plaine for working ballasters" for stairs), gouges, chisels, gimlets, and files. Investing in tools, Sharples could work on his own and hire assistants. During 1804 Sharples made several short visits to Philadelphia, and in the fall of 1804, the house carpenter "Rented a Shop." Conscious of the significance of the event for his autonomy (and to remind himself to pay his landlord), he recorded the exact day—October 5—in his book.[5]

Engaging work space coincided with preparations for Sharples's first independent project, a three-story brick house on Eleventh Street near Market Street. In December 1804, the mechanic bought 600 feet of plank and spent the winter converting it into sashes, doors, and window frames for the dwelling. Throughout 1805, he shepherded construction's numerous stages, engaging specialists for bricklaying, plastering, painting, papering, tinwork and ironsmithing. To finance the $2,000 the house cost, Sharples swapped work and promises of future carpentry for labor and materials, and borrowed money at interest. To meet everyday expenses and demands for cash, he pressed on with minor business.[6]

Labor, however, was now shared by a small and fluid contingent of assistants that Sharples retained for his own construction site and for the contracts he secured. Brooks Matlock, David Davis, and Malan Jackson, all journeymen carpenters, worked for Sharples at various times during 1805; their punctuated employment reflected the master's tenuous hold on independence. Sharples paid principally cash wages, but also with tools, "sap boards," Irish linen, hardware, and ironmongery—items leftover from construction or tendered to him by clients and contractors. By late October, his house was sufficiently finished, ready for a tenant; Sharples rented it out for $190 per year. Though he had erected it, the dwelling was more expensive than one the carpenter would have inhabited, had he then been married with a family.[7]

Buoyed by success, Sharples repeated the formula in subsequent years, combining subcontracting, repair work, and building for clients to finance houses on his own account. Increasingly, he transformed profits into labor power, hiring a number of journeymen at the height of each building season. To finish a house for Lydia Johnson, Sharples retained four men (and occasionally more hands) in the summer of 1806. In September, the project completed, Johnson paid Sharples and he, in turn, paid and dismissed his men. Two summers later, Sharples's work force peaked at six men engaged in steady, but seasonal, employment. Winter work depended on Sharples's intentions for spring; in times he planned to build, journeymen fashioned joinery. Eager to sell two dwellings he was putting up, Sharples hurried assistants to make shutters, clothes horses, and sashes (by the piece), and to finish interior woodwork (by the day or the "job"). When the master carpenter foresaw a slow start to the year's business, however, journeymen looked elsewhere for work.

Even as a journeyman, Joshua Sharples demonstrated that he could manipulate terms of the trade—terms grounded in longstanding practice, but not immutable—to advance his interests. Like Sharples, journeymen carpenters in the early nineteenth century repeatedly manifested aggressive and innovative behavior bent on rising in economic stature. Business cycles squelched many promising attempts. In times of market growth, however, journeymen mixed high wages, full employment, "overwork," and jobbing to enjoy an income other mechanics would envy.

Journeymen carried enterprising behavior into their roles as master craftsmen, exploiting creative methods to set themselves up in business. At the helm of a shop, masters explored opportunities afforded by Philadelphia's expanding economy. Specialization in either joinery production or heavy carpentry suited an increasing proportion of craftsmen. By the 1830s, shops that produced woodwork for builders but were not directly involved in construction itself had become salient features in the industry. Comparably, subcontracting on the building site increasingly divided the tasks and skills to complete them. As a flexible method of production, subcontracting became an attractive choice for many masters. Most mechanics had learned about its characteristics during journeywork; they had also come to know its risks and rewards, and how tiny or substantial profits could be. But the usefulness of jobbing as a stepping stone to greater ventures made it irresistible.

By 1850, woodworking machines which ran on inanimate energy replaced a large portion of the work done in artisan joinery shops. Manufactories sold window sashes, doors, shutters, and blinds at cheaper prices, produced them faster, and stocked them year round. Mechanization also supplanted hand work on some laborious and low-skilled tasks of house carpentry. This is not to say, however, that craftsmen were stripped of their skill, relegated to mindless operation of smarter machines, and paid accordingly. Wages for employees of sash and door firms compared favorably to carpenters in nonmechanized settings. In fact, employment around the seasons probably raised the standard of living for these workers above their artisan contemporaries.

In spite of the success of mechanized woodworking at midcentury, artisan shops remained tenacious. They focused on specialty work that still required hand expertise. They interwove custom work, alterations, and extensions with stints as jobbers for other builders. The master house carpenter and his journeymen could still aspire to advance, perhaps even trying their luck as contractors. Half a century after Joshua Sharples commenced business, little in the way jobbing carpenters worked—or in their ambitions—would have surprised him.

In Joshua Sharples's world, daylight influenced the hours carpenters labored, activity stretching "from sun rise until dark" and shifting with seasons. "[I]n the longest day in summer," journeymen noted, "there are . . . 15 hours sun, and deducting 2 hours for meals, leaves 13 hours for work." But during winter's shortest days, even the efforts of masters to orient workbenches to maximize natural light allowed for only "9 hours sun, and of course 8 hours work."[8]

Notwithstanding public declarations, masters, journeymen, and apprentices often deviated from strictly diurnal routines. Newspaper reports of fires in carpentry establishments, for example, capture craftsmen toiling after hours. The "spark of a candle" ignited the shop of one master minutes after he departed around nine o'clock on an April evening; the sun had set at half past six.[9] As small business owners, masters might be expected to ignore strict boundaries of working hours. More telling of a drive bent on social and economic advancement, however, is the behavior of apprentices and journeymen. Ambition could be evident from the get-go, leading an apprentice to arrange for the "use of [the] . . . masters shop and tools to work after night for himself."[10] Journeyman Samuel Copeland also spent evenings making shutters and doors, though he had already put in a full day at daily wage. Jobbing, such as that Sharples performed as a mature journeyman, also motivated a young man to reject hourly measures of the workday. Acting as his own boss and getting compensation for the task (not the day), he hurried to complete the job in minimal time. This not-quite journeyman, not-quite master stretched the day at both ends. Likely he also accelerated the tempo of cutting, jointing, and planing.[11]

The road to autonomy would lead journeymen carpenters to labor under different methods of payment during the course of the year (and even in the same week). Henry Moore, retained by Joshua Sharples, worked in December 1807 and January 1808 at piece rates making sash and also at day wages. In March, he jobbed, "finishing 1st & 2nd Story north house on 7th street," but in April he returned to per diem rates. Another journeyman, Isaac Church, worked for Sharples in November 1808 at day rates. Church interrupted his pattern, however, by spending "the other day at sashes."[12] Joshua Yardley (who assisted Moses and John Lancaster) worked half the month of January 1817 at day wages, but another half month at piece rate working floorboards.[13]

The kind of work a journeyman did bore generally on how he and his employer reckoned pay. Figuring by the piece reflected the sort of house carpentry mechanics produced in the colder months, in particular preparing parts for spring. When journeyman Benjamin Rue received piece payment in the winter of 1815, it was to compensate him for "96 lights Sash" (that is, making the wood framework for glass panes). Likewise, Michael Shaffer spent November and December 1819 doing "Piece work at floor & doors."[14] Seasonal specificity of prefabricated items led a visitor to consider one December whether to buy "all the Windows sashes & sundry other light things" for his Carlisle, Pennsylvania house while in Philadelphia. Joinery, he thought, would come "very reasonable in the Winter season and not [cost] much to transport."[15] In the weeks before winter set in, and those leading to spring, completing interiors of buildings raised in warmer weather provided another staple for journeymen; this work they might take on a jobbing basis.[16] Bargaining on temperate weather one mid-November, therefore, Jesse Krewson began jobbing. As April approached, crews of journeymen earning a daily wage erected the supports of the year's new construction. After making shutters, drawers, sashes, and panels by the piece in the winter of 1816-17, Thomas Tash returned to outdoor building and daily wages at the first hint of spring.[17]

In London, piece rates applied to joinery throughout the eighteenth century; American crafts continued to use this measure and value system into the nineteenth.[18] Issues of supervision and sporadic availability of work hint at reasons the practice evolved. When orders were too light to keep to regimented days, what work there was might be distributed among journeymen to ease pressures of underemployment and retain employees. Piece work was discrete and easily assessed; employers did not have to monitor the time or the labor done by journeymen. In contrast to piece work, however, jobbing encompassed a range of miscellaneous actions, including wainscoting rooms, hanging shutters, and completing and attaching cupboards and drawers. For this phase of construction, men could be compensated either by time (daily wage), or by task. When builders had several physically dispersed projects going on at the same time, jobbing was a convenient way to set journeymen to a task and dispense with close superintendence. Skill, too, might have entered into the method applied; not all the master's hands worked on the same basis, though they might be doing similar carpentry. Jesse Krewson's decision to "quit working day work" and to job likely entailed some negotiation with his boss regarding his readiness in skill and reliability.[19]

But seasonal variations and type of woodworking tell only part of the story (at least in the case of piece work). Embroiled in a labor dispute in 1791, master carpenters implied that journeymen could choose between piece and day rates. Journeymen insisted otherwise. They berated masters for paying them by the day in the long summer months but by the piece during the winter months; by this method, masters were not obligated to pay journeymen for idle time.[20] When the economy generated plenty of employment, however, journeymen did not criticize compensation by the item, and averred as late as 1836 that they even preferred piece reckoning.[21] A number of journeymen, moreover, often received daily wages in winter months—Joshua Sharples's hands among them.

How do we reconcile the clashing perspectives of employers and employees, or contradictions between statements made during conflicts with the behavior of workers? Like masters, journeymen shaped their attempts to improve their lots to a specific economic context. The health of the real estate market—and the leverage laborers commanded—influenced the ability of journeymen to negotiate terms and determined the practices they could attack. Master house carpenter William Wagner's crew, for example, had plenty of work during the winters of 1809 through 1812 (and during the warmer seasons as well). Wagner figured the men's pay at a daily wage; his arrangements do not support criticisms journeymen made in less healthy construction seasons.[22] Cycles of the economy shifted advantages between employer and employee, and each was ready to act as opportunity arose. In Wagner's case, journeymen mechanics may have rejected piece work, and the long building boom gave them power to dictate their method of pay.

In other instances, however, journeymen integrated piece work into a strategy to supplement the daily wage, offset inflationary prices, and accumulate capital for their own starts in business. A craftsman "disposed" to labor additional hours and husband his earnings, masters insisted, would not be a "journeyman all the days of his life."[23] (Unwittingly, master craftsmen implied that mobility was often elusive if predicated on regular toil.) If a craftsman declined to do "over work," strong summer and spring construction markets might carry him through the slower winters. In slack seasons, however, both journeymen and master carpenters joined day labor with piece work without the prospect of surpassing average income.

The same rule books that regulated other carpentry also applied to piece work. Masters guarded the price structure. Owing to concealment, laborers struggled with capricious rates; negotiating them collectively was next to impossible. To accept journeymen's protestations over secret prices at face value, however, paints them as far more naïve than they were; most mechanics, afterall, repeated work that they had done before. Discounts, as in the case of agreements among masters, were part of the problem. Journeymen found themselves vulnerable to price slashing—even underbidding each other—especially during slow building seasons. When Isaac Davis did general carpentry at Isaac Ashton's houses in 1798, for instance, the parties added 25 percent to the measurer's calculations to compensate for inflation (from the 1786 price standard). But they then subtracted 50 percent from Davis's charges for making two pairs of shutters.[24] In 1829, to offer another instance, Benjamin Robison agreed to furnish shutters for a house at "50 per cent off." William M'Intyre's work at making doors in the winter of 1835 to 1836 was also reduced by 50 percent after the finished product was valued. Though evidence is fragmentary, joinery bills indicate that piece work discounting persisted as late as the 1840s.[25]

What price did the master carpenter command for the joinery his hands fabricated? Or, in other terms, what was his markup when he passed the components to the next level (either to the master builder or to the house purchaser)? Employers claimed in 1791 that journeymen "generally received four-fifths of the price at which the work has been undertaken." The master carpenter, they asserted, justly earned the remaining 20 percent for "the trouble of procuring materials, superintending the workmen, and giving directions, and likewise the expense of providing tools for different kinds of work, and shops in which it may conveniently be performed."[26] If masters themselves received full price, they were disingenuous about keeping only 20 percent of receipts. (Rather, they could sell the parts for 50 to 100 percent above what they paid the piece worker for his product.) But master carpenters operated in competitive markets and in the same disruptive building cycles that journeymen endured. Masters, too, often discounted their final bills, shrinking their margin on the piece work. Such arguments, however, rarely consoled journeymen piece workers, who countered that employers appropriated the value of their labor.

Piece joinery did have some advantages for the craftsman who executed it. For instance, he could control the pace and independent decisions of handiwork. With necessary tools and a separate place to work, such as journeyman William M'Intyre cleared in his cellar, the master had no supervision over the worker.[27] Also beyond the gaze of fellow journeymen, he could work without fear that his speed would upset expectations of required time to produce an item. Imagine disputes that might arise, for example, over the pair of "sash templates" John Monington made to save repeated measuring and scribing of individual pieces of molding. Techniques craftsmen devised to make stock parts more rapidly (and uniformly) must have led employers to question existing piece rates.[28] If a journeyman shaped parts at his master's shop, however (as many piece workers probably did), he remained under the watchful eye of his employer. Yet piece work done in the shop took on some of the character of an in-house subcontract—perhaps an uneasy arrangement, as master and journeyman negotiated issues of control.

Piece work could also prove more secure than daily wages. When journeyman M'Intyre made doors, compensation was backed by "the custom to pay so much weekly for piece-work, except [when] there is a special contract, and the balance when measured." Consequently and according to "custom," Moses Lancaster paid Joseph Medara installments of $10 over several months as the journeyman progressed with a bulk order of joinery.

Practice thus minimized the losses a piece worker suffered if an employer balked at full compensation. Since the master carpenter provided materials, his investment could induce him to pay for the finished work. If the mechanic failed to extract his money, he could at least sell the joinery. Law, if it came to that route, bolstered the claim of the piece worker.[29]

When reckoned by time, journeyman wages for the fewer work hours of winter fell below those of summer. Mimicking the pattern of his peers, Joshua Sharples's hand Isaac Shunk worked for $1.00 in the short winter days of 1805 to 1806, $1.06 in March and April (as the hours of light increased), and finally $1.12½ in May and June. Similarly, a contemporary master house carpenter varied the wages of his employees by season. He increased daily rates each April and again in June, and decreased them each November. Working for John and Moses Lancaster, Joshua Yardley earned $1.33 daily in the summer of 1816, but only $1.25 in December of that year.[30]

In periods of economic stress, journeymen indicted differential seasonal wages as a cost-cutting ruse that caused them severe hardship.[31] But when journeymen could turn the practice to their own advantage, they endorsed it. Consider the conflict that arose in the winter of 1839 to 1840, when craftsmen from Philadelphia and New York labored on the state capitol building at Raleigh, North Carolina. Northern mechanics led a strike for "different summer and winter pay scales" (a system that they condemned at home), and local stonecutters and carpenters quickly grasped their logic. Workingmen were not keen, of course, on getting lower wages in winter but, rather, raising summer rates without explicitly naming the adjustment a wage increase.[32]

What could a journeyman craftsman earn each year? The question is a vexing one for scholars of early America. Archival sources reveal instances of wage rates, but clues to earnings over a year are sparse and sporadic. (Payments by piece and task complicate the problem as well.) For 1802 and again in 1803, Joshua Sharples calculated his yearly income at journeywork to be at least $290. A few years later, Sharples paid journeyman William Wheeler more than $250 for about eight months of labor, and another assistant $204 for approximately seven months of work.[33] Employment likely tapered off during winter, diminishing the sums Wheeler and his peer anticipated.

An unusually comprehensive record of journeymen house carpenter wages was kept by master William Wagner for the years 1809 through 1812. Spanning a period of good prospects in the building trades, the mechanics who worked for Wagner certainly enjoyed the upper limits of income. (They accrued considerably more than daily laborers and mechanics in most

TABLE 1   Annual Income from Daily Wages for William Wagner's Journeymen
House Carpenters

	1809	1810	1811	1812	Journeyman's average
J. Barron	$319		$302		$311
J. Smith	$351		$247		$299
G. Baker	$246	$323			$285
J. Vanhorn	$276	$241	$243	$284	$261
J. Diamond	$276				$276
Average by year	$294	$282	$264	$284	

Source: William Wagner, "Account Book N° 3, Journemans Wages, 1809[–1812]," Germantown Historical Society. The table includes a total only when employment was recorded for
that journeyman over an entire calendar year (January to December). Because only years of
full employment are included, incomes are the upper range of what a journeyman could earn
at day wages. Amounts are calculated on the basis of sums Wagner actually tendered to his
journeymen.

other crafts.) And while demand for skilled labor resulted in low unemployment and increased wages for journeymen carpenters, inflation nonetheless
cut into their purchasing power.

Five of Wagner's hands, working throughout 1809 and generally five
to six days each week (in winter months as well), averaged $294 income
from wages (Table 1). Wagner distinguished among more experienced men
and other (younger?) hands in wages. Different per diem rates as well as
variations in the total number of days each man worked led income across
the crew to diverge widely. Journeyman Joseph Smith was able to earn
more than $350 in 1809, while George Baker took home only $245. Two of
Wagner's hands continued full time in 1810, averaging $282. In 1810, Baker
bettered his situation, pocketing $323 for the year's toil. In 1811, Wagner's
three steady employees averaged income of $264. The next year, only one
man remained in the master's employ throughout the entire period; his pay
amounted to $284.[34]

Even at steady, year-round employment at high wages, squirreling
away funds to start a business must have been challenging. A single man
spent about $160 each year for board and lodging.[35] That expense alone
would leave George Baker a little over a third of his 1809 income for clothes,
washing, medical bills, tools, and a small reserve fund to cushion him during
illness and unemployment. Prodigious drinking and "treating," legendary
features of the craft workplace, might consume the rest of the money.[36] Fair-

ing much better in 1810, Baker might soon become his own master. (In fact, by 1846, Baker had risen to prominence as a lumber merchant with wealth estimated at $150,000.)[37] Expenses of married coworkers would have exceeded those of Baker, a single man. Contributions, however, that the labor of a wife could make—perhaps to board a fellow journeyman or to do his washing—elevated family prospects.[38]

Baker might look forward to earning more, while still in Wagner's employ, by following the course of peers and working on a jobbing basis. Consider the situation of Jonathan Rubincam and Isaac Shunk, both journeymen who worked for Wagner in 1809. At the close of that year, the two men teamed up, doing house carpentry at various structures that Wagner, as master builder, was erecting (Figure 19). Rubincam and Shunk remained journeymen, however, with Wagner responsible for supplying materials and, on occasion, drawing on their labor (and paying them at a day rate). Jobbing, Rubincam and Shunk each earned an average annual income of about $400 in 1810, 1811, and 1812—nearly 50 percent more than Wagner's men working full time at day wages earned those years.[39] John Moore and Henry Rittenhouse exploited a similar tactic for advancing their careers. In 1809 and 1810, each worked for Wagner at daily rates. In August 1810, Wagner "[s]ettled day work" on their (now joint) account. The pair went on to job, though occasionally Wagner called on them for assistance. In August 1811, for example, Wagner was probably framing houses at one of his sites, and Moore and Rittenhouse put in thirteen and a half days at $1.25 per day. Mostly jobbing, however, the average income of each man for 1811 and 1812 was more than $330—not as impressive a difference as Rubincam and Shunk, but nonetheless about 25 percent greater than the wages fellow journeymen took home.[40]

With continued diligence and luck, any one of Wagner's journeymen might set out on his own while in his middle or late twenties. A portion of the savings he marshaled would outfit a workshop, where house carpenters worked about a third of the year.[41] In the shop, hands enjoyed a sort of efficiency of movement because the carpenter had "his benches and tools so arranged, as to employ his journeymen and apprentices to the best advantage." Men prepared materials there before bringing them to the construction site and integrating them into the structure. Joshua Sharples had window frames carted to his Eleventh Street house—frames assembled in his shop in the winter and required in April by his bricklayers for setting in the walls.[42] Likewise, John and Moses Lancaster ordered "a Load of Workt Stuff" transported "from Shop to new house." Another delivery from the

Rec.d July 27.th 1810 of Franks & Wagner
Four hundred and Fifteen Dollars being
the ammount in full for work done at their
house in Tenth Street Jonathan Rubinkam

$415 .. ..   Issac Shunk

Rec.d July 31.st 1810 of Franks & Wagner
One hundred Dollars on acc.t of
Brick work done in Market Street

$100 .. ..   Abraham Woglom

Rec.d August 5.th 1810 of Franks & Wagner
Twenty five Dollars 75/100 in full
for Lime delivered in both Street

$75 - 75   Alexander Lawton

lumber merchant went "part to Shop and part" to the houses in progress, the latter portion needed for the heavy girders, joists, and rafters shaped on location.[43]

Workshops were usually spare frame buildings—no-nonsense structures built for use, not display—tucked into already cramped spaces behind residences. Small shops measured about fourteen by twenty feet, but some were as large as twenty by forty feet. Materials spilled beyond the spaces into yards and alleyways and were stashed beneath floors and rafters. Cheap construction kept the cost of erecting a workshop low. In 1798, values for carpenter shops in Northern Liberties generally ranged from $300 to $500. Values in other years—and for flimsier spaces—could be even less. In 1815, for example, carpenter William Clayton owned two frame shops appraised at no more than $150. (Yet together they accommodated four workbenches and various tools.) Lack of plaster or embellishment also made frame shops easy to move to building sites or to new locations.[44]

Early in his career a house carpenter typically aimed to build a brick dwelling for the occupancy of his family (and tenants) and to erect as well a wooden shop on the lot. But for the young man who needed to forestall demands on meager funds, renting for the short term enabled him to devote capital elsewhere. The shop and lot that Joshua Sharples engaged in 1806 cost him $24 annually, though to purchase it might have meant laying out at once ten times that amount. Ithames Nickuals, who teetered between the ranks of journeyman and master, resorted to another temporary recourse to reduce cash needs. Nickuals crowded two work tables and numerous tools into his home. Henry Silence set his bench and mechanic's equipment in a small three-story brick house—with his family.[45] Working under constraints of space and financial resources, however, a master lost the advantage of hiring assistants and expanding production.

Equipping the shop also promised to drain the coffers of a novice master. A careful man could stretch his resources by getting supplies gradually. Few craftsmen accumulated implements all at once, but rather added pieces over the span of their careers and from a variety of sources.[46] George Cunningham began his collection early, accepting a set of bench tools upon completion of his apprenticeship; numerous peers accepted cash instead.

19 Mechanics and material suppliers signed for payments that they received from master builders. Jonathan Rubincam and Isaac Shunk acknowledged here the subcontracting work they did as journeymen. William Wagner and Jacob Franks, Receipt Book, 1810–1817. Gift of Louise B. Beardwood to the author.

Moses Clement managed to purchase tools on credit, diminishing the drain on his starting capital.[47] Master carpenter Moses Lancaster took "Two dollars and a saw hatchet and Rule it Being the Ballance due" for his labor. When he built a shop for a plane maker, Lancaster was again paid in tools. He transferred a few to one journeyman and also paid a subcontractor partially "in Planes" for his carpentry. Journeymen working for Joshua Sharples likewise took a combination of implements and cash for their wages.[48]

By meeting payrolls with tools, Lancaster and Sharples avoided the expense of cash, transforming an ample cache of fixed capital (tools) into operating capital to hire labor. Lancaster and Sharples also ensured that journeymen would furnish some of their own equipment, reducing the cost to employers. In straitened circumstances, masters might part with more tools than they wished, but when tendered to journeymen, employers still obtained value from the implements. Notwithstanding an assertion by masters in 1836 that Philadelphia's hands rarely supplied tools ("as is the custom of other cities"), journeymen carried a basic complement "from shop to shop, and from building to building."[49] Without reinforcement from the toolboxes of journeymen, employers might fall short of the demands of construction. Michael Barron, for example, had only "an incomplete set of Carpenters tools," though he had a shop. At twenty-three, his lack of equipment had not barred him from assuming the role of master builder. Similarly, Joshua Sharples had $55 in tools, but few duplicates, and thus could not outfit many hands to assist in any efficient way in fashioning the woodwork for houses he undertook.[50]

It follows, then, that master carpenters provided some, though not all tools for work. A journeyman's chest typically included implements worth between $15 and $50, or the amount which Isaac Neall knew to be "absolutely necessary for him to possess accor[d]ing to the custom for working as a Journeyman."[51] Beyond that, young employees, or journeymen making ornate items (or even commonplace piece work) required the master's gear. Lacking his own equipment or capital to buy it, apprentice Thomas Whitesel used his master's premises to fashion parts he could sell elsewhere. Journeyman Walter Thompson executed piece work in the value of $125—about half a year's potential income—using some of the equipment of his master. A mechanic might have only one chance in his career to assemble necessary implements; if he later lost his collection, the start-up expense could prove too great a hurdle. A journeyman house carpenters' association formed in 1837 recognized this danger and advanced partial compensation to members deprived of their tools by stealth or fire.[52] Master

Benjamin Hannis was not so fortunate. When flames obliterated his shop, stock, and equipment, Hannis endured a "loss he has never been able to make up." Less than three years later, the house carpenter had disappeared from Philadelphia.[53]

After he started his business, a master could expect to take a central place in the manual labor of his shop for a number of years and, perhaps, his whole career. Masters at an early career stage, and those least successful, labored more often beside journeymen in lieu of hiring additional help. Young Evan Lloyd, for example, talked about the "labour of himself and his people" in the houses he was raising. A penurious Walter Thompson emphasized that he, too, had "expended his own labor" when a master.[54] William Clark complained that in "consequence of sickness he had to hire men to do that work which he before was in the habit of doing himself"—implying that he had formerly spent his day at his workbench. But if prospects improved, the master was apt to spend more time administering a growing concern, extending absences from the shop, leaving apprentices' training to a foreman, and producing a smaller proportion of carpentry and joinery with his own hands. As Joshua Sharples's venture took off, for example, he increased the number of men he retained during the cold months of shop labor as well as the more temperate months of outdoor work. William Wagner, too, spent much of his time managing financing, materials, labor, and land transactions for his extensive building concern. Though still young himself—he was only twenty-seven years old in 1809—Wagner employed nine journeymen steadily from 1809 to 1812.[55] Unusual circumstances—a rush of orders, for example—could induce a master to pick up tools, but with a suspicion that his principal duties had been interrupted. "I . . . have foure Hands at work with myself" at assembling sashes, doors, and sundry house parts, one master told his client, emphasizing that efforts to finish the job forthwith led him to break from his routine.[56]

Shop owners could also stretch financial resources by withholding pay from their employees—borrowing, in effect (but without interest) from their journeymen. Laggard payment was endemic to building at all levels, and journeymen, subcontractors, and contractors alike bided time until the sale of real estate. Jobbing created additional problems for journeymen. Acting like subcontractors, they might wait for the bulk of their money until the work was measured.[57] Masters counted on delaying payment in order to reduce demands on their circulating capital, and some took advantage of it to allocate funds to other endeavors. For journeymen, industry conditions generally meant that they would receive most, though not all, pay when due. The practice that house carpenter Peter Crouding outlined in 1797 was applied years later in many shops. Crouding employed four men over "Eight weeks that I allow five Dollars Pr week Each hand." Had Crouding paced wages and payment equally, however, he would have needed six or seven dollars for each worker. Not until completion of the joinery several months later did a final accounting settle the balance due Crouding's mechanics.[58] In 1836, journeymen could still decry (though they perhaps exaggerated the proportion) "an unjust, but almost general custom . . . long . . . established in the city of withholding one third of our wages."[59]

Carpenters also reduced the capital needed to launch a venture by specializing and subcontracting. Recall that Michael Barron, master builder, lacked many joinery tools. He also had few employees. How did Barron and others like him manufacture the numerous shutters, doors, sashes, wainscoting, and sundry handiwork required? A small operator, he needed to parcel out contracts to other shops that specialized in joinery, benefiting from their productive resources. A house carpenter who engaged in framing houses and subcontracting joinery required no molding planes and few bench planes. Conversely, a house carpenter who undertook woodworking but avoided heavy construction invested in a diversity of molding planes, joinery chisels, and gouges, but few mortising instruments.

Two interdependent factors account for the intensification of specialization and subcontracting in nineteenth-century Philadelphia. First, continued commercial success and newfound industrial prominence fed capital markets; in turn, investors seeking outlets for their gains fueled real estate development. Braced by a legal and economic climate that facilitated aggressive speculative building, the ambitions of mechanics rose to the occasion. Yet, an artisan builder could not singlehandedly construct ever larger row developments. To juggle managerial, productive, and financial demands, craftsmen turned increasingly to subcontracting. Subcontracting alleviated—or pushed elsewhere—production problems (e.g., shortage of space or tools, inadequacy or recalcitrance of labor).

As "a means of reducing capital investment and risk," moreover, subcontracting answered the financial needs of an artisan builder.[60] Increasingly, the housing industry made identical items and offered them to consumers as ready-made wares, mirroring in this trend the period's clothing and furniture trades. And, much like these trades, it did so more and more in anticipation of buyers. But advance production accorded craftsmen much less security than work ordered by clients, who covered bills and paid for the carpenter's services in stages. Subcontracting could mitigate hardships caused by lengthy intervals between expenditures and receipts—between money spent on materials and labor, and payment received when the dwellings could be sold. It did so by enveloping other masters—and their employees—in extensive tiers of credit.

Rapid demographic growth, secondly, gave rise to a wide base of customers which specialty craft enterprises could pursue.[61] From 1820 to 1850, the population of Philadelphia County increased nearly 200 percent. Men and women from the city's hinterland, families from throughout the nation, immigrants from Europe, and residents who already called the city home became customers for rental housing and owner-occupied dwellings. Builders struggled to keep pace with demand, succeeding over the long haul though not, necessarily, in immediate intervals.[62]

The market for woodworking crafts not only grew, it broadened. Middle-class homebuyers and renters—expanding segments of urban populations—demanded fashionable styles, but new tastes permeated lower-income households as well. Row houses incorporated new ideals that emphasized interior light and neoclassical conceits in wood, marble, and plaster. An emphasis on delicacy of detail translated into slender window mullions and narrow, varied, and close lines of worked wood to create an overall effect of lightness and grace. The size of the window and its component sashes increased, and builders raised ceilings higher. In keeping with a sleeker, though more ornately refined appearance, designs transformed window shutters and interior and exterior doors. Beginning in the 1790s, for example, shutters displayed four depressed panels in lieu of the formerly popular three-paneled shutters, calling for a greater number of joints on each piece. Doors and windows underwent similar restyling toward elaboration and refinement of line.[63]

Separation of space joined with increased light and room height to remodel the interior of the row house. A rising bourgeoisie endorsed specialized uses of rooms that had hitherto integrated sleeping, cooking, work, and social and business interaction. Urban residents embellished parlors, entry halls, and public rooms accordingly. Greater selections of closets and built-in drawers stored an accumulation of consumer purchases such as clothing, kitchen ware, and dining accouterments. Popularity of mahogany doors, plaster-coated wood mouldings, marble mantelwork, exterior stairs, and watertables manifested the growing affluence of segments of the population. Refinement was a national phenomenon that percolated down into

the households of middling folk throughout early America. Even Philadelphians of limited means incorporated modest versions of up-to-date architecture into their homes.[64]

When construction waxed strong, the sheer volume of orders and capital committed to each aspect of building made alternative organization of
production imperative for master artisans. In response to emerging productive and capital opportunities, craftsmen chose among flexible strategies. A
master weighed the size of his shop, the buoyancy of the building market,
his career stage, and his personal and fiscal health in considering options.
He factored in the particular skills of his work force, and the tools he had
available or was willing to buy. Subcontracting empowered master artisans
to respond quickly to market shifts, but also to the vagaries of orders in individual enterprises. Small concerns could, in essence, share the resources of
several shops, and juggle work or laborers around as the urgency of business
demanded.[65]

Subcontracting did not originate in the nineteenth century. A scholar
who finds subcontracting to have been widespread in the mid-Atlantic iron
industry by 1725 argues that workers were "familiar and comfortable with
various forms of wage labor," subcontracting among them. Jobbing, moreover, "was not forced on laborers, but offered to them."[66] Artisans exploited
the system of production in other trades where capital requirements exceeded the means of individual producers (in shipbuilding, for instance). In
housing construction, craftsmen worked as " 'jobbing carpenters' " (read:
"subcontractors") from the Pennsylvania colony's youth.[67] Throughout
England, from whence many colonial Philadelphians migrated, the "jobbing Master" was widely known. A handbook of trades published in London in 1747 reported that "there are several degrees" of carpenters from
jobbing masters to "Master-Builders."[68]

In home construction, the impetus for subcontracting came as much
from below—from small masters and would-be masters—as from above,
that is, contractors. Jobbing masters did not rule out becoming master
builders as their careers advanced or when the real estate market encouraged them. Locating agency for subcontracting in small and nascent masters does not deny that profit margins for jobbed carpentry were narrow.
Competitive bidding for subcontracts, as well as concealed prices and discounted rates on piece work, meant that jobbing masters and their hands
often operated very close to the brink of financial ruin. Consequently, insolvency beset building mechanics at a higher rate than their proportion in
Philadelphia's population merited.[69]

Among house carpenters, some masters opted to specialize in ornate moldings, windows, doors, closets, and drawers. They pieced out parts to hands and then supplied builders with finished components. Other establishments, moving joinery out of the shop, became their customers. Piece work also proved to be a flexible means of removing labor-intensive joinery from an overly taxed workplace. Master John Carver, "not having room in his shop," engaged journeyman William M'Intyre to make thirty-four panel doors off site for housing Carver was building.[70]

Across the crafts, specialization in joinery or in heavy carpentry proceeded unevenly, alternately quickened and retarded by booms and busts in the economy. By the early decades of the nineteenth century, however, it had taken firm hold among Philadelphia house builders. Inventories recorded for the purposes of shop sale or chattel mortgages (loans secured by personal property) provide a snapshot of firms that concentrated on making joinery.[71] In 1814, for example, master Amos Addis had 300 planes and various carpenters tools, and stocked 200 lights of sash intended for a subcontract or for purchase as ready-made wares.[72] George Mosley's concern in 1831 also illustrates the advance of specialized enterprise. Mosley had room for four workbenches and as many journeymen. At age thirty-three, the house carpenter owned 150 planes of various kinds (probably both bench and molding planes), 20 saws, as well as "sundry tools to[o] tedious to mention." A plentiful collection of bits (nearly 200), chisels (100), and gouges (50) testified to the concentration of the shop on joinery.[73] Focus and organization made shops veritable nonmechanized manufactories. In 1832 Isaiah Hall found space for six workbenches and six "full sets" of bench planes, which allowed several journeymen or apprentices to work simultaneously at similar tasks. The master also owned "A Complete set of Moulding Planes from one inch to two inches and three quarters." With a full assortment of bead planes, Hall could direct his workers to make every popular variation on moldings.[74] Despite the distinct orientation of their establishments, Addis, Mosley, and Hall each continued to call himself a house carpenter.

Changes at the building site echoed developments in the shop. The archetypal image of the colonial artisan places him in charge of a small force of journeymen and apprentices, commanding all facets of erecting a house. One should be skeptical about whether this portrait reflects the way urban crafts functioned most of the time. Certainly by the post-Revolutionary decades, such "traditional" organization of carpentry production applied to fewer enterprises in Philadelphia. Rather, several master carpenters operating through subcontracts contributed to a dwelling or group of dwellings. Labor hidden behind the principal builder is difficult to discern, but several instances hint at widespread practices. David Jones, Richard Robison, and Jacob Seniff, for instance, were all master carpenters who worked on Samuel Ashton's house in 1795.[75] At least three master carpenters labored on brickmaker Peter Bobb's two buildings in 1813. Multiple masters joined forces on French & Roberts' house in 1823, one of whom also made the window frames in his shop.[76]

One way craftsmen divided responsibilities was by outside and inside work. In 1819 Henry Errick "& Co"—the designation implies partners, apprentices, or journeymen—took on "all the carpenter work Required in the finishing of the inside of a Two Story Brick House now Building." In 1829 master carpenter Laurence O'Connor also agreed to do "the Carpenters Work of the Inside" of a new brick house.[77] Accepting a role on one house was not tantamount, in this era, to making a lifetime commitment to either framing or finish carpentry. Joshua Sharples paired up with a fellow journeyman to finish inside work of a house. Two years later as a master, however, he engaged journeymen to do similar tasks, while he undertook framing. Likewise, inside work was a stepping stone for young Samuel Copeland. Copeland did "all the Carpenter work in the 2nd [and] third story and garret of a New house" that his erstwhile employer Moses Lancaster was constructing. Copeland subcontracted with the builder to do portions of two other houses, specifically "to lay the floors and finish the inside work." In subsequent seasons, in contrast, Copeland was master builder, directing the construction of his own houses.[78]

Subcontracting flourished during waves of furious real estate development when builders raised several houses at a time.[79] Exemplary are the activities of house carpenter John Ducker, who in 1811 undertook more than a dozen houses on the land of Edward Burd. Ducker managed the enterprise, supervising the contracts and material purchases. Burd provided money on mortgage and conveyed lots on ground rent to the artisans operating under Ducker. Of the several master mechanics, one (who came with his own crew of journeymen and jobbers) did the house carpentry work on the three southernmost of Ducker's six houses on the west side of Tenth Street. John Bailey billed for "house carpenter's work done in . . . building and erecting" another.[80]

Adjustments on subcontracts figured into this means of organizing construction. For the public, master house carpenters added a charge of 25 percent on their bills, an amount intended to compensate "for their trouble" of "giving directions and superintending the others."[81] When a master made terms with fellow craftsmen, however, the subcontractor usually took the work at cost (a "good price" for his labor included), or at least relinguished the mark-up assessed the general public. This practice thrived not only across the building sector, but within the carpentry trade itself.[82]

Competition for work generally, or for work at an attractive construction project (owing to location or to terms from ground lords), could lead mechanics to bid for jobs. In momentary battle against one another, artisans chipped away at profits by raising the deductions off final bills. Several instances illustrate the nature of discounting in building subcontracting. In Ducker's project, John Bailey's work was valued by measurers from the Practical House Carpenters' Society (PHCS). Though measurers calculated the bill using their current reference, issued a mere few months before Bailey finished the job, they deducted 30 percent from the Society's prices. William Curry, with two other master carpenters, worked on Ducker's two northernmost buildings; each bill was reduced by 30 percent from 1811 PHCS rates. The building climate was lively, and the costs of materials and labor had risen over the previous few years. Competitive pressures, nevertheless, led subcontracting carpenters to consent to a 30 percent deduction off the scale set down in 1811.[83]

Agreements like those between Ducker and his subcontractors were not unusual. During the same period, Robert Andrews had his work for Peter Berry calculated at PHCS standards. (Both Andrews and Berry were members of this society of masters). Appraisers arrived at a final charge of one third off the bill. Those who consulted the Carpenters' Company price book also discounted. William Ellis agreed in January 1819 to do carpenter's work for "one third deduction from the Measurers bill at old Price." The "old Price" had been determined in 1786 and was roughly 15 percent above the 1819 cost of living and of building material. Ellis's real pay, then, was approximately 15 percent less than a carpenter toiling in 1786. His compensation declined even more precipitously if he paid hands to assist him, since nominal wage rates for journeyman carpenters had increased some 25 to 50 percent.[84] (Thus, journeymen working for wages at this time actually enjoyed a better relative position than their bosses.) Throughout the second and third decades of the nineteenth century, "difference between old and present price" (ranging from 25 to 50 percent) continued to be deducted, resulting in a final payment that generally reduced the value of work by measurement.[85]

For journeymen and for masters, shifts in methods of compensation and in organizing the building process netted drawbacks as well as opportunities. Seasonal underemployment and seasonally variant day rates, unpredictable piece pay, and a piece work discount system could threaten independence. A vigorous housing market, however, radically diluted journeymen's public discontent with the belief that capitalist organization could work to their advantage. Rush piece work orders executed after a full day of work, carpentry finished on a jobbing basis, and strategically timed demands for pay increases enabled journeymen to keep their sights on getting out on their own. By subcontracting and specializing, newly minted masters could adapt capital and production constraints to individual and market conditions. More seasoned proprietors likewise chose such methods to preserve and better their status as masters. It was not an easy life, and prospects waxed and waned at least as often as building cycles.

Increasingly, house carpenters shaped a version of independence that insisted less on overseeing the total building process and more on selecting subcontracting. At first, joiners were more likely to do some building from time to time than builders were to engage in joinery—but slowly those who exercised abilities in both categories became less common. As early as 1811 Moses Quimby emphasized that he still possessed the inclination and techniques of "Carpenter & joiner." Though a member of the Practical *House* Carpenters' Society, Quimby emphasized that he could frame buildings as well as work moldings, wainscoting, and sashes.[86] By the 1830s distinctions had sharpened. Practitioners no longer assumed that all master house carpenters *could* or *would* build a dwelling from bottom to top, outside to inside. Exemplary is the circumstance of master house carpenters Caldwell & William. The partners seem to have had little command of heavy carpentry skills. A journeyman in their employ noted that the partners had never "'built a house out & out.'" Rather, they "'were to *finish* the work,'" that is, do the inside joinery and any final carpentry on the dwelling in question. Caldwell & William even lacked certain joinery expertise; they hired another master to build the stairs.[87]

* * *

The work rhythm of joinery fabrication and outdoor construction that Joshua Sharples knew did not characterize the productive world of Abel Reed. Born in Massachusetts, Abel Reed moved to Philadelphia sometime around 1831. He likely hailed from Worcester, a region abuzz with developments in woodworking technology. Woodworking entrepreneurs were thick on the ground in Reed's native region, but in Philadelphia new planing and sawing machinery represented vast opportunities.[88]

In his adoptive city, Reed established himself as a sashmaker and glazier.[89] When Reed set up his joinery shop, he was "one of the pioneers, in his bus[iness]."[90] The novelty of his pursuits derived in part from the scale of enterprise, which was larger than most joinery shops. He also focused on making a narrow range of products, namely window sashes and closely related joinery.

Reed's venture, moreover, combined three trades: that of painter, glazier, and joiner. Prior to Reed's era, the house carpenter assembled the window sashes and, if they were to have glass, sent them on to the painter. The latter treated the frames and, if he also had the skill of a glazier, cut and inserted the glass. The house carpenter then arranged for the finished windows to be carted to the building site or back to his shop for safekeeping until needed in the progress of the structure. Reed may not have been the sole or earliest woodworking pioneer to integrate the three craft processes under one roof, but he was one of the most successful. By no longer hauling sashes hither and fro, or integrating work into schedules of diverse craft shops, house carpenters reduced the wait and cost of building components.[91]

At some point in the 1830s or early 1840s, moreover, Reed began to make components using machines. Initially, he probably bought stuff from lumber merchants, had the wood prepared by power-driven saws at one of Philadelphia's planing mills, then transported it to his shop for cutting, mortising, tenoning, and pinning into sashes, doors, shutters, and blinds. But by midcentury, Reed ran all of the requisite saws for preparing lumber at his steampowered sash and door factory in the Northern Liberties. Not only did Reed use molding, tenoning, and mortising equipment in his plant, but as agent for its makers, he also sold the machines.[92]

Reed's business stood at the crossroads of two developments in woodworking. The first, specialization, was principally an organizational change, while the second, the use of steampowered and waterpowered cutting and planing machinery, was overwhelmingly technological. Specialization within the woodworking industry, as we have seen, predated mechanization (though for Reed, the two came close together). Standardization of building dimensions through price book and measuring practices, moreover, meant that handworkers first, and machines and their operators later, produced closely identical parts. A customer in 1802 found mahogany doors "ready made and for Sale" in various dimensions; "ready made" joinery, however, had probably been available for decades.[93] With standard sizes and

a well designed (albeit hand) process, mechanics could make joinery in diverse shops and yet achieve consistency. Carpenter Horatio Jones, for example, fabricated shutters for the second-story windows of nine four-story
buildings. Working efficiently, Jones " 'framed the shutters for the whole of
the houses pretty much at one time.'" Other piece workers adhered to the
measurements of the remaining parts, "where the work and materials were
to be precisely the same in each [of the buildings], so that the whole, when
finished, might exhibit in front . . . a perfect uniformity of appearance."[94]
Likewise, journeyman William M'Intyre exploited the trade's widespread
conventions of size and type when he threatened to auction off doors he
had made if they were not immediately paid for by the contractor. Neither
M'Intyre nor the builder who ordered the parts doubted a healthy market
for components originally produced for a specific house but fit for other
structures.[95]

Uniformity, efficiency, and interchangeability achieved by small concerns reliant on hand processes nevertheless readied production for centralized mechanized workshops. Woodworking equipment—for instance, a
machine to cut holes in sash parts—was on the market as early as the 1790s.
Powered initially by human muscle (it was treadle controlled), the apparatus nonetheless reduced the amount of hand chiseling necessary to make
joints. That it appeared rarely in carpentry shop inventories, however, suggests that it failed to serve all joinery operations.[96] Revolutionary change
in house parts production came a quarter of a century later. Contemporaneous development of several innovations, among them the Woodworth
planer and the Daniels planer, joined with steampower to dramatically alter
woodworking industries.[97]

By the time William Woodworth patented his cylinder planing machine in 1828, a number of mechanics had already devised methods to saw
or shave lumber to a uniform thickness. No one, however, was as "single-
minded" as Woodworth in identifying and developing a planer's potential.[98] The technical advantages of Woodworth's device were matched by
Woodworth's marketing savvy. Quite soon after Woodworth staked his
patent claim, "planing mills" in New England (where he developed and improved the prototype) and in Philadelphia were using the machine.[99]

The beauty of Woodworth's innovation lay in its ability to cut large
pieces of lumber, of varying width and thickness, to consistent dimensions.
Combining planing with a capacity to simultaneously tongue and groove,
Woodworth's machine answered the demands of floorboard manufacture.
It also could be adapted to diverse joinery tasks, and it ran lumber through

its blades at an impressive speed. As early as 1829, planing millers in Philadelphia (using a competing innovation or possibly Woodworth's patent machine) delivered bulk quantities of machine-prepared flooring directly to construction sites. In addition to arriving planed, the boards were tongued and grooved. The Woodworth planer cut a rib (tongue) along one long edge of a board, and a groove along the opposite edge. By setting the boards side by side and coaxing the tongue of one board into the groove of the next, the carpenter formed a tight joint. Laid in this manner, floorboards resisted warping and made a stronger and more durable landing.[100]

" '[D]ress[ing] floorboards,' " carpenters themselves attested, was " 'laborious work to do by hand.' "[101] In 1817 journeyman Joshua Yardley spent nearly fifteen days planing and finishing floorboards (enough for a small one-and-a-half storied house) by hand. Machines designed to plane lumber drastically reduced the time required to get a house prepped for inside finishing. The new Woodworth planer and two semiskilled operatives could match Yardley's output in about three and a half hours.[102]

Woodworth's creation, however, offered neither immediate nor perfect salvation for builders. Drawbacks to the quality of the finished product as well as its cost persisted. Carpenters often found boards too green to use immediately, requiring that they space flooring out to dry for several weeks before construction progressed. Once laid, workmen might still be occupied for several days "traversing [with a plane] & smoothing all the floors."[103] Lumber planed on Woodworth's machine, moreover, could be prohibitively expensive. Patent assignments and rights that assured a veritable monopoly over the technology lay at the root of the problem. "Patent speculators" and a select group of planing millers dominated the field. (Recall Mark Richards, introduced in Chapter 4.) For nearly three decades, the Woodworth planer stood at the center of industry controversy, cumbrous litigation, and legislative battles. Though at the forefront of mechanized production, Abel Reed pushed to the front lines of Philadelphia tradesmen who were fighting against extensions of Woodworth's patent.[104]

The Daniels machine, patented by Thomas E. Daniels in 1834, and refined and manufactured in Worcester in the 1830s, was a rotary planer better suited to shop use than the Woodworth innovation. Though slower than the Woodworth planer, it was more versatile in the types and dimensions of lumber it could work.[105] Abel Reed prized Daniels's machine highly; an 1850 advertisement placed it first among the devices used in Reed's establishment (Figure 20). Reed also dealt in the apparatus itself, attracting buyers by singing its praises. "This Machine," he assured customers, "needs no rec-

20 To reach a wide market, Abel Reed advertised his steam sash, blind, door, and shutter manufactory in the *Philadelphia Wholesale Business Directory and Circular for 1850*. Courtesy of The Library Company of Philadelphia.

DANIEL'S
Patent Planing Machine,
Built at Worcester, Massachusetts, and for Sale by
A. REED,
At his Steam Sash and Door Manufactory,
Rear of No. 127 North Third Street, above Race,
PHILADELPHIA.

This Machine, where it is known, needs no recommendation, it being used to great advantage for planing, jointing, and squaring all kinds of work for Carpenters, Sash and Door Makers, Millwrights, Machinists, Carr Builders, Cabinet Makers, &c., &c. Also, for Planing hollow logs for Machinery, or Staves for large Tubs or Cisterns.

They may be used to plane boards three-eighths inch thick, or large timber or plank, three feet wide up to sixty feet in length.

FAY, FISHER & Co.'s
TENONING MACHINES,
ALSO—For Sale by A. REED as above.

These Machines are very superior articles for all kinds of Tenoning and Boring, doing the work with great despatch and accuracy.

FAY, DAVIS & Co.'s
PATENT PREMIUM
MORTISE MACHINES,
ALSO—For Sale by A. REED as above.

This Machine for all kinds of Mortising, either in hard or soft wood, is believed to be unequalled by any others in use, and is universally approved where used.

☞ All the above Machines may be seen in use as above, at A. REED'S FACTORY, rear of No. 127 north Third Street, above Race, Philadelphia.

Architects.

Carver, John E., 51 n 6th st, below Arch, Architect and Engineer
Haviland, John, 196 Spruce st, between 5th and 6th
Johnson, William, 101 s 5th st, e side above Prune
Koecker & Husband, s e cor 4th and Walnut sts
Le Brun, N., n e cor Spruce and 13th sts
Riddle, John, 65½ s 3d st

Plastering Hair Dealers.

Smith, John T., corner Beaver and St John sts
Stewart, H. B., corner St John and Willow sts
Stokes, Harvey, n w cor Front and Callowhill sts

ommendation, it being used to great advantage for planing, jointing, and squaring all kinds of work for Carpenters, Sash and Door Makers."[106]

In addition to the Daniels planer, Reed employed equipment for "all kinds of Tenoning and Boring . . . with great dispatch and accuracy," and for "Mortising, either in hard or soft wood." (He sold these machines as well, inviting the curious to come witness them in motion.) In 1850, capital investments in Reed's plant amounted to about $5,000; another $10,000 was spent in lumber for making building parts. Four years later, Reed's factory was burned to the ground, a "[l]oss [of] abt 10M$ [$10,000]." By 1860, $20,000 spent on rebuilding and re-equipping his works gave form to a more ambitious enterprise. In one decade, Reed doubled the number of his employees (to thirty-three men) as well as the value of the "Sash, Doors & Moulding" he turned out (to $40,000).[107]

Reed was the sole Philadelphia sales agent for important woodworking machines, but otherwise the output of a handful of sash and door firms in 1850 was comparable to his venture. Donigan & Gatchell employed a dozen men, declared their capital investment to be nearly $5,000, and boasted joinery sales of $15,000. Lentz & Fisher's manufactory housed equipment (premises included) valued at $12,000. Twenty-five employees turned out goods worth about $23,000.[108]

Remarkably, however, despite the central role played by joinery machines run on inanimate power, setting up in the industry in its initial decades remained within the grasp of those with middling resources. Men with modest pools of capital or access to credit continued to compete. Kensington operators Black & Souders ran a small (four horsepower) engine which, inclusive of premises, machines, and fixtures, amounted to a $1,000 investment. Working with eight men, the firm claimed to have produced 150,000 lights of sash with a market value of $9,000.[109] While a steam engine was virtually indispensable to run equipment, machinists constructed American woodworking apparatus (when monopolistic patent pricing did not prevail) to price cheaply. Surveying nineteenth-century American machinery, an engineer-machinist judged that constant advances in technology made any joinery machine obsolete after a mere half-dozen years. Machine builders consequently preferred to make low-priced devices, shunning durable (i.e., cast iron) frames and auxiliary parts that would outlive the encased technology.[110]

In a number of other ways, Abel Reed's joinery production in 1850 diverged from that which Joshua Sharples knew nearly five decades earlier. Whereas Sharples produced for local customers, Reed cast his gaze beyond

Philadelphia to national and international markets. The manufacturer invited "[b]uilders in the Southern cities" and "any part of the United States" to write for "descriptions" (i.e., dimensions and prices) and to order any item from his line of joinery. Parts sold on "the most favorable terms" vied with the goods craftsmen made in places afar, thanks to extension of transportation networks. Reed also looked for new opportunities, promising satisfaction to customers in South America and the West Indies. To keep windows intact, he offered glass "of all sizes . . . for sale by the box," shipped with sash, the whole to be assembled in distant lands.[111]

Advertising and retailing techniques also separated Reed from his predecessor Sharples. Sash manufacturers hawked merchandise in the city's new commercial registers; Reed filled two pages of Philadelphia's *Wholesale Business Directory* of 1850 with illustrations of typical wares and with text acclaiming the virtues of state-of-the-art machinery. Competitor John Bower likewise accented text with sketches of window sashes and shutters (Figure 21). To attract customers, Reed borrowed from consumer trades. Retailers, as historian Stuart Blumin has shown, increasingly hid disagreeable spaces — where workers made goods — behind embellished showrooms and fashionably dressed clerks. Bulk windows, class counters, and lavish decor all made urban "palaces" more appealing to middle-class shoppers. Reed looked to wholesale tradesmen for his patrons, but nonetheless he distanced production from sales. By 1857, he had established his manufactory in Penn township, but he drew buyers to his "office and wareroom" on Second Street above Race, just a few streets removed from the city's bustling retail heart.[112]

Had a record of Reed's manufactory survived, comparisons between the work experiences of his employees and those of Sharples would reflect critical changes in the woodworking industry. Reed continued to chart schedules according to hours of daylight (though gas lighting was quickly becoming available to an ever-expanding area of Philadelphia). Seasons, however, no longer influenced the selection of carpentry made, and bore less on the irregularity of work.[113] Coal-fired steam engines ran machinery year round, and parts came out of Reed's workshop in any month. Orders drawn from warmer climes helped level the local seasonal swings in demand, and the need to dispatch freight weeks in advance of building could keep production running at the height of winter. Reed's firm, and with it his employees, shared with Sharples's hands continued vulnerability to national business cycles. Since sales were more geographically dispersed, however, local ups and downs buffeted his manufactory less severely.

JOHN BOWER,

Manufactory, 18 south Schuylkill Eighth street,

Dwelling, No. 4 Union Row, George St, between Sch. 7th and 8th,

PHILADELPHIA.

Steam Power Manufactory of

SASH. **BLINDS.**

Rolling Pivot Window Blinds

Plain and Fancy

Window Sash.
Panel Doors
AND
SHUTTERS,
GREEN HOUSE SASH, &c.

N. B---Orders for the City, Country, or Shipping thankfully received, and promptly attended to, on the most reasonable terms.
☞ 8 × 10 Sash constantly on hand, glazed or unglazed.

21 Sash and door manufactories produced joinery that conformed to trade standards, but they also took custom orders for more unusual parts. *Philadelphia Wholesale Business Directory and Circular for 1850.* Courtesy of The Library Company of Philadelphia.

While Reed's workers might have gained more regular employment, did they do so at the expense of wages and total annual income? The tentative answer is that mechanization did not impoverish employees in mid-nineteenth-century woodworking establishments.[114] Producers' responses to federal census inquiries suggest that workers in sash and door manufactories enjoyed a higher daily wage than carpenters in the city's artisan shops. In 1850, the median wage for factory hands was $1.16; for carpenters, it was $1.15. (Among sash and door manufacturers, the average wage of $1.38 in Reed's establishment was the second highest in the industry.) The typical employee of a mechanized woodworking enterprise earned only slightly less than the typical hand of a master house carpenter or builder. (The latter's median wage was $1.21.) [115] With sash and door works running a greater part of the year, employees could catch up to or surpass the more seasonally fluctuant income of craftsmen in outdoor building (albeit by toiling a greater number of hours).

The fact that sash and door employees earned good relative wages underscores the reliance of mechanized woodworking operations on skilled labor. While Reed's enterprise produced parts that were ready to hang, it also did a lively trade in custom sash and doors that required deft execution.[116] Even two decades later, engineer John Richards could describe machine hands "as a rule, [as] men who have learned wood work to begin with; generally as joiners, and then gathered some knowledge of machine fitting and millwrighting." [117] Some of the techniques a mill carpenter learned contrasted with those Sharples taught and with skills cultivated by contemporaries in nonmechanized settings. A carpenter in a mechanized works might still exercise traditional expertise and familiar tools in "finishing off, after the several parts of the article have been put together"; until the final steps, however, the "ordinary tools of the carpenter" would be "seldom seen." [118] Yet, to "understand machine fittings so as to direct and make repairs" — even on reputedly "self-acting machines" — ranked among new tasks unknown to journeymen carpenters in the early nineteenth century.[119]

To paint mechanization as a process that robbed a craftsman of his skill, then, does not precisely or usefully capture transformations in the woodworking trades. Specialization in housing parts production already ensured that the call for manual expertise had narrowed before the extensive use of machines. Witness carpenter William Probasco at work in 1841. Probasco made 182 pairs of window shutters and "Dr[ove] Hooks in 114 [window] frames" — tasks that gave him no opportunity to exercise a breadth of techniques.[120] Hand joinery entailed repetition that honed certain skills while sacrificing others; much of the labor usurped by machines was precisely of the monotonous and quickly learned sort. Cutting and chiseling scores of mortise and tenon joints, or planing floorboards, did not demand the dexterity of a seasoned artisan. Both specialization before mechanization, and mechanized production in specialized articles, encouraged the same result: a narrower range of abilities that a carpenter might thereafter be expected to have.

The tempo and volume of production in sash and door enterprises was also apparent to employees and to commentators. The pace of mechanized production was insistent and quicker than hand carpentry. British observers of the industry returned home astonished at the speed with which identical pieces poured out of establishments. "In one of these manufactories," they acclaimed, "twenty men were making panelled doors at the rate of 100 per day"—about ten times the production of a hand worker. They remarked, too, on the many "special manufactures" of the trade, "where only one kind of article is produced, but in numbers or quantity almost in many cases incredible."[121]

Success of sash and door manufactories did not relegate all mechanics to the factory floor nor did it efface small producers. In the 1830s and 1840s, piece work executed by hand—or partly by hand—continued alongside steam-driven mechanized woodworking. Hand processes survived initially owing to an array of economic and technological factors. The depression of the late 1830s, for instance, limited capital available for new ventures and curtailed the optimism of aspirants. Patent machines that enjoyed initial periods of exclusive control could not satisfy demand. New woodworking machines failed to cut hardwoods as cleanly and effectively as they shaped pine and other popular softwoods. At least for a time, the craftworker's expertise in hand tools remained critical.[122] A few sash and door establishments did business as late as 1860 without recourse to machine power.[123]

Production in house carpenter William Eyre's shop captures the contemporaneous interplay of hand and machine methods in joinery. At various times from 1849 to 1851, Eyre and his journeymen were engaged in making, "pinning up," and "smoothing" window sash and "getting out stuff for . . . doors." For one job they made as many as twenty-six doors. They also made window shutters "in speculation," that is, in anticipation of later projects. During these years, however, Eyre called "at A Reeds shop" several times and bought "sash doors & shutters." He even ordered "sash for [the] inside of [a] Bulk Window casing" (for a storefront window) and for a skylight, suggesting that he valued the abilities of Reed's joiners highly. Eyre, principally a custom builder on a modest scale, availed himself of sash and blind firms in much the way masters in the early nineteenth century used piece work or subcontracting. In months of peak outdoor construction, "not having time to make them at [the] shop," Eyre bought prefabricated and custom wares from specialty manufacturers. He moved work out of his space, but only when the press of construction fully occupied his journeymen with other tasks.[124]

Manual skills remained particularly important in building stairs, yet increasingly production of even these structures took place in specialized, nonmechanized workshops. Stairmaking had long been a highly prized occupation, requiring great ability and commanding commensurate pay. Thus, in 1835, Jonathan Pennell worked with another man to cut out risers, work the steps, glue the strips, strike out the horses, and do all tasks necessary to erect stairs. Each earned $1.50 per diem, twenty-five cents more than other carpenters on the site received.[125] Two decades later, craftsmen still made stairs with nonmechanized techniques. Charles Smith, for example, ran a "Stair Case Man'y" using hand labor of two employees. In 1860 Smith made fifteen sets of mahogany staircases, fitted with balusters bought from turning shops. Jonathan Yeager headed one of the larger establishments, yet he employed only four men and produced thirty cases. A product with so many intricate bends, angles and diverse pieces—and one so massive and unwieldly—required resources spent in assembly that outweighed that of cutting and jointing. As late as 1860, stairmaking shops found the savings in labor afforded by steampowered equipment insufficient to warrant owning it. Instead, they used lumber worked at planing mills in constructing their staircases.[126]

The small carpenter shop continued to exist into the late nineteenth century, capturing a niche opened between makers of prefabricated parts and builders. Generally employing three or four men, craft shops did custom work, special orders, renovations, and repairs. They remained ready to step into big ventures as subcontractors and bided time until they could undertake their own projects. These traits characterized C. C. Alvora's operation in 1860. Alvora, a "Job Carpenter & Builder," employed four hands at "Jobbing & Build'g" amounting that year to $5,000. Craft enterprises like those of Alvora shifted in and out of subcontracting as the building economy warranted.[127]

Much as Sharples and his crew did, house carpenters at midcentury also subcontracted or hired out at construction sites. Small producers, however, could no longer rely on much winter work at joinery. In making standard windows and doors, they could not compete with specialized firms. Mechanized workshops now supplied parts to builders "at a much cheaper rate than [artisans] can produce them in their own workshops without the aid of such machinery."[128]

Neither master nor journeymen carpenters raised hues and cries against technological innovations. Demand for new housing in Philadelphia apparently generated enough work that tradesmen did not confront potential ramifications of mechanized woodwork production. Journeymen who organized at the height of new activity in joinery mechanization were silent on the subject of threats posed by manufactories to their jobs and skills. Instead, their protests revisited presumably unrelated issues of wages and shop control.[129] Absence of critique testifies to the subdivision of the carpentry trades that had evolved since Sharples's era, and the distance journeymen house carpenters in artisan shops now put between themselves and skilled and semiskilled factory labor.

Disappearing from house carpentry at midcentury was the fluidity within the trade that existed for Joshua Sharples in 1800. Sharples moved easily between the shop where he shaped sashes and doors in winter months, and the lot where he mortised and tenoned framing joists and rafters in temperate weather. A joiner-machine operator from Reed's labor force could not step onto a building site and erect a house—but neither could Sharples readily take his place operating steampowered equipment.

Mechanized woodworking alone was not responsible for the division of house carpentry. Specialization of hand workshops, responding to urban markets and opportunities of speculative construction, preceded (and moved closely alongside) machine innovations. On the building site itself, skills increasingly separated house carpenters into men who framed and men who finished the structure's inside. Such boundaries in Sharples's time were permeable. By the 1830s, however, a growing proportion of craftsmen failed to master the complexity of building a house "out & out."

Specialization narrowed the range of skills exercised by numerous mechanics while it developed capabilities within concentrations. Workers and small masters enjoyed some positive effects of the differentiation of the trade. New specialties (e.g., stairmaking) and new skills (machine operation) became central to the industry. Subcontracting, which house carpenters used in the colonial period, continued as a sometimes lucrative, sometimes disastrous, but nonetheless flexible mode of organizing production and being one's own master in the mid-nineteenth century. Planing, mortising, and tenoning machines removed many laborious and tedious tasks from workshops; in the midst of a growth economy, wages and jobs kept pace.

Though production methods in joinery changed, much of what went on at the building site in Reed's time would have looked familiar to Joshua Sharples. The scale was now bigger, and a dizzying array of subcontractors labored on the dwellings. Divisions of skill, too, were more pronounced. Men who now performed what were once the most time-consuming tasks of house building—making doors, window sashes, shutters, and moldings—might never visit the site. The process of raising a house, however, varied little from practices Sharples used to erect his first dwellings.

SIX

Final Assembly

IN AUGUST 1849, house carpenter Joseph Montgomery commenced building thirty-two brick row houses near Broad and Spring Garden Streets. The site Montgomery chose lay virtually on the doorstep of Mathias Baldwin's manufacturing plant for steampowered locomotives. At midcentury, Baldwin employed six hundred men and boys and was quickly garnering an international reputation for his products. When he established his factory in the Spring Garden neighborhood in the mid 1830s, the locomotive maker picked a spot convenient to the terminus of the Philadelphia and Germantown Railroad (one of his first customers). Around both Baldwin's plant and the railway depot, industrial and service activity swirled. An omnibus line along Thirteenth Street carried passengers from their homes to jobs, errands and entertainments. Montgomery's houses would be well placed to connect to a thriving local economy with far-reaching networks.[1]

A national depression in the early 1840s followed (after recovery) by intermittent disruptions in the economy stalled development of the Spring Garden section for several years after Baldwin located to the vicinity. By August 1849, however, prices were rising modestly from all-time lows, and business appeared to be pulling out of its doldrums. Closer to home, declining numbers of deaths from cholera allowed Philadelphians to celebrate the end of an epidemic that had plagued the city that year.[2] The climate for speculative development and the likelihood of engaging subcontractors and employees encouraged Montgomery.

Born in Ireland, Montgomery had for some decades plied his trade as house carpenter-builder in the Quaker City. He acquired the Spring Garden land on a ground-rent conveyance from George Cadwalader, scion of an old Philadelphia dynasty. The house carpenter borrowed a third of the projected cost of the project from Cadwalader, who promised to pay him at predetermined stages of construction. While Cadwalader's participation as ground lord and mortgage creditor encouraged him to monitor the progress of de-

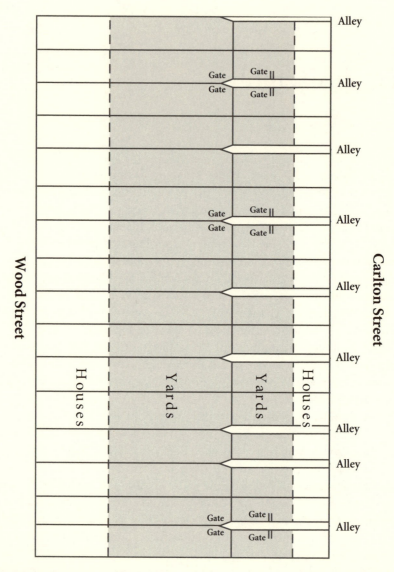

22 Builder Joseph Montgomery constructed houses with one room to each floor on the narrow alley of Carlton Street. The dwellings on Wood Street, a more prominent street, featured two rooms to each floor and commanded higher rents and purchase prices; Wood Street residents also enjoyed larger lots after the parcels were subdivided. Residences of both classes of houses, however, shared privies that they reached by gates between yards. After Ernest Hexamer, *Insurance Maps of the City of Philadelphia* (Philadelphia, 1859).

velopment, he also might have intended to purchase the finished houses from Montgomery. Capitalist and craftsman shared a target value for the properties and a sense of the pool of potential residents. It would have been a poor business decision to build expensive dwellings where most well-to-do Philadelphians were unlikely to live. Up-and-coming families, however, among them respectable mechanic households, were moving into Spring Garden with each passing day. Montgomery's housing designs could accommodate them and offer still more affordable quarters for households with slimmer resources.[3]

In Montgomery's scheme, sixteen of the houses fronted on Wood Street, and the remaining sixteen on a parallel but narrower passage called Carlton Street (formerly Bloom Alley). The backyards of the two rows adjoined (Figure 22). The house carpenter planned the dwellings on Wood Street to be fifteen feet wide and twenty-eight feet deep—that is, with two rooms on each floor. The houses fronting on Carlton Street, in comparison, would be cheaper (as befit budgets of prospective alley dwellers) and smaller. Montgomery designed them to be nearly the same breadth but only half the depth of the Wood Street structures, accommodating only one room to each story. By building for the lower price ranges, Montgomery tapped two tiers in the house-buying market. Beginning in August 1849 and extending throughout the subsequent year and a half, Montgomery, commanding the movements of carpentry assistants as well as those of subcontracting tradesmen, erected the houses.[4]

Until now, the phrase "erected the houses" has escaped close scrutiny, examined only to elucidate obstacles that individual builders encountered. The strategy has been to treat the pieces of the structure separately, to consider each independent of the undertaking of which it was a part. Now, however, attention focuses on connecting the building blocks required to raise and finish a house—or in this case, thirty-two houses. In this chapter, the multitude of steps completed prior to or simultaneous with other elements of building come to the fore. This story emphasizes management of on-site production, that is, coordinating subcontracting tradesmen and overseeing carpentry assistants.

Montgomery's project points to potential economies of scale in production. Assembling the pieces of a house demanded time between steps. It required that the master builder bring together mechanics so that each could do his job without interruption, yet without delays waiting on other tradesmen. By working on several adjacent dwellings, Montgomery could shift men and tasks easily from one to another. Erecting party walls and chimneys on contiguous dwellings simultaneously, and moving scaffolding, tools, and stock among structures also led to savings in building multiple houses. In addition to productive economies of scale, Montgomery was able to spread administrative costs—getting permits, employing conveyancers, advertising properties—over a greater number of houses. The possibility of finding one buyer-landlord for all the dwellings alleviated concerns over costs associated with drawn-out sales and sweetened the attraction of ambitious endeavors. Supervisory advantages emerged from keeping journeymen and subcontractors close at hand, rather than dispersing them over Spring Garden or Philadelphia's many neighborhoods. Subcontractors, too, sought business at a single location and priced desirable jobs at discounts.

Economies of scale in construction, however, were limited, hampered by the nature of materials and production. Montgomery's Spring Garden development opens to view continuities as well as changes in building houses between 1790 and 1850. Wood framing methods remained critical to masonry structures which constituted the majority of building forms in Philadelphia at midcentury. New styles and amenities (plumbing, heating, lighting), however, prompted the master builder to adjust his management of assembly. He now chose among a wider array of materials and processes, and expanded his grasp of new products and techniques. Montgomery and his contemporaries might engage a subcontractor with a novel expertise, or make minor modifications in construction. Neither product innovations nor "modern conveniences," however, overhauled the residential building process in this period.[5]

Problems of construction resonated with builders active throughout the early nineteenth century. Accidents, constraining properties of material, bad weather, and human limitations handicapped the generation of mechanics active in 1790, as well as Joseph Montgomery's peers working in 1850. Conflicts between journeymen and masters—sometimes personal and short-lived, sometimes collective and structural—ignited at moments throughout these years. The ramifications for master builders facing looming deadlines—financial failure, for example—were familiar though more spectacular in Montgomery's time.

Site development acquired a growing administrative character as the nineteenth century progressed. Urbanizing sections of Philadelphia implemented ordinances requiring property owners to retain "regulators" to survey land, divide parcels into lots, and mark out building lines. In 1815, for example, surveyor Reading Howell regulated a lot on Fourth Street, also "[w]riting [a] permit" for a vault (that is, a masonry arch, in this case beginning in the cellar and extending under the common walkway).[6] Formal procedures added to the arrangements and costs incurred preliminary to breaking ground. House carpenters henceforth had to call at the city surveyor's office to "g[i]ve an order for getting the lines of the lot" drawn.[7] The munipical urge for control sometimes fell short of government's capabilities, however, especially in hot real estate markets. In 1833, for example, builders complained that the shortage of active experts caused them "much difficulty in getting their lots regulated ready for building."[8]

In the decades that marked Montgomery's maturity, the administrative and legalistic tenor to urban expansion extended beyond regulators and surveyors. Nuisances of work sites and concerns over safety gave rise to a system of construction permits. For the right to pile materials in public spaces and thoroughfares, a builder needed the imprimatur of local commissioners. To transgress lot boundaries and dig up the street to lay water or gas pipes also required their sanction. Municipal control offered more than regulation; it provided public revenue. No unified constituency would balk at the fees, usually folded into much greater sums months later when builders submitted their final bills; consequently, rates might rise sharply. In 1850, one builder marveled that he "had to Pay $1.00 instead of 25 cents, the old charge, a new ordinance having been recently made, changing the price."[9] Anticipating that bulky materials would block passersby, Montgomery secured permits at the Wood and Carlton Street sites to coincide with outside work in the fall of 1849. That year, Spring Garden commissioners issued permits for 417 three-story dwellings and stores, providing a rough indicator of construction activity in the year Montgomery undertook his development. The figure was a slight rise over the previous year's applications and an encouraging sign for the neighborhood's prosperity.[10]

At the time Montgomery made his deal, cheap two- and three-story houses were scattered throughout the immediate neighborhood of Cadwalader's Spring Garden parcel. Among homeowners and tenants were persons of color who labored as carters, porters, and washingwomen. The presence of Philadelphia's African-American working poor hints at why Cadwalader and fellow landowners had paid little regard to the area—and explains, too, their willingness to clear the lots once lucrative development beckoned. It was a formula repeated as the prosperous or fashionable neighborhoods advanced amoeba-like and absorbed the former edges of the city. Cadwalader's tenants would have to seek shelter and work space farther away from Philadelphia's core, or tucked into the congested alleys of the

inner city. If they had no means of taking away "improvements," Montgomery would have to see to clearing the lots himself. He could salvage
materials, setting his men to "pulling down frames" (that is, wooden buildings) that stood in the way of construction.[11] Newspaper advertisements
announcing the sale of frame structures at locations throughout Philadelphia, "to be removed immediately off the premises," invited tradesmen to
pick over what builders did not deem useful.[12]

With the lots regulated and cleared, Montgomery's superintendence
of site work began in earnest. Even in projects as large as thirty-two houses,
a complete distinction between builder and worker did not exist. At times
Montgomery picked up tools in making joists and raising rafters, as he "was
a master carpenter and builder—worked at the houses himself—and employed journeymen and apprentices to assist him."[13] If he mimicked other
builders, however, he also frequently left his employees to their tasks after
"giv[ing] directions." The business of building took Montgomery away
from the Wood and Carlton Street lots for hours, time spent applying to
Cadwalader's bookkeeper for advances, getting permits, ordering materials, paying bills, soliciting supplementary work, and drafting and revising
framing designs. When men other than his own journeymen and apprentices wielded their tools, a builder stopped to "see how the labourers were
coming," for instance, or to give the stonemasons "the lines & the heights."
He did not often linger, however, or interfere with mechanics skilled in
crafts besides carpentry. House carpenter William Eyre got "the Mason to
work at the celler wall about 9 o'clock" one spring day in 1849, but only
"staid there myself till noon." Likewise at another time, Eyre "believe[d]
the Bricklayer commenced on new wall . . . this morning." As the stage of
construction lay in the bailiwick of a different master craftsman, however,
Eyre had no cause to attend the site that day, and could only surmise.[14]

The master builder next "staked off the ground," and focused his initial attention on the crew of laborers engaged to dig out cellars. For the
three-story houses Montgomery was building, diggers would remove earth
several feet below ground level. (The appropriate support for the walls and
the desired height of the cellar determined the depth that laborers would
excavate.) Carters took the dirt away to become landfill on the city's river
banks or to dump in "brickponds"—gaping holes where clay had once been.
Builders also sold or traded the dirt to artisans who employed it in producing bricks or mortar.[15]

Montgomery might have found the ground on his parcel soft and unstable, as it lay near the northern remnants of Pegg's Run. He strove, there-

fore, to create a strong base to anchor the foundation walls. To this end, he threw any manner of rubbish and construction debris into the cellar and rammed it into the earth. On top of firm ground, a builder typically set a dirt or mortar floor, sometimes with lumber "sleepers" to provide a platform for wood flooring.[16] A mason built up the cellar walls. Random-sized foundation stone—mica schist from Germantown and Roxborough quarries, or gneiss from Delaware County lodes—made sturdy, durable bracing for the above-ground structure. Unless it began to "rain, & they were compelled to quit," masons could complete cellar walls for one of Montgomery's alley dwellings in a mere two days.[17]

Contemporary newspapers occasionally reported construction accidents, and these episodes hint at dangers in excavating and walling the cellar. While site disasters were not frequently covered in the press, what incidents did occur show that cave-ins were among the most devastating. Typical of known cases was an accident that transpired in 1827, while men were digging a foundation: "[T]he earth fell in, and crushed beneath it two of the workmen." One man died, while the second "was very severely injured." Laborer Isaac Townsend survived "a cellar falling" on him, but with injuries that led to a "long confinement," impoverishment, and a spell in debtors' prison. Torrential rains compromised partially completed cellars and raised the risks of excavating and walling foundations.[18]

Most master mechanics superintended their crews to complete foundations without catastrophe. The builder then proceeded to "arrang[e] the lines" and corners of the house "for starting the brick work." Bricklayers followed stonemasons immediately to bring the walls up to the level of the first floor. But weather could hamper activity at this juncture, just as it did in setting the foundation. As a matter of course, a builder could expect that from time to time there would be "showers all day, preventing the bricklayers from doing much."[19] Once underway, however, the structure rose quickly. Mortar became less plastic the longer it set and had to be applied within a few hours after mixing. Consequently, each master bricklayer worked optimally with two assistants: one (a boy) to mix mortar, and another to carry the heavy hod (the wooden trough for mortar and bricks) to the spot where the bricklayer shaped the wall (Figure 23). Laboring with his crew on plain tasks, a master craftsman might lay one thousand bricks in a day; with the assistance of his mixer and hod carrier, he could raise a wall the length of the Carlton Street houses (fifteen feet) about five feet. But the bricklayer was careful not to pile bricks any greater than that height in a single spot, lest the wall shrink in drying, and throw off level and tightly worked masonry.[20]

23 Brickmasons built walls a few feet at a time. Note the hod carrier balanced precariously on the ladder and the ready supply of mortar on the scaffold platform. Alexander Anderson Scrapbooks. Print Collection, Miriam and Ira D. Wallach Division of Art, Prints and Photographs, The New York Public Library, Astor, Lenox and Tilden Foundations.

In designing adjoining houses, Montgomery saved in materials and labor by using "party" (shared) walls. Exterior walls for dwellings the size Montgomery was building were typically nine inches thick. A shared wall need only measure thirteen inches—sparing half as many bricks required in two distinct walls. Constructing two rows of sixteen dwellings, with as many as fourteen party walls (as shown in Figure 22), economized significantly on bricks and bricklaying. Had none of the houses adjoined, Montgomery would have increased his expenses by approximately $500 for the entire project. While Montgomery reaped all advantages to scale, builders of one or two houses could also benefit from similar strategies by supporting joists in part with an existing wall. Under these circumstances, the developer of the new lot paid the owner of the neighboring building half the value of the existing masonry (and half the charge for measuring it).[21]

The bricklayer worked in tandem with the house carpenter. When the former reached the level where the first story was to begin, the latter had to be ready with framing joist to insert into the walls. The builder was responsible for "[m]aking plans . . . to ascertain the number & size of joist," so as to accommodate the weight-bearing needs of each story, the dimensions of the rooms, and the position of interior doors, staircases, and chimneys. Having toured area suppliers "hunting up Joist" for his buildings, Montgomery might send his men to the lumberyard, where (out of the way of the bricklayers) they had ample space to cut and lay out the bulky pieces. At the construction site, he and his journeymen then joined the newly worked framing members to girders and horizontal supports. If he was short of laborers or his supervisory capacity was stretched, however, Montgomery could subcontract the framing. Regardless of the path he chose, "being anxious to keep the Bricklayers steady at work," the master builder pressed on to finish the floor of joist and place it within the brick walls.[22]

For each point where two pieces of lumber met, carpenters shaped strong mortise and tenon joints. A joint could entail a simple mortise and tenon—a socket chiseled out of one piece of lumber and a projecting form in the second member sized to fit the socket. Some frames used "through" joints, with the tenon extending completely through the mortise and set into joist holes in the brick wall. More elaborate contacts, such as tusked or double tusked tenons, added indentations within the joint for greater solidity. Once satisfied with the fit of the tenon in the mortise, a carpenter drilled an auger hole through the assembled members. Temporary hook pins held joints together while carpenters coaxed and adjusted the frame to make it square. "[L]evelling up" the joist, they subsequently hammered wooden pins into the auger holes to pull the framing members together tightly.[23]

Coordination and timing were key to placing supports for windows and doors as well. The bricklayers "started the front [wall] . . . yesterday afternoon," one carpenter noted, and "I set the 1st story w[indow] frames about 6 o'clock this evening." Window frames and sills came out of his shop, where he and his journeymen spent days "lining out stuff," "cutting out & planing [it] up," and finally "putting window frames together." By the following week, the bricklayers had advanced to the second story, and the carpenter set more window frames. Working in this way, bricklayers and carpenters, putting on the floor joists and inserting the door and window frames, progressed gradually around and up the dwelling. If the design specified marble window and door sills, mechanics might bump elbows with the stonemason. In setting the water table—the course of bricks or stone that projected slightly outward from the plane of the house and shielded the foundation from damage by rain—the stonemasons, bricklayers, and carpenters worked closely together. At midcentury, the marble course used machine-sawed slabs produced in highly capitalized steampowered firms.[24]

Next to excavating the cellar, working on scaffolding as the stories rose seems to have been the second most dangerous aspect of construction. Merely erecting and dismantling it opened numerous occasions for "very near[ly] causing [one's] end." Men who mounted scaffolding day after day in pursuit of their trades played the odds. Hugh Brown, a day laborer who "carried the hod, for such Bricklayers as imployed him for 6 or 7 years past," was one such gambler. At work one September day, "a scafling one story gave way with the hod on his shoulder, and in the fall thereof [he] got his arm broken, which deprived [him] of following his daily avocation for 3 months and upwards." A "black man" who carried the hod fared worse in his fall from greater heights. The laborer "ascended the ladder, and throwing the contents of the hod suddenly upon the staging, the whole gave way and two of the men [who were working on the chimney] came to the ground." The hod carrier "lodged on a projecting platform . . . and was greatly injured," while one of the masons "struck against a post some distance from the ground" and was killed.[25]

With physical and productive risks ever present, completing walling and framing without incident signaled an important achievement; mortgage creditors recognized progress toward a valuable structure by opening their purses. They advanced funds "when the first floor of joist" was set in the brickwork, "when the second floor of joist are on," and, depending on the specific house and deal, upon completion of the third-story joist. Thus, Cadwalader agreed to pay Montgomery $100 for each house brought up to the first level and a like installment at the second-story marker. Montgomery used the sums to pay material creditors a portion of their existing demands and place deposits on supplies he would need at future points of construction. His journeymen would have relished a payday but awaited full settlement until Montgomery sold the buildings.[26]

The garret joist, heralded as the "raising floor," marked the final major step of outdoor work. Once secured in place, the house carpenters cut roof posts and rafters, and assembled trusses (the triangular end framework) and connecting beams. Bricklayers "finished topping out the walls & chimneys," enabling carpenters to "set up the Rafters & set the cornice." For his row houses, Montgomery would have chosen the simplest trusses and benefited from the scale of his project. He could have treated the roofs of two dwellings as one structural problem, positioning trusses on the alley walls but omitting them along the party walls. Given the combined span of two buildings (thirty feet), additional trusses were not critical to roof strength.[27]

If Montgomery put dormer windows in his houses, he would need the upper framing members to bear considerable weight. He might place the rafters closer together or bridge (i.e., brace) the roof timbers with additional support. Inclusion of dormer windows enabled house occupants to use attics for sleeping quarters (for household labor, apprentices, or boarders, for instance); the master builder might then construct the garret frame so it was ready to floor.[28]

For roof work, the master carpenter equipped his crew with boards and putlocks, and with poles to "plant" in the ground and support the scaffolding platforms.[29] He would direct his carpenters to lath the roof, that is, nail narrow strips of lumber to the rafters. The laths served as a basis for the protective material that would cover the roof and shield the inside of the house from the elements. If the design specified a shingle roof, the carpenters continued the work, the application of cedar shingles resting within their domain. At this stage, the master builder pressured his men to move quickly and toil long hours to get the structure "under roof," that it not remain "uncovered . . . and liable to injury from the weather."[30] One master house carpenter testified to the urgency of this task, working beside his men on inclement days. "[B]y close application and hard work," he and his men finished the roof "just as it commenced raining." Another time, they worked four hours "in the snow shingling" to get "the roof closed up" before winter halted outdoor work—"a cold job it was." [31]

Cedar shingling was but one of the materials from which Montgomery could choose to finish the roof. Tin or slate cost more, and the requisite skill to handle either lay beyond the scope of his journeymen carpenters. Least expensive—but most daring for a dwelling—was "composition roofing," a conglomeration of pitch, rosin, and tar that manufacturers developed in the 1830s. Makers claimed that the material "costs half less than Slate, or Tin and 1/4 less than shingles, and wears as long." They promoted it as well because it "dispenses with high gable walls, the roofs requiring an inclination of not more than three quarters of an inch to the foot." The stuff could be laid on the ceiling joists, and the cost of rafters spared. [32] Some builders liked it well enough to use it on their own residences, but Montgomery rejected the lower-end product for his buildings. To make an impression on the house buyers he had in mind, he selected slate tiles. His decision raised the total cost of roofing for the rows by a few hundred dollars. [33]

By late December 1849, four months after he made his purchase from Cadwalader, Montgomery appears to have roofed those properties on which he had broken ground. He had reached a good point for suspending any new construction until the early spring. He had not operated haphazardly but organized tasks so that he might cover the unfinished buildings before winter. Frigid days in January, February, and March restrained builders from certain activities. Frozen ground made digging cellars brutally hard work and laying foundations nearly impossible. Carters labored with difficulty when hauling stones over partially frozen roads, and delays in delivery retarded walling cellars. If builders could procure bricks in late winter— when they were both scarce and expensive—bricklayers could rarely put them to use. On cold days, "the mortar froze on the bricklayers' trowels." [34] Freezing temperatures, moreover, barred new mortar from hardening correctly and caused it to remain dangerously unsound. Any moisture that fell on exposed brick or stone walls could lead to cracking when the mercury plummeted, proving disastrous for the building.

Construction was at best an intermittent venture in winter, squeezed in opportunistically on mild days. Like Montgomery, builders exerted themselves to prepare their houses for indoor work before late December. But work that mechanics could accomplish inside, too, was restricted by cold. Plaster, for example, became unstable if frozen before it dried. Painters considered the biting, wet winter months of January through March undesirable for painting (and, incidentally, avoided hot months as well). Consequently, James Hopkins complained about the "extreme cold weather" that contributed to his underemployment as a painter in the severe winter of 1831 to 1832.[35]

Human limitations, as Hopkins implied, also curtailed labor for prolonged periods on raw days. Thomas Hazzard was a bricklayer who could "only work at his trade in the summer season and the little he earned beyond keeping his family in the summer time was soon eaten up in preparation for winter." Hazzard's personal burden, that he "has been afflicted with the inflamatory rheumatism . . . [and was unable] to use his hands to work" exacerbated nature's severity. Repeated exposure to winter chills led to Hazzard's malady. Conditions common in construction, however, caused many fellow mechanics — such as house carpenter Isaac Britton, who was "laid up with rheumatism & other sicknesses" for eighteen months — to commiserate.[36]

The compounded difficulties of making progress in winter encouraged some builders to close up their properties and await warmer weather. Carpenters weeded through their shop's castaways, or visited second-hand dealers, to collect doors, window sashes and shutters to seal the dwellings. Such precautions could minimize damage from nature's storms or the city's vandals. Fearing, too, that arson posed a particular threat to deserted properties, at this juncture builders frequently bought fire insurance.[37]

Many builders moved ahead with inside work throughout the winter, however, accommodating their expectations to the season's vagaries. One of the first interior tasks carpenters faced was to floor each room, nailing the boards to the joists. Building in 1849, Montgomery would have purchased stuff at the lumberyard, and had it sent directly to a planing mill for working into floorboards with tongued and grooved edges. Laying a tight and level floor was a challenge, particularly if the materials were still green, or if they had warped after machine planing. Carpenters had to judge how well seasoned the lumber was and adjust the tightness of the boards to anticipate shrinking. Finally, they planed the floors to level the surface; skilled craftsmen thereby employed an inexpensive hand process to improve upon products made with state-of-the-art technology.[38]

During the winter, Montgomery might hope to get the properties "ready for plastering" (and demand another advance from Cadwalader). Carpenters tacked wood laths onto the brick and to the ceiling supports to provide a base for the compound. Come March, when temperatures had risen, the plasterer slathered these narrow strips with a lime, sand, and hair mixture, working more precisely as he applied successive coats (numbering

in all two or three). Plaster seeped into the spaces between the laths, form-
ing "keys" that locked it into place. For fine plaster mortars, the craftsman
mixed pure lime with water only. For ornate stucco work—for ceiling or
fireplace front decoration, for example—he daubed a gypsum or "Plaster of
Paris" substance on molds carved or planed from wood.[39]

Plaster demanded quick action to take advantage of its plasticity; once
applied, however, each coat required several days to dry. Wet plaster stalled
mechanics from going forward on any other work inside the building. Carpenters adjourned to the shop, where they continued to prepare moldings
or put together window frames for new construction. Superintending a
house at the plastering stage, one master carpenter ventured out of town
for a few days, "in as much as but little could be done . . . untill the . . . plastering should dry." Weather forwarded or impeded drying time. The plaster
might harden "very fast, with the high wind," or remain tacky on humid
and calm days.[40]

In dwellings where plaster had set, Montgomery's crew renewed its
work on interiors, likely mixing jobbing with daily wages in calculating
compensation. Inside carpentry involved finishing door and window cas-
ings (the visible trim surrounding the frames), studding and putting up par-
tition walls, completing stairs, and putting in the washboard (baseboard),
chair rails, and cornice moldings. The crew built chimney closets, trimmed
the chimney, made pediments on interior doors, and shelved the vaults. Carpenters also put in stair rails, and hung window sashes, doors, and shutters.

Builders who plied their trades in the early decades of the nineteenth
century fashioned joinery in their shops in the winter (recall activity on
Joshua Sharples's premises), or subcontracted it to specialized nonmechanized woodworkers. Montgomery, in contrast, built in an era when
steampowered sash and blind manufactories in Philadelphia turned out
standardized pieces. Montgomery bought his "sash work" from one such
manufacturer, and his "doors & shutters" from a second firm. His crew
of carpenters installed the prefabricated features. As builders bought more
prepared parts, they abdicated control to sellers of these wares. When suppliers failed to meet the orders as promised, the delay upset the plans of
builders. At the same time, however, securing punctual deliveries became
even more critical to superintending extensive construction and "keeping
the hands . . . continuously employed." Stymied waiting for supplies, a carpenter at one building site admitted that "we were not doing much of any-
thing that day." Poor management turned out to be a symptom, if not the
cause, of the sheriff's sale that ensued on the unfinished property.[41]

Dwellings of the vintage of Montgomery's houses were often plastered with a "white coating," dispensing with the necessity of painting the walls and ceilings. Likely, however, Montgomery at least had joinery painted or varnished to seal and protect the raw wood. (Sash and blind manufacturers did not yet sell their wares prepainted). The painter's familiarity with linseed oil, drying oils, spirits (turpentine), white lead, and dyes equipped him to adjust his recipes and techniques to particular surfaces. For his supplies, he tapped Philadelphia's rich stock of chemical products, for example those marketed by Wetherill & Brothers paint manufactory and Harrison Brothers white lead works. He anticipated how different grains would react to mixtures and tints, and "killed" knots in lumber (to inhibit sap from oozing through to the surface) by coating them with pastes of slaked lime.[42]

Painting captures the advantages subcontractors reaped on large developments. (Bricklayers and plasterers discovered comparable gains.) Working on a series of dwellings enabled the painter to allow plenty of drying time between coats. Yet, with multiple canvasses, he could move his journeymen throughout neighboring houses to an untouched room or a naked sash. Even clean-up was reduced, as his brush rarely had occasion to dry.

A handful of other craftsmen round out the subcontracting expertise collected at a Philadelphia building project at midcentury. Following the plasterers and painters, paperhangers might decorate the dining room and parlors with the finest sheets from France or, by Montgomery's day, American-produced papers (Figure 24). One contemporary builder obliged the tenant of his new house (a more expensive model than Montgomery's) by finishing it with "Glazed papers" on the first and second floor walls, cheaper "unglazed paper" in the "3rd story Chambers," and "Oak paper to be varnished" in the bathroom.[43] Any time after the roof was secured, a tinsmith installed rain gutters to drain into the watercourses in the alleyways between row houses. While carpenters completed interior woodwork, an ironsmith worked to install fireplace grates and hardware. Gas fitters connected lighting fixtures to municipal gas lines in a growing number of existing and new residences (though not yet in Montgomery's neighborhood). A marble mason set chimney mantels (if they were to be done in stone) and also the outside steps. In contrast to decades earlier, however, marble masons at Montgomery's house did not fashion the mantels and dress them at the site. Rather, they installed ready-made items produced in Philadelphia's steampowered marble yards, and selected by builders at the yards' showrooms.[44]

The plumber was an increasingly important mechanic in mid-nine-

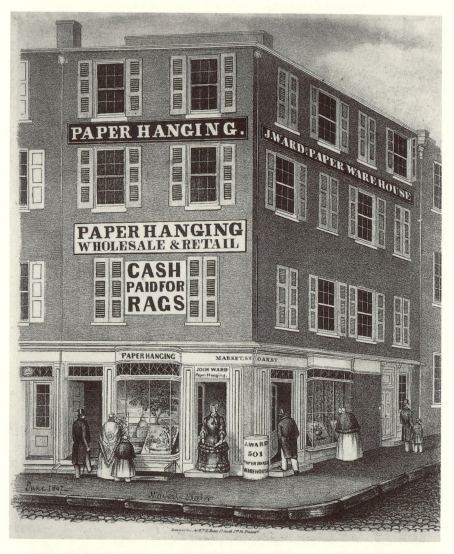

24 Middle-class homebuyers and tenants selected from an expanding array of decorative wallpapers for their residences. John Ward's Western Paper Hangings Establishment, 1848, W. H. Rease (Artist). Courtesy of The Library Company of Philadelphia.

teenth century residential design. Montgomery retained one to lay the pipe joining the public supply to several hydrants located in the yards behind his Spring Garden rows. Each hydrant probably serviced occupants of four houses (two fronting on Carlton Street and two fronting on Wood Street), sparing Montgomery the expense of installing pipe dedicated to each dwelling. Montgomery did not build bathhouses, and provided neither cold nor furnace-heated water indoors. Elsewhere in the city, meanwhile, builders incorporated these "modern conveniences" into new houses and retrofit older dwellings. Montgomery, however, anticipated that high-end customers (many of whom were beginning to embrace new conceptions of the hygienic body) would avoid the Spring Garden development. Instead, his clientele would forego amenities in exchange for lower-priced shelter.[45]

Montgomery pursued a similar strategy of cost savings in sanitation by designing his development to share backyard privies, one for each cluster of four houses. Privies took some trouble to hollow out and render stable. House carpenter William Eyre noted that his twenty-eight-foot deep privy well, with a five-foot three-inch diameter, took ten man-days to dig out. After reaching the desired depth, masons built brick walls to keep the pits from caving in. The supports enabled them to withstand repeated emptying (a task that no doubt fell to laborers at the bottom of the city's socioeconomic ladder). Initial expense and ongoing maintenance for owners prompted Montgomery and contemporary builders to minimize the number of privies they put on their properties.[46]

Compared to Philadelphia's court dwellings, Montgomery's allotment of privies was ample, though they were less private and convenient than those designated for more expensive houses in prime residential neighborhoods. "Water-closets" were novelties that had only begun to intrigue American housing consumers. In 1850, Moyamensing, a neighborhood comparable to Spring Garden in population and development, boasted a mere six water closets among more than 4,000 dwellings.[47] At the basest extreme of sanitation (and health) stood a class of dwellings that shocked well-intentioned Philadelphians. In 1833 reformers visited sixty-four dwellings in a destitute section of the city's Delaware riverfront. Thirty houses had no privies, a deficiency residents dealt with by tossing human effluvium into the nearby river and public thoroughfares. The privies of the remaining thirty-four buildings were located in cellars and in vaults that ran under the street.[48]

The cellars in Montgomery's Carlton Street dwellings served a different purpose, incorporating cooking (and cleaning) space for residents. The first-floor rear room in houses that extended two rooms back typically served as a kitchen—in as much as it had a hearth, a masonry floor, a dry sink and, on occasion, a water source and outlet. Residents of Montgomery's larger and more prominent houses (on Wood Street) found the kitchen facilities in the rear more convenient than the accommodations in the cellars of their Carlton Street neighbors. What Montgomery's plan lacked, however, were innovations such as ranges, which by the mid 1840s had become features common to houses marketed with "every convenience."[49]

In the final weeks before mechanics and laborers finished a dwelling entirely, there seemed always to be "a few little jobs still to do." Builder Eyre, consequently, rallied his "Bricklayers, Stone cutters & Plasterers & also the Plumbers [to endeavor] to draw their respective portions of the work to a close." If a fence was to be put up and painted, or the yard to be paved with a footpath, the carpenters, painters, and brickmasons—"all requiring nudging up"—would need to attend to the tasks. Some builders even sodded the yards to the houses they built, albeit for the more costly dwellings. Montgomery enclosed his lots to prohibit use of the water hydrants and the privies by households beyond the bounds. In the yards of every four dwellings, he built gates for inhabitants to reach their designated facilities (see Figure 22). General clean-up of construction debris also took a day or two and might be parceled out to a carter or an unskilled laborer; any salvaged materials supplemented the low wages men and boys in these occupations earned.[50]

Weather, production snafus, stretched finances, and labor strife thwarted precise schedules in construction, but builders knew the approximate time required between the groundbreaking and finishing touches of a modest residence. Ground-rent contracts bound the grantee to erect a "substantial" (three-story) brick dwelling, usually within one year of the conveyance—suggesting that builder and ground lord considered the term ample opportunity. Both parties understood, however, that the artisan would not begin outside work on a project between December and early March. Typically, a small operator could count on two cycles of construction within twelve months. In the first cycle, he broke ground in late summer (or early fall) and carried the inside work through the initial months of the new year. He could then take advantage of a second cycle of building by digging a foundation in the early spring and working through the temperate months, completing the second structure in midsummer. Montgomery's peer William Eyre found this timetable fit his business, an enterprise that integrated custom house building with repairs and alterations. At any one time, the carpenter rarely carried on more than one new construction.

Eyre's work routines provide an approximate sense of the progress in production that a modest builder could expect to make. It took six weeks to get a house the size of Montgomery's Wood Street structure under roof, another three or four weeks before it was ready for plastering, and an additional eight to twelve weeks until completion—in all, it took five to six months, without counting the initial weeks spent in ironing out the contract and drawing the plans. Large builders might stagger groundbreaking throughout the year, though winter always constrained them; they, too, had to roof their houses by late December. By creating locations where stages of production varied, builders were able to shift their men from house to house. The strategy was increasingly useful as prefabricated parts became central to the industry and replaced hours that men had once spent laboring in the craftshop. Expanding the number of properties in progress, without necessarily increasing the number of hands, smoothed out some of the fluctuations in employment that might have otherwise affected a house carpenter's crew.

Given the time that builders knew would be lost to uncooperative weather, they were often impatient when subcontractors or suppliers upset their calculations. Eyre criticized a stonemason who twice failed to appear when expected, "thus causing me much loss of time [in tracking him down], as well as delay to the building." Postponement of one phase of construction hindered each subsequent—or simultaneous—process. Consequently, when a subcontracting framer failed to move "fast enough to keep the Bricklayers at work," Eyre was "obliged to take 6 of my own hands to assist him." Better to shift the tasks of his own journeymen, than chance that the bricklayers would begin another job and be unavailable when Eyre needed them.[51]

In addition to weather and poor coordination of subcontractors and suppliers, "[j]ourneymen not going on with the work" could disrupt construction schedules and devastate a builder's finances.[52] Master house carpenters complained that "[t]he time selected [for journeymen to strike] is when their employers have large contracts on hand."[53] Perhaps Montgomery, like others before him, battled with union mechanics. A strike in the summer of 1850 and its reprise the following spring could have crippled Montgomery as he finished the last of the Spring Garden houses. The experience of builder William Eyre, however, indicates that trade unionists failed to win all journeymen to their cause. In May 1851, when "many of the

Journeymen house carpenters" were "walking about having struck for $1.75 per day" (a raise of twenty-five cents per day), he noted that "my hands have not joined them."[54]

Associations of workingmen periodically pushed the conflict of interest between employers and employees to the forefront. The daily routine of work in Montgomery's time, however, still allowed masters and journeymen to reproduce a kindred culture of craft—one that could be instrumental in overriding the divergent interests of employer and employee. Consider the tradition of the "Raising Supper," which commemorated skill and cooperation upon completion of a building's garret ("raising") floor. In the eighteenth century, clients who had contracted for building hosted the party. "Went to the supper of Robert Erwin given to a few friends and his workmen on the raising of his house," a diarist recorded in 1795, underscoring the role of the client.[55] Raising celebrations continued into the nineteenth century, albeit in a modified form. The repast in the nineteenth century was more likely to mark the framing of churches, schools, unique residences, and public structures, than average dwellings.[56] Speculative building, however, meant that there was no paying customer on hand. Extensive row development, too, diminished the momentousness of this rite. In custom building craftsmen continued to hold modest raisings. Eyre and his journeymen initiated one in 1849: "we all partook of a collection in our shop prepared as a little raising supper."[57]

The small size of Eyre's enterprise (in 1849, five journeymen and several apprentices) may have intensified its paternalistic character and inhibited the workers from simply seeing themselves as employees. Like Montgomery, a builder on a larger scale, Eyre often labored alongside his journeymen. And while he criticized them on occasion for "botched" work, he also deemed some employees "invaluable." Eyre even shared spontaneous celebrations of achievement with his men. Having finished a roofing job on a pleasantly mild February day, for example, journeyman "Charles & I took our dinners on the roof." A craft culture that emphasized the commonalities between master and employee, rather than their divergent interests in a competitive capitalist economy, survived in many quarters of the trade.[58]

A builder might be spurred to sell any or all his houses as quickly as possible in order to plow proceeds back into the remaining incomplete structures. A quick infusion of funds placated mortgage and artisan creditors and journeymen hands until the builder could parlay another property into cash. If the market was brisk or his resources exhausted, a builder of a speculative house attempted to line up a buyer even before he began interior work, much as house carpenter William Hamitton did by offering for sale seven three-story brick houses, "now finishing."[59] Similarly, one house carpenter sold his dwelling, but bonded himself to "finish the two coats of painting pave the passage to the privy in the yard lay the foot way in the front of the House, make an entry on the second floor in order to make the room private paper the lower room . . . & finish the cellar window."[60]

In the 1790s, builders had two ways to market their real estate. They could attempt the business on their own, or they could commit the matter to agents. Rather than pay the commissions of brokers or relinquish power to negotiate, artisans frequently chose the first option and advertised their properties in Philadelphia's newspapers. They enticed potential residents with promises of their houses' desirability and attracted would-be landlords with claims of good rental prospects. Two building partners, for example, alerted readers to the "new 3 story brick house [with a] furnace in the cellar, gas, hot and cold water up to the 3rd story, with every convenience" that they wished to sell.[61] Another pair hoped that the rents paid by the "good tenants" in their four new buildings in Spring Garden would attract an investor. The appeal of the real estate was compounded by the fact that it was "[c]lear of all incumbrances" (that is, ground rent, mortgages and liens), and could be "bought at a bargain."[62] When builders failed to attract buyers for their houses, they retained them for rentals, used them as loan collateral, and sold them at a later date. Desperate for cash to ward off creditors or fuel another enterprise, however, a builder could not always afford to keep abundant rental properties. He might settle for less favorable terms if he needed to sell. Carpenter Sebastian Root, for example, took a mortgage in payment for one of his houses because he had no cash offers. He needed liquid funds badly, however, and in order to sell the bond quickly, took a loss of several hundred dollars.[63]

Dwellings that artisans could not dispose of obstructed their flow of operating capital. As speculative projects grew in scale, expeditious turnover of houses became more vital, leading builders to engage professional agents more readily. Closely linked to the conveyancing business, real estate specialists were not new to Montgomery and his contemporaries. John Girard used "House Broker" and conveyancer Edward Bonsall when he arrived in Philadelphia in November 1794, so that "he would see the whole of that kind of property that was for Sale in town, that he could there take Notes of the places, look at them . . . and make his purchase."[64] Five decades later, much of a broker's business consisted of selling row developments on behalf of builders. Emlen & Fisher, for example, hoped to sell "[t]wenty-one three story brick Houses, about 16 feet front, in one block."[65] A quick and neat transaction—with a purchaser looking to acquire a conservative investment—would have suited the brokers (and builders) well. Recall that Montgomery might hope to be relieved of marketing his properties by Cadwalader's interest in acquiring the entire development.

A buyer had best beware that the property—particularly new construction—was clear of debts. A search of court records would turn up outstanding mortgages. Acting on behalf of a client, conveyancer James Carmall initiated a search for any mortgage by bricklayer and builder Jonathan P. Smith on his newly finished buildings in Northern Liberties. The Recorder of Deeds consulted the public documents and responded promptly: "I do not find any unsatisfied Mortgage on Record given by Jonathan P. Smith" on the property.[66]

Carmall took further precaution by having each artisan who had worked on the buildings sign a release exempting the properties from any construction debts owed them by Smith.[67] The release preempted subscribers from pursuing unpaid bills under Pennsylvania's mechanics lien laws. Philadelphia instituted its first lien statute in 1803; with subsequent revisions, the laws enabled master craftsmen and suppliers to reserve a creditor priority in suits, fictively holding the building until debts were settled. Master mechanics still followed ground lords and mortgage lenders, but reserved a right to the value of labor and materials that other creditors of the principal builder could not override.[68]

Under the lien laws, creditors had no more than six months from the time of their labor or material delivery to file claims. Within a few years of the provisions, mechanics took to filing claims regularly, almost habitually, to insure their rights in the event the builder defaulted. By 1811 the vast majority of artisans hired attorneys-at-law to weave through the technicalities of liens. Few claimants seemed to hesitate in pressing their suits, though public sale of the building ensued. Chasing after unpaid debts was among the business tasks of master builders, and they could expect to appear in court on litigated lien cases a few times a year. Not surprisingly, the precaution that Carmall took in 1819 to ward off lien claims was far more common four decades later. By 1850, contracts often stipulated that builders were to deliver completed structures with a release signed by all mechanics and material men. Montgomery's mortgage agreement with Cadwalader, too, stipulated that he would receive the last installment only after he presented Cadwalader with a release from all subcontractors and suppliers.[69]

In a final twist, however, Montgomery could not accomplish this feat. The economic recovery that had looked promising in August 1849 when Montgomery began his venture proved elusive afterall. Several mechanic lien claimants, impatient with Montgomery's failure to find homebuyers and pay his debts, forced the sale of the Spring Garden dwellings. In a sheriff's auction held in April 1852, Cadwalader, as the highest bidder, bought the buildings. He paid from $282 to $574 for each lot (which included two houses); the total fund from the sale amounted to $11,415. Despite the protest of lien claimants, the mortgage creditor (whose agreement with Montgomery predated their debts) also collected the funds raised in the auction—less court fees ($66) and overdue taxes ($420). Set against his advances, the thirty-two completed houses cost Cadwalader $13,071. The price to the mortgage investor averaged a little more than $408 for dwellings probably worth around $2,000 each.

A decade later, Montgomery still worked as a house carpenter in Philadelphia, but his ambitions never again matched the Spring Garden development.[70] Artisan colleagues and suppliers would have been slow to forgive the complete losses on Montgomery's enterprise and reluctant to extend him trade credit and material advances. He learned, moreover, that economies of scale alone could not assure the financial success of a builder. The pressures and incentives to undertake big developments, nevertheless, were substantial. Productive savings—achieved in superintendence of his labor force and construction of party walls, for instance—could enable a builder to rein in his costs. He could, moreover, spread administrative, sales, and marketing expenses over a greater number of properties, price his real estate more competitively, and augment his chances of gain in speculative construction.

Greater availability of prefabricated parts contributed as well to the mushrooming size of building projects. Factory-bought window sashes, doors, and shutters did not speed up assembly at the construction site. By drastically curtailing their preparation at the shop, however, the master builder could dedicate an increasing proportion of labor hours to house carpentry; conversely, only if he engaged to build more houses could he keep his work force fully occupied. Nonetheless, no matter how inventive and persistent, he could discover only a finite variety of techniques to create advantages of scale. Seasons, the inherent character of materials, and the cumbersome and varied nature of construction continued to guide the industry's rhythms and constrain scale gains of on-site assembly in 1850, as they do even today.

Conclusion

ARTISANS—both masters and journeymen—were central players in economic change between 1790 and 1850. Philadelphia's real estate industry grew increasingly complex in these years, paralleling trends of specialization, differentiation, professionalization, and scale that transformed the American economy at large. Building tradesmen maneuvered within this economic maelstrom to place their imprint on the organization of credit and production. They acted creatively to anticipate markets and to secure the means necessary to pursue their ends. Though grander forces periodically swept the trade's practitioners into turmoil, they persisted in buying land, building on their own account, implementing new technologies, and investigating new markets. Their behavior was part and parcel of what it meant to be independent men in the first half of the nineteenth century.

The particular nature of legal and financial institutions in Philadelphia shaped its capitalist economy. Ground-rent tenure exercised a critical role in the expectations and actions of artisan builders and enabled small producers to persevere in construction to Joseph Montgomery's day. From the nation's early bull markets—such as the one John Munday rode in 1794— the ability to get land with no money down encouraged artisans to build on speculation. It compelled mechanics like John Munday and Moses Lancaster to inject a dynamic ingredient into their conception of "competence." These men could not avoid aggressive market behavior; immediate rewards and disappointments necessitated both short-term speculative behavior and long-term goals of accumulation. As veteran craftsmen, they assisted journeymen attempting to rise from wage work to subcontracting and finally to master status. At the same time, they cast themselves as entrepreneurs, always ready to exploit an opportunity—or to concoct one. Sometimes in concert with capitalists, sometimes in contestation with them, and often as capitalists themselves, they sketched the parameters of property instruments and credit vehicles. Just as quickly, however, artisans tested those limits through practice and through legal avenues. They discovered new ways to raise funds in pursuit of building interests and juggled craft credit with mortgages, notes, and cash resources. Continued access to credit invested the master craftsman-builder with the means to survive as a self-employed artisan; as a consequence, there was little proletarianization in the Philadelphia construction trades.

The immersion of building mechanics in an inherently unstable capitalist economy, however, exposed them to great risk. Vulnerability to contractions in the market, and international and national phenomena that sent interest rates soaring (and credit evaporating) or property values plummeting plagued nineteenth-century proprietors. Overextension of finances, job estimates upset by sudden increases in real estate prices, and poor calculations about consumer demand led to crises in many careers. Fellow artisans whose mismanagement reduced outstanding trade balances to worthless debts, regional shortages in labor and material, and production difficulties in construction itself cut off promising men in their prime. While their colonial counterparts had never been immune to such problems, the magnitude of later real estate ventures and the increasingly integrated national economy worsened the impact of business disruptions.

Assisting mechanics in erecting an infrastructure for Philadelphia's real estate industry were innovators of many stripes. Brokers mediated property and money transactions, carving out niches of financial, technical, or sales specialties. At the nadir of Warnet Myers's career in 1840, differentiation of the industry enabled the erstwhile builder to set himself up as a broker exclusively dedicated to real estate deals—raising start-up funds, but also marketing finished houses. Lawyers, too, made their marks in the building industry. They deciphered an ever more inscrutable body of statutes, procedures, and judicial opinions that governed ground rent, mortgages, insolvency, and mechanic liens. By the mid 1800s, attorneys-at-law (stressing specialties in property issues) counseled capitalists and building mechanics routinely in property transactions.

Running a business pulled the master mechanic in diverse directions in Montgomery's era. Raising money, controlling funds, soliciting jobs, ordering supplies, and finding subcontractors consumed much of a builder's time. Also on the artisan's plate (and heaped higher with each decade) were preconstruction tasks in design and contracting. In the first half of the nineteenth century, architects expanded their influence in building although they rarely usurped artisan control over residential construction. Taking the lead from these up-and-coming professionals, mechanics perpetuated some of their architectural and business practices. Applying techniques learned as apprentices and expanded through self-education and practice, an independent man marketed his expertise. No longer did simple sketches suffice to win a client's commission. Now, architectural drawings—plans, elevations, renderings—showcased the facility of a master. Conjoined with estimates and specifications, drawings also satisfied the new legalistic tenor of the building enterprise—even as textual language was gaining authority over graphic expressions. Accords between master builders and subcontractors acquired a similar character and more precisely outlined the obligations of both parties as older generalities failed to withstand the pressures of a competitive business.

In addition to honing his graphic talents and contractual aptitude, the master builder had to keep current with new designs, technologies, and products to persuade clients to walk in his door. Forced to stretch his craft expertise and business oversight, a builder might have found in his extended schedule grounds to reject the traditional measure and value systems of pricing work. The centrality of advance housing construction to the trade, moreover, made measurement less common and critical. The streamlining of pricing methods to further facilitate the speed and cost of getting houses to market encouraged contract building and eluded the scrutiny of craft associations.

Innovation and change also characterized the regional industries that supported urban construction. Artisans, material suppliers, and men of commerce brought together immense sums of labor and capital to convert nature's wealth into producer goods. Local knowledge and experience, as well as political lobbying for transportation projects that extended the geographic range for supplies, were critical in exploiting geological deposits. New fuels, new machines, new processes, new organization, new markets, and new occupations transformed the way that some materials—marble, for example—got to builders in Philadelphia.

By 1850, a wide spectrum of business organizations, productive processes and technologies existed simultaneously in lumber, brick, lime, and marble production. Uneven developments had far-reaching implications for artisan ownership and the viability of petty entrepreneurs. Some sectors, in particular marble, integrated ownership of scarce geological sources with finishing the materials for producer and consumer markets in Philadelphia. The availability and cost of land, as well as the expense of extraction and final processing, barred small capitalists from entering the marble trade and other similarly developed sectors. In contrast, operations with minimal land

and equipment expenses—brickmaking, for example—continued to hold out opportunities for men operating on a modest scale. Other trades bifurcated and developed different markets that small and large producers served independently. By this method, the lime industry supported both seasonal producers tending a few kilns, and year-round highly capitalized ventures. In the lumber business, likewise, commercial sawmillers failed to force out farmer-millers until the latter part of the nineteenth century. Once shipments reached Philadelphia, however, the ability of small retailers to enter and survive in the business was tenuous at midcentury. The expense of stock in retail lumberyards and the high cost and limited availability of planing technology confined these arenas to a narrow group of capitalists.

The unevenness of technological change and the opportunities for petty capitalists also characterized the fabrication of joinery for houses. John Munday's generation worked with the rhythms of the seasons to make doors and windows in winter months and to frame houses in temperate weather. At the zenith of Moses Lancaster's career, many craft shops extended the year for making house parts, forsaking outdoor construction altogether. Two decades later, Joseph Montgomery and his peers bought pieces from manufactories that turned out sash, doors, blinds, and related woodwork exclusively. Mechanized planing mills converted lumber into floorboards and molding that carpenters could readily cut and install; prefabricated parts required only modest finishing by the trained hand. Dexterous journeymen remained essential to carpentry in 1850, however, even in mechanized contexts—although the value of their labor fluctuated with construction's health. In good times, they used piece work, jobbing, overwork, and occasional strikes to their advantage. For several decades, moreover, machine-made wares existed side by side with joinery that journeymen carpenters made by hand. So long as the demand for housing made Montgomery and his contemporaries hustle, builders bought joinery from specialized manufactories because crews were too busy to make it. When business was slow, however, shops retreated momentarily into more general production and fashioned pieces for use in their own projects.

Good relative wages for shop work, site labor, and, at midcentury, production in mechanized manufactories kept the expectations of journeymen mechanics high. So did the ease with which young men could become subcontractors on their own in a good economy. The flexibility of production characterized by subcontracting, specialization, and the simultaneous use of hand- and machine-crafted pieces created variable thresholds of entry. Small producers, therefore, were able to set up and compete in otherwise capital-intensive trades. Some carved their spots as masters at the head of shops devoted to joinery or stairmaking. Others moved in and out of outdoor subcontracting and speculative building on their own account as the economy warranted. Like their predecessors, these men viewed themselves as independent artisans. In charge of their own crew, making their own contracts and productive decisions, exercising craft skill and judgment, and reaping the profits of business ownership, flexible production enabled men with a little capital to resist dependent wage labor as a permanent condition of their trade.

Both in the shop and on the worksite, the master artisan rarely severed himself completely from craft labor. Working in 1850, Montgomery superintended operations on thirty-two houses but also framed joist now and then. His everyday actions and those of his contemporaries exhibit the continued coexistence of craft culture and capitalism. Without a doubt, pursuing legal claims, conforming to municipal regulations, arranging for public services, and estimating projects diminished the manual tasks the master had occasion to perform in the company of his journeymen and apprentices. Ambitious operators in 1850 maneuvered through a more regulated city and sophisticated industry than John Munday or Moses Lancaster knew. Nevertheless, several conditions kept craft culture alive in a capitalist environment. Tasks shared by boss and crew at the construction site reinforced mutuality. Fluidity between the ranks of the trade united the efforts of employee and even large builders. Finally, subcontracting and piece work afforded the master a self-interested occasion to assist journeymen in striking out on their own.

Having embarked on business with an initial speculative row development, however, the new master found the field very competitive. Raising money, pursuing debts, drafting plans, navigating municipal agencies, keeping abreast of products, marketing houses—these pursuits came at a cost. Builders at midcentury met the increasing expenses of industry complexity by expanding the size of their developments. Dividing administrative expenses over larger projects, builders could compete more effectively in selling their houses. If one had an image of a big undertaking in Munday's prime, it would reveal a builder commanding work on six houses. A depiction of a construction scene in Lancaster's heyday would show twelve dwellings in progress. Attending Myers's site in 1828, a visitor would notice walls rising on eighteen lots, and two decades later Montgomery's project would reveal thirty-two houses designed to accommodate Philadelphia's middling families.

The small producer did not disappear—he is still a fixture today—but the transformations in the business of construction made it more difficult for him to succeed. He could subcontract, specialize, do alterations, or find some other market niche. New building on a small scale, however, could not return the gains necessary to compete with extensive operators. Small construction was never completely out of the question, of course; the nature of housing assembly in the mid-nineteenth century checked productive advantages of big developments. Properties of materials, the centrality of on-site work, the weight and awkwardness of the building process, and the seasonal constraints on natural and human inputs constricted builders. These obstacles persisted in construction despite prefabricated joinery parts, machine-planed flooring and molding, and ready-sawn or cut water tables and marble mantels. Productive limits to scale mitigated against administrative and managerial advantages and kept avenues open to novices entering the business. So long as boom markets reappeared and bust periods rearranged the persons engaged in construction, men with no capital could build speculatively.

In 1854, one of the bulwarks of speculative building crumbled. State legislation put a stop to new perpetual contracts generally and—almost inadvertently—ended ground rent as Philadelphians knew it. Thereafter, ground lords could no longer create new rents payable "forever." The complications of ground rent, however, had already become evident by mid-century and had hastened the demise of the system. After several generations of urban use, purchasers struggled to locate the heirs or assignees of the original ground lords. New legislation, consequently, set out procedures to extinguish obligations when diligent efforts failed to turn up owners of rent charges. The problems heralded the growing incongruence of a system with feudal roots and a fast-moving property market. Ground rent, furthermore, was no longer critical to artisan entrepreneurship in Philadelphia. By the mid-nineteenth century, credit markets had expanded and matured. An army of brokers and conveyancers linked lenders and borrowers, and financial institutions had entered the mortgage market. Building and loan associations mushroomed to fill the vacuum left by ground-rent transactions and to provide capital to members in the tradition of the city's past.[1]

Without missing a beat, financiers and builders who came after the ground-rent building business utilized methods that drew from previous experience. They linked delayed advance money mortgages and building agreements to place row houses on the landscape. In the boom following the Civil War, single projects of several hundred dwellings rose in rapidly urbanizing sections of the county. Financing flowed in a series of first and second mortgages—not unlike the attachments that ground rent and mortgages had exercised when Warnet Myers was active. An enterprising builder now organized sites as Myers had done—on subcontracts to master craftsmen, each of whom undertook the number of houses that he could handle with his own crew, or with other masters subcontracting under him. A tradesman in 1869 called this arrangement a "huge partnership, in which each operator . . . takes whatever interest in the houses may be agreed upon"; Myers and later "extensive operators," however, endeavored to be first among equals in earning rewards for organizing men, materials, and capital.[2]

The history of building craftsmen in Philadelphia during the first half of the nineteenth century thus challenges the dominant narrative of industrializing America. For a major constituency of the urban working population—its tradesmen in construction—the picture of resistance to competitive capitalism blurs. Despite the cataclysmic failures of some artisans, the field never lacked for men intent on mimicking the routes of successful peers. Capital did not fuel the exploits of manufacturers or merchants alone, but flowed to artisans and small material men as well. Workingmen thus established themselves as self-employed operators—even in presumably mechanized trades—well into midcentury. The transformations in the organization of capital and production, moreover, were not imposed by powerful capitalists onto desperate laborers. Together, journeymen and master mechanics wielded creative methods to persevere in the dynamic landscape of nineteenth-century America.

Abbreviations

ADI	Affidavits, Depositions and Interrogatories
APS	American Philosophical Society
BCHS	Bucks County Historical Society
ChCCCP	Chester County Court of Common Pleas
ChCHS	Chester County Historical Society
DCCCP	District Court of the City and County of Philadelphia
Deeds	Philadelphia County Deed Books, PCA
DelCCCP	Delaware County Court of Common Pleas
DSB	Debit Sans Brève Docket and Claims
GHS	Germantown Historical Society
GSP	Genealogical Society of Pennsylvania
HSD	Historical Society of Delaware
HSMC	Historical Society of Montgomery County
HSP	Historical Society of Pennsylvania
IP	Insolvent Petition(s)
LCP	Library Company of Philadelphia
LSCC	Lewis S. Coryell, Correspondence
MCCCP	Montgomery County Court of Common Pleas
MFP	*Mechanics' Free Press*
MfrCen	U.S. Census of Manufactures (year specified)
Misc Bk	Miscellaneous Books, Philadelphia County, PCA
Mortgages	Mortgage Books, Philadelphia County, PCA
NARA	National Archives and Records Administration
PA Sup Ct	Pennsylvania Supreme Court
PCA	Philadelphia City Archives and Records
PCCCP	Philadelphia County Court of Common Pleas
PMHB	*Pennsylvania Magazine of History and Biography*
PSA	Pennsylvania State Archives
PopCen	U.S. Census of Population, Manuscript Returns

(year specified)—Philadelphia County, except as
indicated

USDC ED PA   U.S. District Court of the Eastern District of
Pennsylvania

CASE REPORTERS

Browne   Peter A. Browne, *Reports of Cases adjudged in the*
               District Court for the City and County of Philadelphia
               and the Court of Common Pleas, Pennsylvania (St.
               Louis, 1871)

Miles   John Miles, *Reports of Cases determined in the District*
               Court for the City and County of Philadelphia
               (Philadelphia, 1836–1842)

Rawle   William Rawle, et al., *Reports of Cases argued and*
               adjudged in the Supreme Court of Pennsylvania
               (Harrisburg and Philadelphia, 1828–1835)

PA   *Pennsylvania State Reports* (Philadelphia, 1859-)

S & R   Thomas Sergeant and William Rawle, *Reports of Cases*
               adjudged in the Supreme Court of Pennsylvania
               (Philadelphia, 1818–1829)

W & S   Frederick Watts and Henry J. Sergeant, *Reports of*
               Cases adjudged in the Supreme Court of Pennsylvania
               (Philadelphia and Pittsburgh, 1841–1845)

Wharton   Thomas I. Wharton, *Reports of Cases argued and*
               determined in the Supreme Court of Pennsylvania, in the
               Eastern District (Philadelphia, 1836–184?)

Notes

Introduction

1. As a portion of products the economy was generating, construction represented about one tenth of national output in nineteenth-century America. (The statistic is for 1839.) Lance E. Davis et al., *American Economic Growth: An Economist's History of the United States* (New York, 1972), 252. On population and number of houses see J. Thomas Scharf and Thompson Westcott, *History of Philadelphia, 1609–1884*, 3 vols. (Philadelphia, 1884), 3: 1762; see also Chapter 5.

2. Bruce Laurie, *Working People of Philadelphia, 1800–1850* (Philadelphia, 1980), 4–5; Bruce Laurie and Mark Schmitz, "Manufacture and Productivity: The Making of an Industrial Base, Philadelphia, 1850–1880," in Theodore Hershberg, ed., *Philadelphia: Work, Space, Family, and Group Experience in the Nineteenth Century* (New York, 1981), 43–92; Billy G. Smith, *The "Lower Sort": Philadelphia's Laboring People, 1750–1800* (Ithaca, N.Y., 1990), 65, 78; Eric Foner, *Tom Paine and Revolutionary America* (New York, 1976), 19–28. On carpenters particularly, see Lisa Beth Lubow, "Artisans in Transition: Early Capitalist Development and the Carpenters of Boston" (Ph.D. dissertation, University of California, Los Angeles, 1987); Catherine W. Bishir, et al., *Architects and Builders in North Carolina: A History of the Practice of Building* (Chapel Hill, N.C., 1990).

3. Ethel Elise Rasmussen, "Capital on the Delaware: The Philadelphia Upper Class in Transition, 1789–1801" (Ph.D. dissertation, Brown University, 1962), 40–43; Richard Webster, *Philadelphia Preserved: Catalog of the Historic American Buildings Survey* (Philadelphia, 1976); Ivan D. Steen, "Philadelphia in the 1850s As Described by British Travelers," *Pennsylvania History* 33 (Jan. 1966): 32–46; Beatrice B. Garvan, *Federal Philadelphia, 1785–1825: The Athens of the Western World* (Philadelphia, 1987), 14–17; William John Murtagh, "The Philadelphia Row House," *Journal of the Society of Architectural Historians* 16 (Dec. 1957): 8–13. Margaret Tinkcom sees row houses as having been "built all at once and all alike as a speculative enterprise." I apply the term more generally, allowing for more staggered land purchasing and building dates and to convey a general impression of domestic architecture. Margaret B. Tinkcom, "Southwark, a River Community: Its Shape and Substance," *Proceedings of the American Philosophical Society* 114 (Aug. 1970): 327–42, 337.

4. Sean Wilentz, *Chants Democratic: New York City and the Rise of the American Working Class, 1788–1850* (New York, 1984); Ron Schultz, *The Republic of Labor: Philadelphia Artisans and the Politics of Class, 1720–1830* (New York, 1993); Howard B.

Rock, *Artisans of the New Republic: The Tradesmen of New York City in the Age of Jefferson* (New York, 1979); Laurie, *Working People*; Lubow, "Artisans in Transition"; Robert Max Jackson, *The Formation of Craft Labor Markets* (Orlando, Fla., 1984), 105–10; John R. Commons et al., *History of Labour in the United States*, 4 vols. (New York, 1918); William Haber, *Industrial Relations in the Building Industry* (Cambridge, Mass., 1930).

5. A few studies of artisans treat them as small businessmen. See particularly Gary J. Kornblith, "From Artisans to Businessmen: Master Mechanics in New England, 1789–1850" (Ph.D. dissertation, Princeton University, 1983); see also Susan E. Hirsch, "From Artisan to Manufacturer: Industrialization and the Small Producer in Newark, 1830–1860," in Stuart W. Bruchey, ed., *Small Business in American Life* (New York, 1980), 80–99; Mansel G. Blackford, *A History of Small Business in America* (New York, 1991); Rosalind Remer, *Printers and Men of Capital: Philadelphia Book Publishers in the New Republic* (Philadelphia, 1996). For the centrality of entrepreneurs to economic change, see Joseph A. Schumpeter, "The Creative Response in Economic History," *Journal of Economic History* 7 (Nov. 1947): 149–59.

6. For a critique of artisan literature, see Richard Stott, "Artisans and Capitalist Development," *Journal of the Early Republic* 16 (Summer 1996): 257–71; Richard B. Stott, ed., *History of My Own Times or, the Life and Adventures of William Otter* (Ithaca, N.Y., 1995). Several accounts shed light on unpalatable ingredients of artisan ideology and culture—virulent racism, engendered and racialized definitions of independence, violent misogyny; see Paul A. Gilje and Howard B. Rock, eds., *Keepers of the Revolution: New Yorkers at Work in the Early Republic* (Ithaca, N.Y., 1992); Christine Stansell, *City of Women: Sex and Class in New York, 1789–1860* (New York, 1986); David R. Roediger, *The Wages of Whiteness: Race and the Making of the American Working Class* (New York, 1991); see also Peter Way, *Common Labour: Workers and the Digging of North American Canals, 1780–1860* (New York and Cambridge, England, 1993).

7. Thomas M. Doerflinger, *A Vigorous Spirit of Enterprise: Merchants and Economic Development in Revolutionary Philadelphia* (Chapel Hill, N.C., 1986), 15–16; Philip Scranton, *Proprietary Capitalism: The Textile Manufacture at Philadelphia 1800–1885* (New York, 1983); Thomas A. Heinrich, *Ships for the Seven Seas: Philadelphia Shipbuilding in the Age of Industrial Capitalism* (Baltimore, 1997). Even the paradigm of New England industrialization is now under assault. That absentee capitalists and large-scale centralized and mechanized manufacturing of cheap goods may not characterize New England industrialization, much less textile production, is a tantalizing indication of how important small producers and particularly artisan entrepreneurs continued to be in the early nineteenth-century economy. François Weil, "Capitalism and Industrialization in New England, 1815–1845," *Journal of American History* 84 (Mar. 1998): 1332–54.

Chapter 1. Men on the Make

1. John Munday, Deposition, Oct. 21, 1801, and Schedule A, List of Debts, Case of John Munday, Bankruptcy Cases, 1800–1806, USDC ED PA [hereafter

"Bankruptcy Cases"]; see also Judgment Bill, John Munday to Jonathan Robinson, Apr. 12, 1785, Robinson-Elliot Papers, Folder 1, HSD. To convert Pennsylvania pounds to dollar currency, multiply by 2.68. James Hardie, ed., *The Philadelphia Directory and Register for 1793* (Philadelphia, 1793).

2. Munday, Deposition. Munday first purchased building lots in Philadelphia in July 1791. Deeds, D32: 100.

3. On the cycles of the economy in the early nation, see Willard Long Thorp et al., *Business Annals* (New York, 1926), esp. 112–25; John J. McCusker, "How Much Is That in Real Money? A Historical Price Index for Use As a Deflator of Money Values in the Economy of the United States," *Proceedings of the American Antiquarian Society* 101, pt. 2 (Oct. 1991): 297–373; see also Joseph A. Schumpeter, *Capitalism, Socialism and Democracy*, 3rd ed. (New York, 1950), 81–86; Peter Mathias, "Entrepreneurs, Managers, and Business Men in Eighteenth-Century Britain," in Peter Mathias and John A. Davis, eds., *Enterprise and Labour: From the Eighteenth Century to the Present* (Oxford, 1996), 12–32.

4. Scharf and Westcott, *History of Philadelphia* 1: 94–97; Hannah Benner Roach, "The Planting of Philadelphia: A Seventeenth-Century Real Estate Development," *PMHB* 92 (1968): 3–47, 143–94; Gary B. Nash, "City Planning and Political Tension in the Seventeenth Century: The Case of Philadelphia," *Proceedings of the American Philosophical Society* 112 (Feb. 1968): 54–73.

5. William Robert Shepherd, *History of Proprietary Government in Pennsylvania* (New York, 1896), 17–22; Elizabeth Gray Kogen Spera, "Building for Business: The Impact of Commerce on the City Plan and Architecture of the City of Philadelphia, 1750–1800" (Ph.D. dissertation, University of Pennsylvania, 1980); Sam Bass Warner, *The Private City: Philadelphia in Three Periods of Its Growth*, 2nd ed. (Philadelphia, 1987); Matthew Clarkson and Mary Biddle, "Philadelphia," 1762; "Plan of the City and Suburbs of Philadelphia," 1794. For a recent reinterpretation of the grid, see Dell Upton, "The City as Material Culture," in Anne Elizabeth Yentsch and Mary C. Beaudry, eds., *The Art and Mystery of Historical Archaeology: Essays in Honor of James Deetz* (Boca Raton, Fla., 1992), 51–74.

6. Carl Bridenbaugh and Jessica Bridenbaugh, *Rebels and Gentlemen: Philadelphia in the Age of Franklin* (London and New York, 1942, 1962), 1–13; Cynthia J. Shelton, *The Mills of Manayunk: Industrialization and Social Conflict in the Philadelphia Region, 1787–1837* (Baltimore, Md., 1986); Gary B. Nash, *The Urban Crucible: Social Change, Political Consciousness, and the Origins of the American Revolution* (Cambridge, Mass., 1979), 312–38; Arthur Jensen, *Maritime Commerce in Colonial Philadelphia* (Madison, Wis., 1963); Doerflinger, *Vigorous Spirit*; Marcus Rediker, *Between the Devil and the Deep Blue Sea: Merchant Seamen, Pirates, and the Anglo-American Maritime World, 1700–1750* (New York, 1987).

7. Warner, *Private City*, 13; Smith, *"Lower Sort,"* 43; "Plan of the City," 1794; Thomas Samuel Gentry, Jr., "Specialized Residential and Business Districts: Philadelphia in an Age of Change, 1785–1800" (Master's thesis, Montana State University, 1988).

8. The 1794 urban plan also reveals settlement on the edge of the city at Callowhill and Eighth Streets, reflecting the area's early ironworks. "Plan of the City," 1794; Spera, "Building for Business"; John F. Watson, *Annals of Philadelphia*,

and Pennsylvania, in the Olden Time, revised by Willis P. Hazard, 3 vols. (Philadelphia, 1909), 1: 226ff; Warner, *Private City*, 3–21; Smith, *"Lower Sort,"* 7–39.

9. Shepherd, *History of Proprietary Government*; Anthony N. B. Garvan, "Proprietary Philadelphia as Artifact," in Oscar Handlin and John Burchard, eds., *The Historian and the City*, (Cambridge, Mass., 1963), 177–201.

10. Foner, *Tom Paine*; Garvan, "Proprietary Philadelphia," 190–99; Bridenbaugh and Bridenbaugh, *Rebels and Gentlemen*, 12; Doerflinger, *Vigorous Spirit*, chpt. 7.

11. Susanna Dillwyn to —— Dillwyn, March 1792, quoted in Rasmusson, "Capital on the Delaware," 40–43.

12. Road Petitions (1796), Packet 17: 286, Philadelphia Court of Quarter Sessions, PCA; For an overview of the decade's speculative euphoria, see Doerflinger, *Vigorous Spirit*, 314–39.

13. Smith, *"Lower Sort,"* 81–84.

14. For an example of one house carpenter who spent a very short time as a journeyman, see Case of Evan Lloyd (1803), Bankruptcy Cases; Roger William Moss, Jr., "Master Builders: A History of the Colonial Building Trades" (Ph.D. dissertation, University of Delaware, 1972).

15. Guardians of the Poor, Almshouse Indentures, 1804–1812; see also *MFP*, June 13, 1829; Richard B. Morris, *Government and Labor in Early America* (New York, 1946), 363–89; Sharon V. Salinger, *"To Serve Well and Faithfully": Labor and Indentured Servitude in Pennsylvania* (New York, 1987). Several sources suggest that upper age limitations were flexible, especially in the eighteenth century. Joseph Baker, Deposition, Mar. 17, 1792, *Lessee of William Ogden* v. *Thomas Fitzgerald* (PA Sup Ct, 1791), PSA; *Case of Pidgeon*, 1 Browne 374, note (PA Sup Ct, 1811); *Commonwealth* v. *Sturgeon*, 2 Browne 205 (PCCCP, 1812); Indenture of Charles Doyle, Mayor, Apprentice, and Redemptioner Indentures, 1800; see also Ian Quimby, *Apprenticeship in Colonial Philadelphia* (New York, 1986). Terms for black youth, for example, often extended beyond the age of twenty-one; Gary B. Nash, *Forging Freedom: The Formation of Philadelphia's Black Community, 1720–1840* (Cambridge, Mass., 1988), 77–78.

16. For example, William Ellis, Charles Conard, and Charles Noble were all apprentices for master house carpenter Moses Lancaster, who later employed them as journeymen. See also *Stevenson* v. *Stonehill*, 5 Wharton 301 (PA Sup Ct, 1840); *MFP*, June 14, 1828; Smith, *"Lower Sort,"* 6–27.

17. For annual income of journeymen house carpenters, see Chapter 5.

18. George Sockworth, Misc Bk, IH1: 489 (1824).

19. David Buckman, Dec. 8, 1814, and June 7, 1815, Insolvent Petition [hereafter "IP"], PCCCP; see also Mortgages, IW3: 83.

20. Bright Huggs, Sept. 23, 1819, IP, PCCCP.

21. Indenture of Thomas Whitesel, Mayor, Apprentice, and Redemption Indentures, 1806. Samuel Garrigues called himself a carpenter, but was engaged at the time in building houses—more specifically the expertise of a "house carpenter." Samuel P. Garrigues, Sept. 23, 1819, IP, PCCCP; see also Philip Justus, June 16, 1835, IP, PCCCP.

22. DSB, Mar. term 1829, no. 158, DCCCP.

23. Thomas Kelly, *The New Practical Builder and Workman's Companion* (London, 1823), 105, 159. Moxon described joiners' tables as "exactly flat and smooth, and [joiners] shoot their Joint so true, that the whole Table shews all one piece: But the Floors Carpenters lay are also by Rule of Carpentry to be laid flat and true, and shall yet be well enough laid, though not so exactly flat and smooth as a Table." Joseph Moxon, *Mechanick Exercises: Or the Doctrine of Handy-Works* (London, 1703; rpt. Morristown, N.J., 1975), 117–18; see also Edward S. Cooke, Jr., *Making Furniture in Preindustrial America: The Social Economy of Newtown and Woodbury, Connecticut* (Baltimore, Md., 1996).

24. Tom W. Smith, "The Dawn of the Urban-Industrial Age: The Social Structure of Philadelphia, 1790–1830" (Ph.D. dissertation, University of Chicago, 1980), 43.

25. Smith, *"Lower Sort,"* 84–91, 129–39; Laurie, *Working People*, 11; Richard G. Miller, "Gentry and Entrepreneurs: A Socioeconomic Analysis of Philadelphia in the 1790s," *Rocky Mountain Social Science Journal* 12 (1975): 71–84; Sharon V. Salinger and Charles Wetherell, "Wealth and Renting in Prerevolutionary Philadelphia," *Journal of American History* 71 (Mar. 1985): 826–40.

26. John Munday, Deposition; Cornelius W. Stafford, ed., *The Philadelphia Directory for 1798* (Philadelphia, 1798).

27. See Chapter 2.

28. Richard M. Cadwalader, *A Practical Treatise on the Law of Ground Rents in Pennsylvania* (Philadelphia, 1879); Vincent D. Nicholson, *A Treatise on the Law Relating to Real Estate in Pennsylvania*, 3rd ed. (Philadelphia, 1929).

29. On price levels using commodity prices, see McCusker, "How Much Is That in Real Money?," 316–32. Shippen also contracted with Munday for a large house, "containing four Rooms on a floor with Kitchen stables, &c for £3,362..8..6 [approximately $9,000] to be finished in the best manner and with the best materials." Munday, Deposition; Munday to Shippen, Receipts, June 28, 1794 and Aug. 1, 1794; Deeds, D50: 13, D50: 2, D50: 6; Kenneth Roeland Kimsey, "The Edward Shippen Family: A Search for Stability in Revolutionary Pennsylvania" (Ph.D. dissertation, University of Arizona, 1973).

30. Munday, Deposition; Deeds, D54: 132.

31. Deeds, D66: 108, D65: 365; Munday, Deposition and Schedule of Debts; John Munday, IP, Mar. 9, 1801, PA Sup Ct (reproduced in the Petition of Bankruptcy). For labor and wholesale material costs, see Donald R. Adams, Jr., *Wage Rates in Philadelphia, 1790–1830* (New York, 1975), 9–10; U.S. Department of Labor, Bureau of Labor Statistics, *History of Wages in the United States from Colonial Times to 1928*, Bulletin no. 604 (Washington, D.C., 1934); Anne Bezanson et al. *Wholesale Prices in Philadelphia, 1784–1861* (Philadelphia, 1936), 1: 113–19.

32. Munday, Deposition.

33. Munday, Deposition; Deeds, D59: 396, D63: 352, D64: 92, D65: 365; Munday, IP.

34. Munday, Deposition.

35. Munday, Deposition; Munday received £2,000 ($5,360) for the frame houses, which he built on a lot on the southwest corner of Filbert and Eleventh Streets. In conveying the property to Sarah Lea, he exempted the lots from ground-

rent payments due both Steinmetz and Cooper, holding the remaining parts of lots subject to the ground rent. Such an arrangement indicated that Munday wanted both a quick sale, and also that the frame houses may have been of insufficient value to secure the ground rent. Deeds, D74: 62, EF12: 262, EF15: 376, D63: 352. Sarah Lea was the widowed daughter of Edward Shippen. Kimsey, "The Edward Shippen Family," 235.

36. U.S. Direct Tax of 1798, Philadelphia: East Northern Liberties, Schedule A.

37. Charlotte Burns, Deposition, Dec. 3, 1803, *Correy* v. *Riffetts* (PA Sup Ct, n.d.), PSA.

38. Emma Jones Lapsansky, "South Street Philadelphia, 1762–1854: 'A Haven for Those Low in the World'" (Ph.D. dissertation, University of Pennsylvania, 1975), 58–69.

39. In Kensington, for instance, frames represented 70 percent of the dwellings. In contrast, the number of frame and brick dwellings was nearly equal in the Northern Liberties section. Within the city proper frame residences comprised 28 percent of the total—a smaller proportion than outlying neighborhoods but a warning sign of poor housing. James Mease, *The Picture of Philadelphia* (Philadelphia, 1811).

40. Local regulation and refusal by insurance companies to sell policies discouraged frame construction. Spera, "Building for Business." Where the ban applied, authorities controlled new construction closely; see *Douglas* v. *Commonwealth*, 2 Rawle 262 (PA Sup Ct, 1830).

41. James Robinson, ed., *The Philadelphia Directory for 1806* (Philadelphia, 1806).

42. Murtagh, "The Philadelphia Row House."

43. Stuart M. Blumin, *The Emergence of the Middle Class: Social Experience in the American City, 1760–1900* (Cambridge and New York, 1989), 38–58; see also Smith, *"Lower Sort"*, 27–33, 158–65. Sharon V. Salinger's recent work suggests that during the eighteenth century, residential space for the poorest Philadelphians declined, while residences of the wealthy grew in size. Salinger, "Space, Inside and Outside, in Eighteenth-Century Philadelphia," *Journal of Interdisciplinary History* 26 (Summer 1995): 1–31.

44. Munday, Deposition; Munday, Schedule of Property, IP.

45. Munday, Deposition; Elizabeth Munday, Affidavit, Feb. 20, 1800, *Joseph Hampton* v. *John Monday*, ADI, ChCCCP.

46. Elizabeth suggests that John paid for the merchandise with "some flour, some hams & some lard" that he took with him from Philadelphia. Elizabeth Munday, Affidavit.

47. *Hampton* v. *Monday*, Feb. term 1800, Continuance Docket D, ChCCCP; Munday, Deposition; Ann Norris, Deposition, Oct. 1, 1801, in Munday, Bankruptcy Cases; John Munday, 1803 no. 44, Administrations, Philadelphia County; Sheriff's Deeds, F7: 46, PCCCP; James Robinson, ed., *The Philadelphia Directory, City and County Register* (1803–1807, 1810, 1811); Cemetery Returns, Apr. 14, 1812, Board of Health, Philadelphia.

48. Norman B. Wilkinson, *Land Policy and Speculation in Pennsylvania, 1779–*

1800 (New York, 1979 [rpt., Ph.D. dissertation, University of Pennsylvania, 1958]);
Doerflinger, *Vigorous Spirit*, 310-33.

49. Walter B. Smith and Arthur H. Cole, *Fluctuations in American Business,
1790–1860* (Cambridge, Mass., 1935).

50. I am drawing here on hundreds of insolvency petitions, and find quite
divergent definitions of "competence" among mechanics. See also Daniel Vickers,
*Farmers and Fishermen: Two Centuries of Work in Essex County, Massachusetts, 1630–
1850* (Chapel Hill, N.C., 1994), 14–23; Ric Northrup, "Decomposition and Reconstitution: A Theoretical and Historical Study of Philadelphia Artisans, 1785–1820"
(Ph.D. dissertation, University of North Carolina, 1988), chpt. 4.

51. Green Street Monthly Meeting Minutes, Sep. 1817, and Membership Records, 1815–1836+, Friends Historical Collection, Swarthmore College.

52. Ibid., Sep. 1833.

53. Evan Lloyd, Deposition, May 24, 1803, Case of Evan Lloyd, Bankruptcy
Cases; Philadelphia Southern District Monthly Meeting, Minutes, Nov. 21, 1799; I
am indebted to Mark Lloyd and James M. Duffin for the Meeting citation.

54. Lancaster's wife Susanna Jordan was the sole heir to her father's estate
and stood to inherit modest property after her mother's death. Robert Jordan, 1797,
no. 448, Wills, Philadelphia County Registrar; Deeds, IH1: 462; Moss, "Master
Builders." Susanna was not a birthright Quaker but was admitted to membership
in 1819. The oldest children of Moses and Susanna also were admitted upon appli-
cation. Harry Fred Lancaster, *The Lancaster Family: A History of Thomas and Phebe
Lancaster and Their Descendants* (Columbia City, Ind., n.d.); Clarence V. Roberts,
Early Friends Families of Upper Bucks (Philadelphia, 1925), 334. Religious Society of
Friends, Richland Monthly Meeting, Dec. 1801, and Green Street Monthly Meeting
Minutes and Membership Records.

55. Green Street Monthly Minutes and Membership Records; Deeds, EF26:
348 and IC26: 107; Mortgages, EF11: 173, IC3: 527, and IC4: 251.

56. Eight years older than Moses, John had preceded him to Philadelphia
and completed his apprenticeship with a Quaker member of the Carpenters' Company. James Robinson, ed., *The Philadelphia Directory, City and County Register, for
1802* (Philadelphia, 1802); Lancaster, *Lancaster Family*; Philadelphia Monthly Meeting, Northern District, Minutes, April 1791; Carpenters' Company of the City and
County of Philadelphia, *An Act to Incorporate the Carpenters' Company. . . .* (Philadelphia, 1873).

57. Deeds, IC2: 563, IC8: 340, IC8: 6, MR5: 464, MR5: 465, MR5: 466,
GWR17: 514, and GWR17: 517; Mortgages, IC3: 621, IC8: 244, and MR1: 432;
Moses Lancaster, Receipt Books, 1812–1836 [hereafter "Receipts"], HSP.

58. Reliance Fire Company, Minutes, 1812–1821, Roll Book [n.d.], and
Ledger, 1800–1822, HSP; Scharf and Westcott, *History of Philadelphia* 3: 1910–1912.
Laurie, *Working People*, 63ff; Wilentz, *Chants Democratic*, 256–63, 300. John Lancaster was elected to the Carpenters' Company at the same time; Carpenters' Company, *An Act to Incorporate*.

59. Thomas C. Cochran, *Frontiers of Change: Early Industrialism in America*
(New York, 1981), 27, 42.

60. Browne credited the "diversion of a large capital from mercantile specu-

lations, to those connected with the landed interest." Peter Arrell Browne, *A Summary of the Law of Pennsylvania, Securing to Mechanics . . . Payment for Their Labour* (Philadelphia, 1815).

61. Mease, *Picture of Philadelphia*; *The Philadelphia Directory and Register for 1813*.

62. Quoted in Louis Martin Sears, "Philadelphia and the Embargo: 1808," *Annual Report of the American Historical Association for the Year 1920* (Washington, D.C., 1925), 257.

63. DSB, Dec. term 1812: no. 178.; Dec. term 1813: no. 34; Sep. term 1814: no. 187; June term 1813: nos. 125 and 197; Dec. term 1813, nos. 101, 120, and 121; June term 1814: no. 183, DCCCP. On Northern Liberties and development, see Garvan, "Proprietary Philadelphia."

64. Lancaster, Receipts; *American Daily Advertiser*, May 14, 1791; Commons, et al., *History of Labour*, 1: 127–28; *Pennsylvanian*, Mar. 17, 1836; *MFP*, June 13 and July 18, 1829; John and Moses Lancaster, Account Book, 1812–1820, HSP.

65. Guardians of the Poor, Almshouse Indentures; Minutes of the Managing Committee of the Carpenters' Company of the City and County of Philadelphia, Book 15: 9, 45, 57, and 84, on deposit at APS; Lancaster, Receipts (5/4/1813).

66. A Quaker boy from Bucks County was also apprenticed to Lancaster. Green Street Monthly Meeting, Minutes, February 1817, and Membership Records; John and Moses Lancaster, Account Book; Lancaster, Receipts (4/17/1819); PopCen, 1810.

67. John and Moses Lancaster, Account Book; Deeds, MR11: 471, IH6: 178, GWR8: 617, MR22: 70; *Harker* v. *Conrad*, 12 S & R 300 (PA Sup Ct, 1825); *Hopkins* v. *Conrad*, 2 Rawle 316 (PA Sup Ct, 1830).

68. Cochran, *Frontiers of Change*, 42; Thorp, *Business Annals*, 116–18; *Moroney* v. *Copeland*, 5 Wharton 407 (PA Sup Ct, 1840). Ellis married the daughter of lumber merchant George Woolley, who was also in the Green Street Monthly Meeting; Marriages, Green Street Monthly Meeting; Federal Bankruptcy Cases, 1841–1843, USDC ED PA.

69. Agreement, John and Moses Lancaster, Account Book.

70. Lancaster made identical arrangements with other artisans and then sold the rent charges (including those of the house lots he had developed). He also mortgaged the developed properties for $6,000. Deeds, MR11: 471, IH6: 178, GWR8: 617, MR22: 70, MR23: 176; Mortgages, IW3: 478, IH4: 525.

71. *Hinchman* v. *Lybrand*, 14 S & R 31 (PA Sup Ct, 1825).

72. Lancaster, Receipts (8/2/1815); Margaret Morris Haviland, "In the World, but Not of the World: The Humanitarian Activities of Philadelphia Quakers, 1790–1820" (Ph.D. dissertation, University of Pennsylvania, 1992); Robert W. Doherty, *The Hicksite Separation: A Sociological Analysis of Religious Schism in Early Nineteenth-Century America* (New Brunswick, N.J., 1967), 42–50, 77–89; H. Larry Ingle, *Quakers in Conflict: The Hicksite Reformation* (Knoxville, Tenn., 1986). I am grateful to Margaret Haviland for sharing her notes on the Lancaster daughters.

73. Lancaster, Receipts; Carpenters' Company, *An Act to Incorporate*; Abraham Ritter, *Philadelphia and Her Merchants* (Philadelphia, 1860); Roberts, *Early Friends*; DSB, Sep. term 1829, no. 67, DCCCP.

74. Lancaster, Receipts (12/7, 12/10, and 12/28/1821; 3/4 and 3/16/1822); Carolyn C. Cooper, "A Patent Transformation: Woodworking Mechanization in Philadelphia, 1830–1856," in Judith A. McGaw, ed., *Early American Technology: Making and Doing Things from the Colonial Era to 1850*, (Chapel Hill, N.C., 1994), 278–327; M. D. Leggett, *Subject Matter Index of Patents for Inventions, 1790–1873* (Washington, D.C., 1874), 1057–58.

75. Lancaster, Receipts; John and Moses Lancaster, Account Book; Plat Book of Northern Liberties, 1824–1828, on deposit at the APS.

76. Lancaster, Receipts; PopCen, 1810 and 1820.

77. PopCen, 1830; Lancaster, Receipts (8/4/1829). On the transformation of master households, see Paul E. Johnson, *A Shopkeeper's Millennium: Society and Revivals in Rochester, New York, 1815–1837* (New York, 1978); Salinger, *"To Serve Well and Faithfully."*

78. Susanna, of course, may have influenced the decision, since it is she who would have been most burdened with the duties required to board young men. Lancaster, Receipts (1/12 and 3/14/1835); Matthias Krauter, Sep. 22, 1834, Declaration of Intent, and Oct. 31, 1836, Petition of Naturalization, Philadelphia Court of Quarter Sessions, PCA.

79. Mortgages, GWR3: 712, GWR8: 171 and 289, MR10: 225, IH1: 193, IH4: 525 and 585, IW3: 671.

80. Roberts, *Early Friends*; Green Street Monthly Meeting, Membership; DSB, Dec. term 1829, nos. 213, 223, and 224, and Mar. Term 1830, no. 31, DCCCP; Deeds, IH1: 462; Lancaster, Receipts (10/30/1820, 2/1/1821).

81. Dorothy Large was a member of the nearby Society of Friends Northern District Monthly Meeting. Lancaster had previously done business with the Large family, having bought property and obtained a mortgage from her son in 1816. Philadelphia Monthly Meeting, Northern District, Membership; Deeds, MR8: 484, MR11: 471, IH6: 178; Mortgages, MR6: 36; DSB, Sep. Term 1829, no. 296, DCCCP.

82. George Rogers Taylor, "Comment," in David T. Gilchrist, ed., *The Growth of the Seaport Cities, 1790–1825* (Charlottesville, Va., 1967), 38–39; Warner, *Private City*, 51, 56–57.

83. Laurie, *Working People*, 10; Diane Lindstrom, *Economic Development in the Philadelphia Region, 1810–1850* (New York, 1978), 25–29; DSB, Sep. term 1826, nos. 82 and 121, and Mar. term 1827, no. 25, DCCCP; Warner, *Private City*, 51.

84. Lancaster, Receipts (3/19, 3/21, 4/4, 4/11, 4/18, 5/2, 5/9, 5/15, 5/23, 6/6, 6/13, 6/20, 6/27, 7/3, 7/18, 7/25, and 8/22/1829). For subcontracting and piece work in construction, see Chapter 5.

85. William Meredith to William M. Meredith, Mar. 15, 1828, Meredith Papers, Correspondence, HSP; Commons et al., *History of Labour*, 1: 170–71, 215–16; Sidney Homer, *A History of Interest Rates* (New Brunswick, N.J., 1963), 280–81.

86. Deeds, AM22: 146, AM20: 585; Sheriff's Deeds, E: 559, E: 598, E: 597, E: 599, E: 532, DCCCP, PCA.

87. Sheriff's Deeds, E: 359, 360, 361, 362, 382, 388, DCCCP; Execution Docket, Sep. term 1829, no. 951 and Dec. term 1829, nos. 112, 113, and 115, DCCCP; Appearance Docket, Sep. term 1829, no. 950, DCCCP; Mortgages, IW3: 671;

Deeds, GWR8: 289. On the heavy proportion of insolvent building mechanics for these years, see Chapter 2.

88. Lancaster, Receipts (1/23, 3/11, 4/4, 8/16, 9/3/1825; 3/12, 4/8, 4/26, 5/11, 6/16, 8/20/1831); Deeds, GWR7: 608; Mortgages, GWR3: 712, GWR15: 33, GWR10: 52, AWC12: 234, AM23: 374, AM24: 189, 191, 193, and 195, AM25: 535; Cooper, "Patent Transformation"; Leggett, *Subject Matter Index of Patents*.

89. Deeds, SHF29: 381; GS7: 32; John and Moses Lancaster, Lumber Day Book, 1823–1829, 1838–1841; *A. M'Elroy's Philadelphia Directory for 1840* and *Philadelphia Directory for 1841* (Philadelphia, 1841); Sheriff's Deeds, R: 119, K: 181, DCCCP. Fragmentary accounts for the oilcloth manufactury are contained in the second part of the Lumber Day Book.

90. County Tax Assessment Ledger, Northern Liberties, Sixth Ward, 1853, PCA; Deeds, 187:20, Bucks County, BCHS; PopCen, 1850.

91. PopCen, 1860 and 1870; Tax Lists, Newtown Borough, Bucks County, 1861–1864, 1866–1867, 1870, 1875, 1876, and 1879; S[olomon] Hersey, ed., *Bucks County Directory and Gazetteer for 1871–1872* (Wilmington, Del., [1871]); *Public Ledger*, Nov. 17, 1879. The real estate Lancaster enumerated in the census was likely the same small plot that he deeded to his daughter a year before his death; Deeds, 187: 20, Bucks County. I am indebted to Phil Scranton for making me rethink the "success" of Lancaster's career by pointing to issues of inflation and the annuity Lancaster could expect with the amount of property listed.

92. William Eyre, Diaries, 1840–1880, Friends Historical Collection, Swarthmore College, entries 11/16 and 11/18/1879; Roberts, *Early Friends*.

93. Catharine Myers, Warnet's mother, was widowed sometime between 1796 and 1803. James Robinson, ed., *The Philadelphia Directory, City and County Register, for 1803*; Mortgages, IW3: 60; *A. M'Elroy's Philadelphia Directory for 1860* (Philadelphia, 1860).

94. Bond, Jan. 6, 1818, Franklin Legacy Bond Book, vol. 1. According to the terms of the fund, the borrower was required to be a married man under the age of twenty-five, and to have served his apprenticeship in Philadelphia. Myers's bond, and the date of the earliest deed to which he was a party, establishes his date of birth between 1793 and 1795.

95. James Paxton, ed., *The Philadelphia Directory and Register for 1818*; County Tax Assessment Ledger, Northern Liberties, Fifth Ward, 1820; Mortgages, MR7: 218, MR8: 501, IH3: 696, GWR2: 589, GWR4: 91, GWR8: 258, IW3: 84, IW3: 263, IH1: 312; Deeds, MR18: 463, MR23: 442, IW5: 707; Bond, January 6, 1818, Franklin Legacy.

96. Edward Whitely, ed., *The Philadelphia Directory and Register for 1820*; McCarty and Davis, *The Philadelphia Directory and Register for 1821*; ———, *The Philadelphia Directory and Register for 1822*. Myers continued to build on at least one lot he bought in 1820. Deeds, IW5: 373; DSB, June term 1820, no. 124, DCCCP; Mortgages, IW4: 244.

97. Joseph Reed and Warnet Myers, Real Estate Ledger, 1824–1829; see "Joseph Reed," *Dictionary of American Biography* (New York, 1929) for his father's entry; Scharf and Westcott, *History of Philadelphia*, 3: 2117; Mortgages, GWR2: 589, GWR4: 91, GWR5: 48, GWR5: 50, GWR5: 51, IW3: 84, IW3: 263, IH1: 312. Reed

served as President of American Fire Insurance Company from December 1824 to June 1829, the dates correspond to his speculative real estate ventures with Myers.

98. Reed and Myers, Ledger; Mortgages, GWR2: 589, GWR4: 91, GWR5: 489, GWR7: 34, GWR7: 615, GWR8: 258, GWR8: 751, GWR8: 753, GWR9: 640, GWR10: 90, GWR10: 333, GWR10: 336, GWR10: 521, GWR10: 529, GWR11: 17, GWR11: 19, GWR11: 599, GWR12: 315, GWR12: 317, GWR12: 434, GWR12: 567, GWR14: 515.

99. Reed and Myers, Ledger; Deeds, GWR15: 689, GWR21: 177; Mortgages, GWR10: 90.

100. Jacob Franks and William Wagner, Receipt Book, 1824–1839; DSB, Sep. term 1828, no. 184, DCCCP; Reed and Myers, Ledger.

101. *MFP*, May 22, 1830; DSB, June Term 1829, nos. 83, 84, 120, 133, 134, 137, 138, 139, 140, 141, 142, 145, 152, 161, 162; Sep. term 1829, nos. 134, 199; Dec. term 1829, nos. 3, 36, 164, 350; Mar. term 1830, nos. 35, 276; June term 1830, nos. 49, 55, 128, 178, DCCCP.

102. Kensington District, Third Division, District Plan, Oct. 1829; "Petition to Open Phoenix Street and Thompson Street in Kensington," Road Petitions, Philadelphia Court of Quarter Sessions, (1830), 52-1091 (P-805); Kensington, Paving Assessment Ledger, 1828–1836; Watson, *Annals*, 1: 436ff and 3: 302; Scharf and Westcott, *History of Philadelphia*, 1: 9; Shepherd, *History of Proprietary Government*, 84–93.

103. William Allen, "Map of Philadelphia, 1828" (Philadelphia, 1828); Kensington, Paving Assessment Ledger.

104. Allen, "Map of Philadelphia, 1828"; County Tax Assessment Ledger, Kensington (East), 1826; Scharf and Westcott, *History of Philadelphia*, 3: 2299. I have used the Kensington East tax assessments from 1826 because no others exist for Kensington until 1841. Myers's houses would have probably been a street west of the Kensington, East division, so they are not far removed from the concentrated development near the Delaware River.

105. State Tax Assessment Ledger, Kensington, Third Ward, 1841, 35–39.

106. *Pennock* v. *Hoover and Myers*, 2 Rawle 291 (PA Sup Ct, 1835).

107. *Pennock* v. *Hoover and Myers*. A number of his other properties were also sold around this time. Sheriff's Deeds, PCCCP, E: 403, F:40, E: 372, F: 18, E: 404, F: 80, E: 465, X: 36.

108. *Pennock* v. *Hoover and Myers*. On Joseph Reed's misdeeds, see [Anon.], "Sweet William; A Tale of Three Chapters of Philadelphia," *Philadelphia Evening Bulletin* (Dec. 15, 1869); Nicholas B. Wainwright, ed., *A Philadelphia Perspective: The Diary of Sidney George Fisher Covering the Years 1834–1871* (Philadelphia, 1967), 554.

109. James Shaw, June 14, 1830, IP, PCCCP.

110. "History of the Fifth Street Methodist Episcopal Church," 1882, HSP; *Allen* v. *Myers*, 5 Rawle 335 (PA Sup Ct, 1835).

111. Commons et al., *History of Labour*, 1: 381–84, 396.

112. *Desilver's Philadelphia Directory and Stranger's Guide for 1835 & 1836*; *A. M'Elroy's Philadelphia Directory for 1837* (Philadelphia, 1837); Mortgages, GS13: 65; Warnet Myers, no. 233, Federal Bankruptcy Cases, 1841–1843, USDC ED PA; *A. M'Elroy's Philadelphia Directory of 1860*.

113. Jonathan Conard and John Lancaster, partners in the lumber business, sued Warnet Myers for a debt incurred in supplying lumber. The debt was settled in May 1825, about the time that Moses Lancaster bought Conard's interest in the business; DSB, June term 1820, no. 124, DCCCP.

114. Deeds, GWR26: 711; Estate of Frederick Forepaugh, Orphans Court, Philadelphia County, Book 31: 219 (Sep. 21, 1827); William Garrigues, 1831 no. 187, Wills, Philadelphia County Registrar; Misc Bk, IH1: 31 (1822); Horatio L. Melchior and Elenor Burk, May 29, 1808, GSP; Misc Bk, GWR1: 23 (1827); PopCen, 1820 and 1830.

115. See also Gary John Kornblith, "From Artisans to Businessmen: Master Mechanics in New England, 1789–1850" (Ph.D. dissertation, Princeton University, 1983).

116. Northrup's argument makes a similar point, though I see the entrepreneurial character of building artisans as much more widespread than he suggests. Northrup asserts that "though a competence implied upward limits on wealth, it also motivated merchants and 'entrepreneurial artisans' to engage in daring enterprises and take speculative risks. Ambitions for a competence consequently provided a continual stimulus to capitalist expansion." Northrup, "Decomposition and Reconstruction," 122; see also Schumpeter, *Capitalism, Socialism*, 81–106.

Chapter 2. By "Credit & Industry"

1. Wainwright, ed., *A Philadelphia Perspective: The Diary of Sidney George Fisher*, 409. Deeds, AM40: 815, AM47: 380, AM52: 606, AM56: 531, AM60: 576, AM62: 6, AM67: 177, 180, 183, 186, 189–228, 231, 235, 238, 241, AWM9: 645.

2. Another mechanic made similar allegations against Loyd. IPs, PCCCP: Michael Barron, Apr. 12, 1837, and Charles B. Deal, Mar. 19, 1838.

3. Frederic Cople Jaher, "Old Elites and Entrepreneurial Activity in New York City from 1780 to 1850," *Working Papers from the Regional Economic History Research Center* 2:2 (1978): 54–78; Stanley L. Engerman, "Elites and Economic Development: A Commentary," ibid., 78–86; Herman E. Krooss, "Financial Institutions," in Gilchrist, ed., *The Growth of Seaport Cities*, 104–35; Gordon C. Bjork, "Foreign Trade," ibid., 54–61; James Weston Livingood, *Philadelphia-Baltimore Trade Rivalry, 1780–1860* (Harrisburg, Penn., 1947); Thomas C. Cochran, "Philadelphia: Industrial Center, 1750–1850," *PMHB* 106 (1982): 323–40; Lindstrom, *Economic Development*, 95–110; Allan R. Pred, *The Spatial Dynamics of U.S. Urban-Industrial Growth, 1800–1914: Interpretive and Theoretical Essays* (Cambridge, Mass., 1966); Walter Licht, *Industrializing America: The Nineteenth Century* (Baltimore, 1995); Scranton, *Proprietary Capitalism*. François Weil challenges the importance of absentee merchant capitalists in the New England textile industry, though he does not suggest any greater participation of artisan entrepreneurs; Weil, "Capitalism and Industrialization in New England."

4. Cochran, "Philadelphia: Industrial Center"; Lindstrom, *Economic Development*, 95–110.

5. Elizabeth Blackmar, *Manhattan for Rent, 1785–1850* (Ithaca, N.Y., 1989);

Lubow, "Artisans in Transition." A recent study suggests that in London tradesmen and men and women in the middling ranks exercised a great deal of "economic confidence" (350) and participated widely in small-scale speculative building "in their own right, for their own ends" (346); Lisa Margaret Bowers Isaacson, "The Building Society: Speculative Building in the West End of London, 1660–1760" (Ph.D. dissertation, Princeton University, 1992).

6. Lubow, "Artisans in Transition"; Rock, *Artisans of the New Republic*. Blackmar points to the development of a new entrepreneurial class of small scale landowners that capitalized on the escalating land prices through the accumulation of housing. She does not focus on those engaged in building and the consequences of the city's property relations for these artisans; Blackmar, *Manhattan for Rent*.

7. William Penn conveyed large tracts of land to each of the colony's investors, in return for which the purchasers agreed to pay a nominal quit rent (a yearly token of fealty). Many of these landowners then conveyed land to colonists in fee simple, reserving an annual rent payable to the themselves as ground lords. At the close of the American Revolution, the commonwealth of Pennsylvania eyed title to the twenty-four million acres of land held by the proprietors. The Divesting Act of 1779 agreed that the Penn family would retain lands that were considered the personal property of the proprietary. Title to the remaining tracts passed to the commonwealth. While the Divesting Act did not treat ground rents directly, it provided confirmation of title to ground owners, and specifically converted quit rents on the remaining private Penn lands to ground rents. Richard M. Cadwalader, *A Practical Treatise on the Law of Ground Rents*; Bernard Dougherty to Colonel McPherson, March 19, 1799, Provincial Delegates, 5: 31, HSP; Joseph N. Smith, "Tenures in Pennsylvania and Their Relation to Ground Rents," *Temple Law Quarterly* 5 (1931): 279–87; William R. Vance, "The Quest for Tenure in the United States," *Yale Law Journal* 33 (1924): 248–71; Rainer Jacobs, *Die Quit-Rents in den USA und ihre Wurzeln in der Geschichte des Englisch-Amerikanischen Real-Property-Law* (Berlin and New York, 1971); Robert Grey Bushong, *Pennsylvania Land Law* (Newark, N.J., 1938), 121–25; Christopher Fallon, *The Law of Conveyancing in Pennsylvania* (Philadelphia, 1901), 459–61; Edward P. Allinson and Boies Penrose, "Ground Rents in Philadelphia," *Quarterly Journal of Economics* 2 (April 1898): 297–313; Garvan, "Proprietary Philadelphia"; Wilkinson, *Land Policy and Speculation in Pennsylvania*, 2–5; Shepherd, *History of Proprietary Government*, 19–25; Robert L. Brunhouse, *The Counter-Revolution in Pennsylvania* (Harrisburg, Penn., 1942), 79–80.

8. Chief Justice of the Pennsylvania Supreme Court John B. Gibson explained that "[a] sale on ground rent differs from an ordinary sale only in this, that in the first the consideration [purchase price] is an annual sum perpetually charged on the land, instead of a gross sum paid or secured [by mortgage], as in the second." *Juvenal v. Jackson*, 14 PA 519, 523 (PA Sup Ct, 1850).

9. Taxes and assessments often proved considerable, as the city added streets, pavements, water, and gas to its municipal improvements. For example, one owner of property on ground rent paid $324 rent per year, plus an additional $32 per year (10 percent) for taxes. Samuel R. Fisher to Esther Fisher, January 20, 1820, Morris Family Papers—Samuel B. Morris, HSP; see also John William Crum, "The Citizen

vs. the City: Municipal Bureaucracy in Nineteenth-Century Philadelphia" (Ph.D. dissertation, University of Delaware, 1980).

10. Cadwalader, *A Practical Treatise on the Law of Ground Rents*; Nicholson, *A Treatise on the Law Relating to Real Estate in Pennsylvania*.

11. William Bingham (probably the richest man in Philadelphia in the decades before the Revolution) inherited lands, married a woman of property, and also bought extensive urban properties. Edward Shippen Burd inherited much of his landed wealth through his associations with the Shippens, a family of Pennsylvania's "First Purchasers." Emlen, Cresson, Pemberton, Cadwalader, Coxe, Penrose — these are among the old Philadelphia families that owed much of their fortunes to landed investments. Henry Simpson, *The Lives of Eminent Philadelphians, Now Deceased* (Philadelphia, 1859); Gustavus Myers, *History of the Great American Fortunes* (Chicago, 1911); Ritter, *Philadelphia and Her Merchants*; Stephen Brobeck, "Changes in the Composition and Structure of Philadelphia Elite Groups, 1756–1790" (Ph.D. dissertation, University of Pennsylvania, 1973); E. Digby Baltzell, *Philadelphia Gentlemen: The Making of a National Upper Class* (Philadelphia, 1958). For a useful analysis of the frequency of ground-rent transactions, see Robert E. Wright, "Ground Rents against Populist Historiography: Mid-Atlantic Land Tenure, 1750–1820," *Journal of Interdisciplinary History* 29 (1) (Summer 1998): 23–42.

12. For example, Edward Shippen Burd, Apr. 4, 1823, Society Collection, HSP.

13. Cadwalader, *A Practical Treatise on the Law of Ground Rents*, 65.

14. Some leases stipulated that the tenant could remove any buildings on the ground at the end of the term, although the expense and inconvenience did not always make the trouble worthwhile. The long-term leasehold system was also used in later periods in Chicago and Detroit: "The Long Term Ground Lease: A Survey," *Yale Law Journal* 48 (1939): 1400–1414. It is still frequently used for commercial properties and was popular in New York City in the 1970s when land values were low and owners wanted to lock in rents in anticipation of further decline. Community land trusts, an attempt to redevelop old housing stock in urban areas for private ownership by low-income residents, are the newest form of long-term leasing.

15. Morton J. Horwitz, *The Transformation of American Law, 1780–1860* (Cambridge, Mass., 1977). Preference toward ground-rent creditors was probably based on priority of contract; Cadwalader, *A Practical Treatise on the Law of Ground Rents*, chpt. 5; *Morton v. Sibley*, DCCCP, 1835, Judge John Cadwalader, Legal, Cadwalader Collection.

16. For example, see *Annual Statement of the Funds of the University of Pennsylvania as Reported by the Committee of Finance* (1828), and Journal and Ledger Books, 1779–1803, University Archives, University of Pennsylvania; Journal, Ledger, and Land Record Books, Thomas Cadwalader, Cadwalader Papers, HSP. (Cadwalader was the agent for the Penns and looked after their land interests in Pennsylvania.) See also Robert Blackwell, Property Record, Business Papers, Winterthur Library; Deeds, EF23: 218 for institutional ground rents (for the use of the Friends Monthly Meeting). Until 1854 trusts, however, were barred from investing in ground rents without permission from Orphan's Court, although it is unclear that the prohibi-

tion was followed in the early part of the century; Miscellaneous Docket, 1856–1867, PCCCP; Miscellaneous Papers, 1832–1915, PCCCP. *Christy* v. *McClung*, Dec. term 1844, no. 8, Equity Papers, PCCCP; see also *Cochran* v. *Cadwalader*, June term 1845, no. 4, Equity Papers, PCCCP.

17. William Tilghman, Rent Book, 1810–1835; Edward Shippen Burd, Real Estate, Mortgage and Ground Rent Record, 1830–1834.

18. William M. Evans to Edward S. Burd, Sep. 8, 1823, Edward Shippen Burd, Society Collection.

19. Maria Rockwell to Thomas Blundell, Aug. 19, 1816, Rockwell Letters, Society Collection, HSP.

20. Isaac Elliott to John H. Brinton, Apr. 14, 1826, Brinton Collection, HSP.

21. *Smith* v. *Starr*, 3 Wharton 62 (PA Sup Ct, 1838); Deeds, EF23: 213. House carpenter Moses Lancaster sheltered assets by creating ground rents and assigning them to a trustee to administer for his wife. Deeds, GWR32: 382 and 387. If he were pressed to insolvency, however, the assignments to Susanna would have been deemed fraudulent.

22. Deeds, AM65: 105.

23. Other conservative investment options in the early republic included United States government stocks, state government stocks, bank shares, mortgages, and insurance company stocks; Homer, *History of Interest Rates*; Wright, "Ground Rents Against Populist Historiography," 30.

24. Deeds, EF23: 328; see *Hazard's Register of Pennsylvania* 5 (1830): 399 for typical ground-rent transactions.

25. Allinson and Penrose, "Ground Rents," 311.

26. Wainwright, ed., *A Philadelphia Perspective: The Diary of Sidney George Fisher*, 227.

27. Lancaster first redeemed the original rent on the lot, though as the subsequent example suggests, the action was not always necessary to attract buyers. Deeds, GWR8: 617, MR22: 70, GWR8: 617.

28. Deeds, IC8: 340.

29. Deeds, EF9: 553; *Ingersoll* v. *Sergeant*, 1 Wharton 337 (PA Sup Ct, 1836).

30. Blackmar, *Manhattan for Rent*. Baltimore leases were made for ninety-nine years, but with an option exercised by the tenant to renew, which made them similar to perpetual ground rents. Baltimore, in economy and housing, bears much similarity to Philadelphia. At present, such leases are sold in Baltimore on a secondary market.

31. Tilghman, Rent Book. Similarly, if many years later the buyer of William and Ealy Green's house chose to redeem the rent charge owed to Loyd, he would pay the amount William and Ealy Green could have paid in 1834. The Green brothers could have paid Isaac Loyd $1,800 in 1834, or their assignee could pay that amount years later. Deeds, AM65: 105.

32. Edward Shippen Burd, Will, Philadelphia, 1848, Judge John Cadwalader, Legal, Cadwalader Collection; Nicholson, *A Treatise on the Law Relating to Real Estate in Pennsylvania*, 66–67; Cadwalader, *A Practical Treatise on the Law of Ground Rents*, 298–301.

33. S. Fisher to E. Fisher, Jan. 20, 1820; John H. Brinton to Edward S. Burd, Nov. 25, 1814, Edward Shippen Burd, Society Collection, HSP; see also James Trimble to Thomas Cadwalader, Dec. 2, 1820, Penn Estate Correspondence, HSP.

34. Tilghman, Rent Book.

35. Over time, deed specifications for the value of the requisite quality of the building became more specific; compare, for example, Deeds, D68: 486, D39: 492, EF23: 326. Although the occupant might not be the grantee in the ground-rent assignment, he was not shielded from disruption. The property of the "terre tenant" could be seized by the sheriff, although the grantee in the ground-rent deed might be the debtor; Cadwalader, *A Practical Treatise on the Law of Ground Rents*, chpt. 9 and pp. 259–60; William Duane, *A View of the Relation of Landlord and Tenant in Pennsylvania* (Philadelphia, 1844).

36. Misc Bk, MR 1: 175 (1817).

37. William Logan Fisher to Emma Kimber, Jan. 5, 1832; see also S. Fisher to E. Fisher, Jan. 10, 1820, Morris Family Papers—Samuel B. Morris.

38. Jeffrey A. Cohen, "The Queen Anne and the Late Victorian Townhouse in Philadelphia, 1878–1895" (Ph.D. dissertation, University of Pennsylvania, 1991), 65–77 summarizes the late nineteenth-century discussions on the persistence of Philadelphia's row house tradition. Contemporary comparisons with New York offer a variety of overly enthusiastic Philadelphia boosterisms, but the point comes clear. In 1884, for example, 2,700 building permits were issued in New York City compared to about 3,800 in Philadelphia. New York had roughly 50,000 single-family dwellings, while Philadelphia had about 165,000.

39. Historians who have explored British tenure systems (most of which are long-term rather than perpetual leases) disagree over their effects on the quality, nature, and cost of housing stock. Dan Cruikshank and Neil Burton, *Life in the Georgian City* (London and New York, 1990) and Donald J. Olsen, *The Growth of Victorian London* (New York, 1976) and *Town Planning in London: The Eighteenth and Nineteenth Centuries* (New Haven, Conn., 1982); compare M. J. Daunton, *House and Home in the Victorian City: Working Class Housing, 1850-1914* (London, 1983); "Rows and Tenements: American Cities, 1880–1914," in Daunton, ed., *Housing the Workers, 1850–1914: A Comparative Perspective* (London and New York, 1990). Daunton uses Martha Vill's work on Baltimore (where ninety-nine-year leaseholds renewable by the tenants dominated) to analyze American row house development. Martha J. Vill, "Building Enterprise in Late Nineteenth-Century Baltimore," *Journal of Historical Geography* 12, (1986): 162–81; on Baltimore, see also Mary Ellen Hayward and Charles Belfoure, *The Baltimore Row House* (New York, 1999).

40. Edwin T. Freedley, *Philadelphia and Its Manufactures . . . in 1857* (Philadelphia, 1859).

41. Addison B. Burk, "The Philadelphia Building Societies," *The Banker's Magazine* (Oct. 1881): 287–92.

42. Lorin Blodget, "A Building System for the Great Cities.—The Business and Social Influences of Building Systems Illustrated," *Penn Monthly Magazine* (Apr. 1877): 285–304, 293.

43. Blackmar, *Manhattan for Rent*, see particularly pp. 185, 192–99; Lubow,

"Artisans in Transition," 66–128. The assertion rests on the assumption that build-ers passed this "savings" on to the purchasers of housing. For a contrary argument for Baltimore, see Daunton, "Rows and Tenements." The overall purchasing price of a house and lot, however, would be higher over time if the ground rent was not redeemed.

44. Based on summaries of permits issued for placing construction materi-als on public passageways. See *Journal of the Select Council of the City of Philadelphia* (Philadelphia, 1841–1852): 1840–1841, App. 3; 1842–1843, App. 7; 1843–1844, App. 5; 1844–1845, App. 3; 1845–1846, App. 3; 1846–1847, App. 3; 1847–1848, App. 5; 1848–1849, App. 9; 1849–1850, App. 31; 1851–1852, App. 13. (1841–1842 and 1850–1851 reports are missing.); see also Theodore Hershberg et al., "The 'Journey-to-Work': An Empirical Investigation of Work, Residence, and Transportation, Phila-delphia, 1850 and 1880," in Hershberg, ed., *Philadelphia: Work, Space, Family*, 128–73.

45. J. Sharples, Account and Day Book; Eyre, Diaries, 3/29/1868. For the suc-cess of the two-story single house in the late nineteenth century, see Blodget, "Build-ing System"; A. F. Davies, *Land Values and Ownership in Philadelphia*, U.S. De-partment of Labor, Bureau of Labor Statistics, Bulletin no. 50 (Washington, D.C., 1904); Cohen, "Queen Anne and the Late Victorian Townhouse," 65–77.

46. Rockwell to Blundell, Sep. 20, 1810. See also Depositions, *Meredith* v. *Peters*, Oct. 1803, DelCCCP. For subsequent decades, see William Meredith, Rent Book, 1821–1830, Meredith Papers, HSP; *MFP*, Jan. 30, 1830; Edward Shippen Burd, Real Estate, Mortgage and Ground Rent Record, 1832; Isaac Bedford, Papers, 1827–1846, HSP; William Bell, Folder 1833–1836, Society Small Collection, HSP; Moses Lancaster, Receipt Book, 1828–1844 (notations on inside covers).

47. Blackmar, *Manhattan for Rent*, 87–88; Freedley, *Philadelphia and Its Man-ufactures*, 98. Daunton traces the critical divergence between Philadelphia and New York land tenures and rents to the antebellum period and offers figures for post-bellum New York to emphasize land costs in building. Skilled laborers spent a larger proportion of their wages on rent in New York than in the cities of Philadelphia, Boston, and Chicago (according to Daunton's statistics beginning 1909); Martin J. Daunton, "Cities of Homes and Cities of Tenements: British and American Com-parisons, 1870–1914," *Journal of Urban History* 14 (1988): 283–319.

48. Smith, *"Lower Sort,"* 160–62. Elsewhere, families used the same strate-gies, but with smaller spaces. Blackmar, *Manhattan for Rent*, 61–63, 67–68, 122–26; Stansell, *City of Women*; Jeanne Boydston, *Home and Work: Housework, Wages, and the Ideology of Labor in the Early Republic* (New York, 1990). Compare Salinger's por-trait of eighteenth-century housing in Philadelphia; Salinger, "Space, Inside and Outside."

49. Rockwell to Blundell, Oct. 15, 1815; see also J. Sharples, Account and Day Book.

50. William F. Miskey, Autobiography, 1816–1892, HSP. Recall, too, that Elizabeth and John Munday sold goods out of the house of Elizabeth's sister.

51. Rockwell [Bushell] to Blundell, Nov. 3, 1805; Deposition of Catharine Litle, *Vandyke* v. *McFadden*, Sep. term 1840, no. 13, Equity Papers, PCCCP.

52. Daniel T. Glenn, Sep. 5, 1835, IP, PCCCP.

53. John Munday, Deposition, Bankruptcy Cases, 1800–1806, USDC ED PA; John A. Miskey, Mar. 27, 1837, IP, PCCCP.

54. J. Sharples, Account and Day Book; see also Sebastian Root, Dec. 22, 1840, IP, PCCCP.

55. These estimates should be used cautiously. [Anonymous], *Memoirs and Autobiography of Some of the Wealthy Citizens of Philadelphia* (Philadelphia, 1846); see also William Miskey, Autobiography, on brickmakers Benjamin Davis and Amos Ellis.

56. Browne, *A Summary of the Law of Pennsylvania, Securing to Mechanics*, introduction; Fisher to Kimber, Jan. 5, 1832, Morris Family Papers—Samuel B. Morris.

57. Proportions and statistics were compiled from a number of sources, including the following: Robert Desilver, ed., *Philadelphia Directory and Stranger's Guide* (Philadelphia, 1830); [Anonymous], *Insolvent Register for the Last Five Years; Being a Complete List of Cases in Philadelphia Court of Common Pleas Advertised in Newspapers* (Philadelphia, 1830); Pennsylvania Septennial Census, 1800, City of Philadelphia [microfilm]; *Hazard's Register of Pennsylvania* 3 (1829): 224; 4 (1829): 85, 336; 8 (1831): 65–72; 11 (1833): 415 . Extant petitions for the PCCCP cannot be used to determine occupational proportions of insolvents because only a fraction of the original petitions have survived, and occupations are frequently omitted.

58. IPs, PCCCP: James Ayers, June 8, 1822; William Haydock, June 10, 1819; Jacob Stone, Sep. 29, 1820; see also James Butler, Sep. 30, 1815; Adam D. Burkart, Oct. 18, 1820; Peter Bob, Mar. 6, 1817; Garrigues; Alexander McAllister, Sep. 23, 1819. Butler's and McAllister's occupations are not given, and they might not be building artisans.

59. Barron, March 13, 1835, IP, PCCCP.

60. James Shaw, IP.

61. Glenn, IP; see also Sebastian Root, Jan. 15, 1841, IP, PCCCP.

62. Edgar Shivers, Dec. 13, 1836, IP, PCCCP.

63. Annual rates assume monthly compounding. Munday, Bankruptcy Cases; James Shaw, IP; Reed and Myers, Real Estate Ledger; see also Wainwright, ed., *A Philadelphia Perspective: The Diary of Sidney George Fisher*, 81, 84.

64. Justus, IP.

65. Munday, Bankruptcy Cases.

66. Glenn, IP.

67. Mortgages consisted of three parts. The mortgage itself stated the terms of the obligation and the property that was the security for the bond. The mortgage bond testified to the amount of the debt and the provisions for interest payments, and the warrant of attorney facilitated foreclosure or other legal actions in the event of nonpayment of the debt. The warrant of attorney functioned as an admission to the debt and enabled the lender, or mortgagee, to obtain judgment against the debtor without the delay or inconvenience of a protracted legal proceeding. Nicholson, *A Treatise on the Law Relating to Real Estate in Pennsylvania*, 245–86.

68. Mortgages AM14: 495, AM17: 600, SHF7: 589. For the connection between Green and the mortgage creditor Susanna Lyndall, see Green's household in PopCen, 1860. Similarly, Joshua Sharples tapped sisters and cousins to outfit his

workshop and prepare for speculative building. In short order, Sharples borrowed $1,000 at interest from three different female relatives; J. Sharples, Account and Day Book.

69. Cochran, *Frontiers of Change*, 32, 35; Krooss, "Financial Institutions," 106. Founded in 1816, Philadelphia Saving Fund Society (PSFS) had $35,000 invested in mortgage loans by 1820. Though the amount represented more than half the portfolio of PSFS, it would fund the credit needs of only a handful of midcareer building artisans. By 1836, the savings bank had increased its mortgage lending to nearly $900,000. James M. Willcox, *A History of the Philadelphia Saving Fund Society, 1816–1916* (Philadelphia, 1916). On the investment (i.e., lending) policies of comparable institutions, see Lance E. Davis, "United States Financial Intermediaries in the Early Nineteenth Century: Four Case Studies" (Ph.D. dissertation, Johns Hopkins University, 1956).

70. Based on sampling of recorded mortgages in Philadelphia County in several periods, the latest in 1841; business documents of building artisans, including insolvency and bankruptcy petitions, support the observation. Capital artisans obtained from private lenders, however, often came indirectly from institutional sources in the form of secondary loans. For the local nature of real estate development and financing in the nineteenth century, see Alexander Von Hoffman, "Weaving the Urban Fabric: Nineteenth-Century Patterns of Residential Real Estate Development in Outer Boston," *Journal of Urban History* 22 (2) (Jan. 1996): 191–230; J. W. R. Whitehead, "The Makers of British Towns: Architects, Builders and Property Owners, *c.* 1850–1939," *Journal of Historical Geography* 18 (4) (1992): 417–38.

71. When building associations did take hold, they became an integral part of the "Philadelphia Building System"; Burk, "Philadelphia Building System," 288. The societies favored the ground-rent system; it minimized their capital needs because the principal of the ground rent would not be called in if the buyer defaulted.

72. *Philadelphia Gazette & Daily Advertiser*, July 13, 1802; Harry Toulmin, *Clerk's Magazine and American Conveyancer's Assistant* (Philadelphia, 1806); Benjamin Lynde Oliver, *Oliver's Practical Conveyancing, a Selection of Forms of general utility. . . .* (Boston, 1816).

73. *Poulson's American Daily Advertiser*, June 21, 1827, and Apr. 16, 1833. Brokers also lent money on securities, leading Frederick Erdman, a contractor on public works, to turn to one for credit. *Erdman* v. *Davis*, Mar. term 1845, no. 13, Equity Cases, PCCCP.

74. John Bonsall, Day Book, 1815–1831, HSP; see also William M. Evans to Edward S. Burd, Sep. 8, 1823, Edward Shippen Burd, 1821–1825, Society Collection.

75. See also Report on John S. Hoffman, Philadelphia, Penn., vol. 3, p. 532, R. G. Dun & Co. Collection, Baker Library, Harvard Business School [hereafter cited as "R. G. Dun & Co."].

76. Robert McKnight, Deposition, Apr. 18, 1786, in *Lessee of Mary Flick* v. *Kelly* (PA Sup Ct, [Philadelphia, n.d.]), PSA; Deposition of John Bosler, *Rump* v. *Williams*, Mar. term 1849, no. 16, Equity Papers, PCCCP.

77. In addition to advance money mortgages, builders frequently used developed properties as security to raise money for further undertakings. For a builder,

then, a mortgage was a means to raise capital at the outset of construction, an instrument to provide creditors with security for debts after the fact, or a means to raise capital for other projects.

78. IPs: Barron and Glenn.

79. For example, Edward Shippen Burd to Hannah Emlen, Assignment of Bonds and Mortgages as Collateral Security, Dec. 22, 1813, Society Miscellaneous Collection, HSP; Root, IP.

80. Deeds, GWR12: 756, AM61: 334; see also EF23: 193 and EF23: 268.

81. Answer of Defendant, *Hodge* v. *Stewart*, Dec. term 1847, no. 2, Equity Papers, PCCCP.

82. *Philadelphia Gazette & Daily Advertiser*, Mar. 6, 1804.

83. Nicholson, *A Treatise on the Law Relating to Real Estate in Pennsylvania*, 285–86; for example, see *Gorgas* v. *Douglas*, 6 S & R 512 (PA Sup Ct, 1819); *Twelves* v. *Williams*, 3 Wharton 485 (PA Sup Ct, 1838). If, in rare cases, construction began prior to the execution of a mortgage, the mechanics were preferred to mortgage creditors; *American Fire Insurance Company* v. *Pringle*, 2 S & R 138 (PA Sup Ct, 1815).

84. *Morton* v. *Sibley*; *Heston* v. *Ridgway* (PCCCP, Sept. 1811); *Pennock* v. *Hoover and Myers*. The importance of mortgage priority to inducing investment was made clear in the decades before the Civil War. Through paper exchanges, investors worked to circumvent the priority of mechanics' lien claims by establishing a mortgage prior to building. Allinson and Penrose, "Ground Rents," 308–9.

85. Deeds, AM47: 385, AM58: 722.

86. Jonathan A. Glickstein, *Concepts of Free Labor in Antebellum America* (New Haven, Conn., 1991).

87. There were exceptions, for example, Sarah Lea, widowed daughter of Edward Shippen, for whom John Munday built; see Chapter 1. Lea, however, probably employed a male agent to transact the deal on her behalf. See also *Mason* v. *Davis*, June term 1848, no. 1, Equity Cases, PCCCP. In the early republic, individual personality and social vision account for some of the men of wealth who asserted exceptional control over property development. A striking instance is Stephen Girard, a vastly wealthy and eccentric man. Girard functioned as a general contractor on houses built on his land, taking bids, ordering supplies, and contracting with individual master craftsmen. Stephen Girard Papers, APS. William Sansom, intent on maintaining air space and gardens in Penn's city, also took a hands-on approach to houses he financed. (Unlike Girard, Sansom did sell the lots on ground rent, but he withheld deeds until building was finished.) See William Sansom to David Jackson and Edward Burd, Dec. 1, 1797, UA General, no. 906, University Archives, University of Pennsylvania.

88. Garrigues, IP.

89. Josiah Bunting, Lumber Ledger, 1812–1813, HSP.

90. George F. and Franklin Lee, Ledger, 1813–1852, Franklin Lee Papers; John and Moses Lancaster, Receipts, 1812–1836. For excellent accounts of the nuances of book debt and exchange see Christopher Clark, *The Roots of Rural Capitalism; Western Massachusetts, 1780–1860* (Ithaca, N.Y., 1990), 30ff; Bruce H. Mann, *Neighbors and Strangers: Law and Community in Early Connecticut* (Chapel Hill, N.C., 1987),

11–41; W. T. Baxter, *The House of Hancock; Business in Boston, 1724–1775* (Cambridge, Mass., 1945), 11–38.

91. *Croskey* v. *Coryell*, 2 Wharton 223 (PA Sup Ct, 1837). The material man's information was correct. Glenn would lambaste his detractors from debtors' prison less than two years later.

92. Henry B. Venn to Samuel Fox, Aug. 15, 1841, Samuel M. Fox Correspondence, HSP.

93. *McCall* v. *Eastwick*, 2 Miles 45 (DCCCP, 1836).

94. *Croskey* v. *Coryell*. Arrangements for Colonnade Row, the 1830s buildings designed by architect John Haviland, used labor and material exchange to pay for construction costs. The building artisans "each one of whom became owner of a single building," appear to have taken labor and materials provided for their buildings in exchange for their own product. *Hazard's Register of Pennsylvania* 10 (1832): 94.

95. David Townsend to W. H. Brown, Jan. 6, 1844, ChCHS.

96. *Stevenson* v. *Stonehill*; George and Franklin Lee, Ledger; see also Bill in Equity, *Shultz* v. *Brown*, Sep. term 1849, no. 9, Equity Cases, PCCCP.

97. Munday, Deposition; see also Root, IP; William McDonough, Deposition, July 1, 1800, Case of William McDonough, Bankruptcy Cases, USDC ED PA. A reverse situation (by a nonartisan builder) is presented by Joseph Winter, a tailor and builder. Winter entered "the building business, believing that it would afford him the readiest & most profitable opportunities to dispose of his stock in trade & clothing." He paid his "builders & mechanics by . . . orders" for clothes; Joseph Winter, Sep. 30, 1835, IP, PCCCP.

98. John and Moses Lancaster, Account Book.

99. Haydock, IP.

100. Garrigues, IP; see also Charles Barras, Sep. 18, 1817, and Oct. 18, 1819, IP, PCCCP, and Root, IP.

101. Bunting, Lumber Ledger; Franks and Wagner, Receipt Book, 1824–1839.

102. At least 45 percent of brickmaker John Bosler's $52,000 indebtedness consisted of promissory notes (though he may have included mortgage bonds among them). John Bosler, no. 109, Federal Bankruptcy Cases, 1841–1843, USDC ED PA. For an important discussion of the transition to written instruments, see Mann, *Neighbors and Strangers*, chpt. 1.

103. Francis Douglass, June 6, 1816, IP, PCCCP; Glenn, IP; Nathan W. Ellis, no. 1710, Federal Bankruptcy Cases, 1841–1843, USDC ED PA; on Myers and Lancaster, see Chapter 1.

104. On Montgomery, see *Taylor* v. *Montgomery*, 20 PA 443 (PA Sup Ct, Eastern District, 1853); *Moroney's Appeal*, 24 PA 372 (PA Sup Ct, Eastern District, 1855); and Chapter 6.

Chapter 3. Dimensions of the Master Builder

1. DSB, June term 1828, no. 5, DCCCP; David Evans to John Dickinson, Mar. 22, 1804, Logan Collection. An account of the modern building process, with

some attention to historical issues, can be found in Tracy Kidder, *House* (Boston, 1985).

2. Eyre, Diaries, 1/20, 1/25, and 5/20/1840; 2/17, 3/9 and 12/6/1849; 1/15/50; 2/2/1852; 5/24/1853.

3. *Barnes* v. *Wright*, 2 Wharton 193 (PA Sup Ct, 1837), quotation 194.

4. Matthew Pearce to George Read, Aug. 10, 1797, R. S. Rodney Collection, HSD; Evans to Dickinson, Mar. 22, 1804, Logan Collection; John C. Thompson, Sep. 19, 1816, IP, PCCCP.

5. Eyre, Diaries, 1/22/1850; see also 6/20/1850.

6. Jeffrey A. Cohen, "Early American Architectural Drawings and Philadelphia, 1730–1860," in James F. O'Gorman et al., *Drawing Toward Building: Philadelphia Architectural Graphics, 1732–1986* (Philadelphia, 1986), 15–32; Jeffrey A. Cohen, "Building a Discipline: Early Institutional Settings for Architectural Education in Philadelphia, 1804–1890," *Journal of the Society of Architectural Historians* 53 (June 1994): 139–83.

7. There were exceptions, of course, though the dwellings were not "common" in the sense of style. Architect John Haviland designed a series of at least five stone (rather than brick) houses on Chestnut Street between Twelfth and Thirteenth Streets. DSB, Mar. term 1826, nos. 109, 110, 111, 113, and 114, Dec. term 1826, nos. 15, 16, and 17, DCCCP. Robert Mills designed "Franklin Row," ultimately ten residential dwellings built around 1811. Though they were "row" houses, Mills's conception departed from the city's extant designs. Kenneth Ames, "Robert Mills and the Philadelphia Row House," *Journal of the Society of Architectural Historians* 27 (May 1968): 140–46.

8. Evans to Dickinson, Aug. 4, 1798, and Mar. 12, 1804, Logan Collection.

9. Ibid., Mar. 30, 1804.

10. Ibid., Mar. 22, 1804.

11. Eyre, Diaries, 3/15, 3/16, and 3/30/1849; 1/14, 1/15, and 3/21/1850.

12. Mayor, Apprentice, and Redemptioner Indentures, 1800–1806.

13. For an appreciation of the mathematics involved in surveying, see Joseph Siddall's Plat Book, [n.d.] Third Survey District Office, City of Philadelphia; Alexander Steel, Ledger, 1797–1819, HSP.

14. Moses Lancaster, Receipts (5/26/1820); Webster, *Philadelphia Preserved*, 121. In 1833 when the Carpenters' Company surveyed potential demand for a drawing school for apprentices, two former journeymen of Lancaster agreed to send students; Cohen, "Building a Discipline," 160 n. 87.

15. Cohen, "Building a Discipline," esp. 147 and 151.

16. Eyre, Diaries, 1/14/1872; Matthew Eli Baigell, "John Haviland" (Ph.D. dissertation, University of Pennsylvania, 1965), 12–14; Cohen, "Building a Discipline"; James C. Massey, "Carpenters' School, 1833–1842," *Journal of the Society of Architectural Historians* 14 (May 1955): 29–30; Louise B. Hall, "First Architectural School? No! But . . . ," *Journal of the American Institute of Architects* 14 (Aug. 1950): 79–82.

17. Cohen, ibid.; Moses Lancaster, Receipts (12/15/1818, 5/4/1821).

18. *MFP*, July 18, 1829.

19. Cohen, "Building a Discipline." Dell Upton argues that builders effec-

tively resisted early efforts by architects to wrest control of design from them and to impose their aesthetic and systems. Dell Upton, "Pattern Books and Professionalism: Aspects of the Transformation of Domestic Architecture in America, 1800–1860," *Winterthur Portfolio* 19 (Summer-Autumn 1984): 107–50; see also Louise B. Hall, "Artificer to Architect in America" (Ph.D. dissertation, Harvard University, 1954) for a chronicle of the early history of builders and architects.

 20. Upton, "Pattern Books and Professionalism."

 21. In the British context, David Yeomans argues that early books for carpenters attempted to "make up for the deficiencies in their formal education and provide accurate detail for new architectural styles." David T. Yeomans, "Early Carpenters' Manuals, 1592–1820," *Construction History* 2 (1986): 13–33.

 22. "The Practice of Stone Masonry," *Architectural Review and American Builders' Journal* (Sep. 1870): 172–76.

 23. Helen Park, "A List of Architectural Books Available in America Before the Revolution," *Journal of the Society of Architectural Historians* 20 (October 1961): 115–30; Carpenters' Company Acquisition Records, APS; Janice G. Schimmelmann, *Architectural Books in Early America: Architectural Treatises and Building Handbooks Available in American Libraries and Bookstores through 1800* (New Castle, Del., 1999).

 24. Probably Andrea Palladio, *The Four Books of Andrea Palladio's Architecture* (London, 1738) and Olinthus Gregory, *Mathematics for practical men; being a commonplace book of principles, theorems, rules, and tables . . .* (London, [1825]).

 25. William Pain, *The Practical House Carpenter; or, Youth's instructor: containing a variety of useful designs in carpentry and architecture . . .* , 6th ed. (Philadelphia, 1797); John Haviland, *The Builders' Assistant* (Philadelphia, 1819); Peter Nicholson, *The Carpenter's New Guide: being a complete book of lines for carpentry and joinery . . .* , 8th ed., from the 6th London ed. (Philadelphia, 1818).

 26. Owen Biddle, *The Young Carpenter's Assistant; or, A system of architecture, adapted to the style of building in the United States . . .* (Philadelphia, 1805). William Pain is also credited with *The Builder's Easy Guide; or Young carpenter's assistant*, which could have been the book noted here; Misc Bk, IH1: 358 (1823). These manuals went through a number of editions and reprintings, and various books were available in London editions. Evald Rink, *Technical Americana: A Checklist of Technical Publications Printed before 1831* (Millwood, N.Y., 1981).

 27. Howard B. Rock suggests that guides encouraged the emergence of untrained or partially trained practioners. Rock, ed., *The New York City Artisan: A Documentary History, 1789–1825* (Albany, N.Y., 1989). But trade books enjoyed wide use among Carpenters' Company members—hardly likely to be the jerry builders of the day.

 28. Minutes of the Committee on Attendance, 1830, and Minutes of the Board of Managers, 1834–1851, Apprentices Library Company, Philadelphia, HSP. The Quaker-run lending library considered instructive publications those that shaped morals and character, but mention of a Latin dictionary suggests that the collection contained reference works as well; Apr. 10 and May 11, 1830, Minutes of the Committee on Attendance. For adult members, the Franklin Institute and the Library Company of Philadelphia also provided access to expensive volumes.

29. He also made "plans" (drawings?) for "finishing a vestibule," and for "Marble work," Eyre, Diaries, 1/23 and 5/25/40; 2/15, 2/16, 3/12, 3/15, 6/21, and 8/6/1849; 2/23 and 4/3/1850.

30. A vault was a masonry structure with an arched ceiling, in this case in the cellar (underneath the street), which could be used for storage; *Harker* v. *Conrad*. For a discussion of differences in verbal and spatial thinking by mechanics, see Brooke Hindle, *Emulation and Invention* (New York, 1981).

31. Moses Lancaster, Receipts.

32. Peter Crouding to George Read, Dec. 1, 1797, R. S. Rodney Collection, George Read II.

33. Evans to Dickinson, Aug. 4, 1798, Logan Collection, emphasis added. Hindle suggests an "irrelevance of words" among mechanics; Hindle, *Emulation and Invention*, 134.

34. *Pollock* v. *Moroney*, Dec. term 1843, no. 15, Equity Papers, PCCCP.

35. Sansom then advertized the sale of lots on ground rent. Builders were to receive advance money mortgages and to conform their dwellings to Carstairs's design. Thomas Carstairs, "The Plan and Elevation of the South Buildings in Sansom Street in the City of Philadelphia," LCP; Robert C. Smith, "Two Centuries of Philadelphia Architecture, 1700–1900," *Transactions of the American Philosophical Society*, vol. 43, pt. 1 (1953): 289–303. See also James F. O'Gorman, "The Philadelphia Architectural Drawing in Its Historical Context: An Overview," in *Drawing Toward Building*, 1–13.

36. Michael Pepper and George J. Ewing, May 18, 1829, Society Collection.

37. Cohen, in O'Gorman, *Drawing Toward Building*, 60.

38. Eyre, Diaries, 2/15, 2/16, and 2/23/1849.

39. *Moroney* v. *Copeland* quotation 409. Ashlar (or "ashler") is a squared block of stone.

40. *Moroney* v. *Copeland*, 409; *Mason* v. *Davis*; Evans to Dickinson, Mar. 30, 1804, Logan Collection. Dickinson had owned the Slate Roof House, which was destroyed in 1868. Anthony N. B. Garvan, ed., *The Mutual Assurance Company Papers: The Architectural Surveys, 1784–1794* (Philadelphia, 1976), vol. 1, policy no. 72.

41. John and Moses Lancaster, Account Book; Moses Lancaster, Receipts (12/17/1819).

42. *Hopkins* v. *Conrad*.

43. John and Moses Lancaster, Account Book; see also Bishir et al., *Architects and Builders*.

44. DSB, June term 1828, no. 5, DCCCP; Agreement between Levi Ellmaker and Daniel T. Glenn, James E. Johnson, and William Britton, May 16, 1832, Cadwalader Papers, Judge John Cadwalader, Legal; Lancaster, Receipts (12/17/1819); John and Moses Lancaster, Account Book.

45. Barron, IP.

46. DSB, Mar. term 1822, no. 89, DCCCP; *Barnes* v. *Wright*.

47. Eyre, Diaries, 3/21 and 6/20/1850; see also 3/30 and 6/11/1850; 4/22 and 9/2/1854.

48. John and Moses Lancaster, Account Book; Lancaster, Receipts (11/17/1829); Pepper and Ewing (1829).

49. Lancaster, Receipts (12/14/1827). "Rendering" was the first coat in two coats of plaster work, applied directly to bare brick or stone work. Peter Nicholson, *Mechanical exercises; or The elements and practice of carpentry, joinery, bricklaying, masonry, slating, plastering, painting. . . .* (London, 1812), 304–7.

50. Abraham Strickler, June 14, 1830, IP, PCCCP.

51. IPs, PCCCP: Martin Beck, Sep. 22, 1815, and Joseph Hughes, Mar. 2, 1801; *Clark* v. *Baker*, 2 Wharton 340 (PA Sup Ct, 1837).

52. George and Franklin Lee, Ledger. A perch is equal to 24$\frac{3}{4}$ cubic feet.

53. Article of Agreement, Isaac Ashton and Jacob Vodges, Aug. 31, 1795, Ashton Papers, Winterthur Library; John and Moses Lancaster, Account Book; see also Pamela W. Hawkes, "Economical Painting: The Tools and Techniques Used in Exterior Painting in the Nineteenth Century," in H. Ward Jandl, ed., *The Technology of Historic American Buildings: Studies of the Materials, Craft Processes, and the Mechanization of Building Construction* (Washington, D.C., 1983), 189–220.

54. Roger William Moss, Jr., "Master Builders"; Charles E. Peterson, ed., *The Carpenters' Company of the City and County of Philadelphia 1786 Rule Book* ([n.p.], 1971). The Bricklayers' Company issued rules for "the regulation of measuring and valuing stone mason and bricklayer's work" in 1801, but no complete copy has survived. Rink, *Technical Americana*. Samuel Jones, "Book of Dimenttions of Carpenters Work," 1784, Carpenters' Company. See also Commons et al., *History of Labour*, I: 80–87.

55. The Carpenters' Company published the 1786 rule book for public use *without* the prices filled in, whereas its members received books *with* the prices inserted. Moss, "Master Builders"; Peterson, ed., *Carpenters' Company*; Carpenters' Company of the City and County of Philadelphia, *Articles of the Carpenters' Company of the City and County of Philadelphia, and their rules for measuring and valuing house carpenters work. . . .* (Philadelphia, 1805).

56. Evans to Dickinson, Nov. 11, 1800, Logan Collection; see also Eyre, Diaries, 1/10/1851.

57. Practical House Carpenters' Society of the City and County of Philadelphia, *The Constitution of the incorporated Practical House Carpenters' Society . . . together with the rules & regulations for measuring & valuing house carpenters' work* (Philadelphia, 1812).

58. The 1805 revision converted the Pennsylvania pound currency to U.S. dollars and added some categories to meet fashionable architectural elements. A manuscript supplement had been prepared by the Company in 1795, but no book was published until 1805. Only twelve copies were printed of the 1831 edition. These were kept in Carpenters' Hall and specifications for new styles added in manuscript. Louise B. Hall, "Artificer to Architect in America."

59. DSB, June term 1835, no. 298, DCCCP.

60. Minutes of the Committee on the Book of Prices, Mar. 12, 1827, Carpenters' Company of the City and County of Philadelphia.

61. "Samuel Ashtons Bill," July 27, 1796, and "Isaac Ashtons Bill," Feb. 12, 1798, Ashton Papers. See Chapter 5 for a complete discussion of price discounting in the woodworking trades.

62. Amos Yarnall, Deposition, Mar. 21, 1796, *Jordan* v. *Wetherill* (PA Sup Ct, [n.d.]), PSA.

63. Dickinson to Evans, Aug. 23, 1800, and Moses Rea to David Evans, Sep. 15 and Oct. 16, 1800, Logan Collection.

64. Eyre, Diaries, 6/28/1849, 3/9/1850; 11/26, 12/7, 12/14/1849; 1/2, 8/15, and 12/3/1850; 11/18/1852.

65. Eyre, Diaries, 1/10, 1/21, 1/24, 2/1, and 2/6/40.

66. The 1786 Carpenters' Company book was published complete with prices in a pirated edition in 1801. *House carpenters' book of prices, and rules, for measuring and valuing all their different kinds of work* (Philadelphia: Printed by R. Folwell, 1801). An 1819 edition by the same title also approximated the Carpenters' Company schedules.

67. Measuring one new house took William Eyre several days to complete in 1840—a day and a half at the site, and another day (into the evening) "over Calculations of measurement" at home. It took, however, several weeks to get all appropriate parties together at the house for the appointed measurement. Eyre, Diaries, 1/21, 1/24, and 2/1/1840; 2/25/1853.

68. Employers, meanwhile, attempted to maintain profit margins by getting more product (at the same rate) from workers, leading to "sweating" of labor. See, for example, Commons et al., *History of Labour*, 1: 66–71; Wilentz, *Chants Democratic*, esp. 132–34; Stansell, *City of Women*, 105–19.

Chapter 4. Enterprising Nature

1. DSB, Mar. term 1835, no. 381 and June term 1835, no. 96, DCCCP.

2. J. Sharples, Account and Day Book; Joseph Trotter, "Account of Cost of New House Fourth Street near Green Street," 1829–1830, HSP.

3. William B. Marsh, *Philadelphia Hardwood, 1798–1948: The Story of the McIlvains of Philadelphia and the Business They Founded* (Philadelphia, 1948); Alfred Philip Muntz, "The Changing Geography of the New Jersey Woodlands, 1600–1900" (Ph.D. dissertation, University of Wisconsin, 1959); Harry J. Hartley, "A History of the Lumber Industry in Pennsylvania to 1900," (M.A. thesis, Pennsylvania State College, 1926), 2–26; James Elliott Defebaugh, *History of the Lumber Industry of America*, 2 vols. (Chicago, 1906), 2: 496–507, 530–42, 575–90; Samuel Preston to Lewis S. Coryell, June 26, 1821, Lewis S. Coryell, Correspondence, HSP.

4. Preston to Coryell, Dec. 15, 1821, LSCC. Susquehanna white pine forests were characterized by straight and dense growth (100,000 board feet per acre) and could be harvested at less cost than sparser woods. Marsh, *Philadelphia Hardwood*, 27–28; Cooper, "A Patent Transformation," 283.

5. Defebaugh, *History of the Lumber Industry*, 1: 552; Joseph Watson and Josiah Bunting, Receipt Book, 1821–1825, Friends Historical Collection, Swarthmore College; letters received, William Wagner Papers, 1827–1828, Wagner Free Institute, Philadelphia; *Hazard's Register of Pennsylvania* 13 (1834): 51.

6. William Cronon, *Nature's Metropolis: Chicago and the Great West* (New

York, 1992), 164–71; see, for example, Report of Lippincott, Phillips & Mann, Philadelphia, PA, vol. 2, p. 378, R. G. Dun & Co.

7. Robert Kuhn McGregor, "Changing Technologies and Forest Consumption in the Upper Delaware Valley, 1790–1880," *Journal of Forest History* 32 (Apr. 1988): 69–81; Cooper, "Patent Transformation"; Henry Sampson, no. 760, Federal Bankruptcy Cases, 1841–1843, USDC ED PA; Preston to Coryell, Sep. 4, 1818, LSCC. These categories, however, should not obscure the variety of millers within them. A number of family-owned mills straddled both designations. Passing from generation to generation, family enterprises often accumulated earnings and reinvested fortunes in multifarious commercial and industrial undertakings. Both Lewis Coryell and one of his partner's Daniel Parry stemmed from several generations of local millers. Deposition of Henry K. Paul, Aug. 19, 1829, Case of Abraham Weaver, OC 19667, Montgomery County Register of Wills and Orphans Court, Montgomery County Archives; personal communication from Michael Kennedy to the author, May 24, 1999.

8. Daniel Parry, "Account Book, Lackawaxen Establishment," 1821–[1835], BCHS.

9. Defebaugh, *History of the Lumber Industry*, 2: 500.

10. Preston to Coryell and Hugh Ely, Jan. 13, 1819, LSCC, emphasis added; Cronon, *Nature's Metropolis*, 151–53.

11. Benjamin Chew, Jr., to Coryell, Jan. 12, 1833; William Maris to Coryell, Dec. 9, 1814; William Strickland to Coryell, Apr. 19, 1819, LSCC.

12. William Maris to Coryell, Dec. 9, 1814; Isaac A. Chapman to Coryell, Apr. 8, 1817, LSCC. See also Deposition of Patrick McKelvie in *Reed* v. *Smith* [1799], ADI; Deposition of John Pyle, *Bar* v. *Smith*, 1799, ADI; Deposition of Joseph Pennock, *Baily* v. *Jones*, 1797, ADI, ChCCCP, Chester County Archives and Records; Parry, "Account Book." "Jobbing"—contract cutting and hauling—was widespread in early nineteenth-century Maine, and may also have developed in the Philadelphia region. Richard G. Wood, *A History of Lumbering in Maine* (Orono, Me., 1935), 42–45.

13. Benjamin Stickney to Joseph D. Murray, Mar. 25, 1843, Correspondence, Griffith MSS, Murray Family Collection, 1837–1853, HSP.

14. David Evans to John Dickinson, Mar. 12, 1804, Logan Collection.

15. Preston to Coryell and Ely, Jan. 13, 1819; Preston to Coryell, Dec. 15, 1821, LSCC; Stickney to Murray, Mar. 25, 1843, Correspondence, Griffith MSS.

16. McGregor, "Changing Technologies," 75; Louis C. Hunter, *A History of Industrial Power in the United States, 1780–1930. Volume 1: Waterpower* (Charlottesville, Va., 1979).

17. Preston to Coryell, Oct. 15, 1818; see also Preston to Coryell and Ely, Jan. 13, 1819, LSCC.

18. *Easton Argus*, Apr. 17, 1829, quoted in *MFP*, Apr. 25, 1829; *Poulson's American Daily Advertiser*, Apr. 16, 1833.

19. Stickney to Murray, Mar. 25, 1843, Correspondence, Griffith MSS; Parry, "Account Book"; Preston to Coryell and Ely, Dec. 12, 1818, LSCC. See also Hulce Family Papers for numerous instances, for example Chesley Yauman to M. R. Hulce, June 24, 1847 and Silas D. Hulce to M. R. Hulce, Oct. 3, 1845, Hulce Family Papers,

George M. Lauman Collection, Cornell University; J. W. White to Coryell, Apr. 14, 1830, LSCC; Anthony F. C. Wallace, *Rockdale: The Growth of an American Village in the Early Industrial Revolution* (New York, 1972), 374–80.

20. Strickland to Coryell, May 8, 1820, LSCC; Crouding to George Read, Dec. 1, 1797, R. S. Rodney Collection, George Read II, HSD.

21. Calculated from data for several mills reporting in Montgomery and Philadelphia Counties, MfrCen, 1850, and Bills of Lading, Lehigh Coal & Navigation Company (July 1838), contained in Correspondence of Joseph D. Murray to Thomas Murray, Griffith MSS. Lumber is measured by the thousand feet and is assumed to be a board foot unless "foot running" or linear foot is specified. A board foot is a length of board one inch thick, twelve inches wide, and one foot in length, whereas a running foot is the actual length of a piece of lumber without regard to thickness or width. To calculate board feet, multiply pieces by thickness (inches) by width (inches) by length (feet), and divide the result by twelve. Kornelis Smit, ed., *Means Illustrated Construction Dictionary* (Kingston, Mass., 1985). On amount of lumber for a small house, see Bishir et al., *Architects and Builders*, 198–99.

22. Preston to Ely, Coryell et al., Feb. 18, 1818; Preston to Coryell, June 13 and Dec. 15, 1821, LSCC; Earl J. Heydinger, "Lumber and Its By-Products," *Bulletin of the Historical Society of Montgomery County, Pennsylvania* 10 (1955): 16–30; M. R. Hulce to S. D. Hulce, June 12, 1843, and S. D. Hulce to M. R. Hulce, Apr. 26, 1848, Hulce Family Papers.

23. Preston to Coryell and Ely, Jan. 13, 1819, LSCC; Defebaugh, *History of the Lumber Industry* 2: 499–500; "Account, 1832," M. R. Hulce, and "Bill of Hiram Hulce, 1846," Hulce Family Papers.

24. Lindstrom, *Economic Development*; J[ohn] Finch, *Travels in the United States of America and Canada* . . . (London, 1833), 304; Gasherie Radeker to M. R. Hulce, Apr. 18, 1849; M. R. Hulce to F. S. Truman and S. D. Hulce, May 3, 1842; Gasherie Radeker to M. R. Hulce, Apr. 15, 18, and May 4, 1849, Hulce Family Papers; James Clayton to George Read, Nov. 6, 1797, R. S. Rodney Collection, George Read II; Strickland to Coryell, Apr. 19, 1819, LSCC.

25. Lumber sold as boards, scantling, or plank, the distinctions based on thickness and width. Board referred to pieces not more than one and one-fourth inches thick and two inches or more wide. Scantling applied to general sizes and widths, including small pieces two inches thick and less than eight inches wide, or not more than five inches square. The latter term could also refer to any squared hardwood not of standard dimensions. Plank measured from two to four inches in thickness and six inches or more in width. Kornelis Smit, ed., *Means Illustrated*; Frederic H. Jones, *The Concise Dictionary of Construction* (Los Altos, Calif., 1991); Samuel Moore to Coryell, July 24, 1830, LSCC; *Hazard's Register of Pennsylvania* 5 (1830): 311; Defebaugh, *History of the Lumber Industry*, 2: 579.

26. Moses Bross, no. 841, Federal Bankruptcy Cases, 1841–1843, USDC ED PA.

27. Stickney to Murray, Mar. 25, 1843, Correspondence, Griffith MSS.

28. DSB, Sep. term 1813, no. 16 and Mar. term 1829, nos. 44–47, DCCCP; *Croskey and Clay, Trading as Ashmead & Croskey* v. *Coryell and Jackson*, 2 Wharton 223 (PA Sup Ct, 1837). See also Christopher Powell, " 'Widows and others' on Bristol

Building Sites: Some Women in Nineteenth-Century Construction," *The Local Historian* 20(2) (May 1990): 84–87.

29. Moses Lancaster, Receipts (5/3/1823); John and Moses Lancaster, Lumber Day Book; Crouding to Read, Dec. 28, 1797, R. S. Rodney Collection, George Read II; see also Eyre, Diaries, 5/2/1856.

30. *MFP*, Aug. 23, 1828; see also May 22, 1830; Glenn, IP; Misc Bk AM1: 707 (1834).

31. Bill in Equity, *Cochran* v. *Perry*, Dec. term 1842, no. 2, Equity Cases, PCCCP.

32. Report of David B. Taylor & Co., Philadelphia, PA, vol. 2, p. 100, R. G. Dun & Co.

33. Charles Morris, ed., *Makers of Philadelphia: An Historical Work* (Philadelphia, 1894), 203. Traders charged fifty cents per thousand feet for handling the lumber, 1/2 to 1 percent for insurance, and a sales commission of 5 percent. Marsh, *Philadelphia Hardwood*, 45. Defebaugh suggests that some Philadelphia merchants owned their own upstate sawmills to supply their boardyards, but the timing of this development is unclear from his discussion. Defebaugh, *History of the Lumber Industry*, 2: 575–90.

34. Philadelphia, PA, vol. 2, pp. 349 and 356, R. G. Dun & Co.; see also Report on Taylor, and Report on M. Trump & Sons, Philadelphia, PA, vol. 2, p. 424. Cronon argues that for the nineteenth-century lumber industry in the midwest, individual properties of lumber "made it less suited to the speculative needs of a futures market" than, for example, grain. Cronon, *Nature's Metropolis*, 177–78. Croskey's trade in "Lumber paper" suggests that a lumber futures market (uninstitutionalized) did develop in Philadelphia. The evidence is inconclusive, however, as "Lumber paper" may refer alternatively to the loans that wholesalers and commission merchants made to sawmills.

35. McGregor, "Changing Technologies," 74; Alfred J. Van Tassel, *Mechanization in the Lumber Industry* (Philadelphia: Works Projects Administration, Report no. M-5, Mar. 1940), 1–12.

36. McGregor, "Changing Technologies"; Van Tassel, *Mechanization in the Lumber Industry*, 9.

37. Ibid.; Louis C. Hunter, *A History of Industrial Power in the United States, 1780–1930. Volume 2: Steam Power* (Charlottesville, Va., 1985).

38. By the late 1800s, the requirements of milling machinery and private railways led to a consolidation in the lumber trade that bore close resemblance to mass production industries. Van Tassel, *Mechanization in the Lumber Industry*, 9–12.

39. McGregor, "Changing Technologies."

40. Mark Richards, no. 521, Federal Bankruptcy Cases, 1841–1843, USDC ED PA.

41. Cooper, "Patent Transformation"; James M. Patton, no. 1201, Federal Bankruptcy Cases, 1841–1843, USDC ED PA; MfrCen, Philadelphia Co., 1850; see also *Sloat* v. *Smith*, Mar. term 1847, no. 4, Equity Papers, PCCCP.

42. Report on J. P. Wilson, Philadelphia, PA, vol. 2, p. 22 and Report on Wilson & Lavender, Philadelphia, PA, vol. 1, p. 274, R. G. Dun & Co. George Sloat, who also shared in Woodworth's assignment, was the son-in-law of the senior Wil-

son. Carolyn Cooper finds that carpenters and lumber merchants generally resented the "upstart newcomers" involved in introducing the Woodworth planing machine. Cooper, "Patent Transformation," 303; Gregory K. Clancey, "The Cylinder Planing Machine and the Mechanization of Carpentry in New England, 1828–1856" (M.A. thesis, Boston University, 1987).

43. Thomas C. Hopkins, *Clays and Clay Industries of Pennsylvania*, 2 vols. ([Harrisburg, PA], 1898–1899), 2: 43–47; Richard Neve, *The City and Country Purchaser and Builder's Dictionary; or, the Compleat Builders Guide* (London, [1826?]); Harrold E. Gillingham, "Some Early Brickmakers of Philadelphia," *PMHB* 53 (1929): 1–27. Richard P. O'Connor, "A History of Brickmaking in the Hudson Valley (New York)" (Ph.D. dissertation, University of Pennsylvania, 1987), 53. Susan Mackiewicz points especially to the desire of Philadelphians to build a permanent civic and Christian city as motivating early immigrants to construct brick structures. "Philadelphia Flourishing: The Material World of Philadelphians, 1682–1760" (Ph.D. dissertation, University of Delaware, 1988).

44. Hopkins, *Clays and Clay Industries*, 2: 42.

45. Jacob Cox Parsons, ed., *Extracts from the Diary of Jacob Hiltzheimer, of Philadelphia, 1765–1798* (Philadelphia, 1893); "Plan of City," 1794; Hopkins, *Clays and Clay Industries*, 2: 47; Gillingham, "Some Early Brickmakers"; *Savoy v. Jones*, 2 Rawle 342 (PA Sup Ct, 1830); Thomas Cadwalader to Edward S. Burd, July 7, 1821, Edward Shippen Burd, Society Collection; MfrCen, Philadelphia Co., 1850; Poulson's scrapbooks, Nov. 28, 1849, LCP.

46. DSB, Sep. term 1814, no. 121, DCCCP; Poulson's scrapbooks, Nov. 28, 1849; MfrCen, Philadelphia Co., 1820 and 1850; Crouding to Read, Jan. 14, 1800, R. S. Rodney Collection, George Read II; [Anonymous], *Memoirs and Autobiography of Some of the Wealthy Citizens*.

47. Karl Gurcke, *Bricks and Brickmaking: a Handbook for Historical Archaeology* (Moscow, Idaho, 1987), 1–38; F. E. Kidder, *Building Construction and Superintendence*, 2nd ed., 2 vols. (New York, 1897), 1: 189–90, 200; Harley J. McKee, *Introduction to Early American Masonry: Stone, Brick, Mortar, and Plaster* ([Washington, D.C.], 1973), 41–59; Harley J. McKee, "Brick and Stone: Handicraft to Machine," *Building Early America*, ed. Charles E. Peterson (Radnor, Pa., 1976), 74–95.

48. Quoted in Lee H. Nelson, "Brickmaking in Baltimore, 1798," *Journal of the Society of Architectural Historians* 28 (Mar. 1959): 33–34; Neve, *City and Country Purchaser*; Nathan Sharples, Day Book, 1828, Friends Historical Collection, Swarthmore College.

49. N. Sharples, Day Book. On Gill's career, see Henry Gill, Nov. 4, 1828, and Feb. 3, 1834, IPs, ChCCCP. Clay in West Chester differed somewhat from deposits in Philadelphia. West Chester clays were mostly from gneiss and schistose rocks, whereas Philadelphia offered a limestone clay. West Chester clay also had mineral fragments that could cause the bricks to burst in firing. It also lay closer to the surface (within about three and one-half feet). Nonetheless, Sharples's yard serves well to outline the processes of brickmaking in the region, particularly in small yards. See Hopkins, *Clays and Clay Industries*, 2: 47–48.

50. In larger yards, jobs could be more specialized. "Setters" might load the kiln, and designated workers sort the finished bricks. McKee, "Bricks and Stone,"

82. N. Sharples, Day Book; David Townsend to W. H. Brown, Jan. 6, 1844, ChCHS; Gurcke, *Bricks and Brickmaking*, 5; James Mease, "Method of Making Bricks as Followed in Philadelphia," [1813]. The figures for McCarter's house are derived from brickmakers returns in Penn district, Philadelphia County, MfrCen, 1850.

51. Townsend to Brown, Jan. 6, 1844; Gurcke, *Bricks and Brickmaking*; Andrew Ure, *A Dictionary of Arts, Manufactures, and Mines* . . . (New York, 1842 [from the 2nd London ed.]), 270–79; O'Connor, "History of Brickmaking," 58; see also Deposition of Edward Simon, *Rump* v. *Williams*.

52. N. Sharples, Day Book; McKee, *Introduction to Early American Masonry*, 42; Gurcke, *Bricks and Brickmaking*, 3–12; McKee, "Brick and Stone," 84; O'Connor, "History of Brickmaking," 59; Hopkins, *Clays and Clay Industries*, 2: 56.

53. A mold was a wooden box without top and frequently without bottom, which consisted of two or more rectangular compartments, each approximately 9 1/2 inches long, 4 7/8 inches wide, and 2 1/2 inches deep. With a "strike," the molder removed clay in excess of the eleven pounds or so required for the brick. In the process of drying and firing, the brick shrank roughly 14 percent. The finished size of the brick, after firing, would be approximately 8 by 3 1/4 by 2 1/4 inches. Nelson, "Brickmaking in Baltimore." The mold is prepared by dipping it in either water or fine sand to keep the bricks from sticking to it. McKee, *Introduction to Early American Masonry*, 42; Ure, *Dictionary*.

54. N. Sharples, Day Book. Similarly, when a dispute arose in one brickyard in 1850, one partner of the firm "removed the moulders so that the work might cease"; Answer of George Huhn, *Huhn* v. *Huhn*, Dec. term 1850, no. 14, Equity Papers, PCCCP. For daily production rates, see also Nelson, "Brickmaking in Baltimore."

55. N. Sharples, Day Book; Gurcke, *Bricks and Brickmaking*, 26; see also Jacob Glasgow, Feb. 1 and Mar. 15, 1825, IPs, ChCCCP.

56. N. Sharples, Day Book; MfrCen, Philadelphia Co., 1820; Hopkins, *Clay and Clay Industries*, 2: 56.

57. N. Sharples, Day Book; Gurcke, *Bricks and Brickmaking*, 28; Neve, *City and Country Purchaser*. Attendants needed to recognize the mineral content of the clay by color prior to firing and adjust temperatures accordingly; McKee, *Introduction to Early American Masonry*, 41.

58. Deposition of David Sterritt, [no date], Industry-Brickmaking File, ChCHS; N. Sharples, Day Book.

59. R. C. McCormick to Samuel Fox, May 2, 1838; James M. Fox to William P. Fox, Sep. 17, 1838, Samuel M. Fox, Correspondence.

60. Michael Fox and Stephen Girard, Articles of Agreement, Aug. 5, 1823, Real Estate Accounts, 1817–1828, Stephen Girard Papers; McKee, *Introduction to Early American Masonry*, 43; Gurcke, *Bricks and Brickmaking*, 35–38; see also Mordecai Churchman to Coryell, June 28, 1814, LSCC.

61. Crouding to Read, Jan. 14, 1800, R. S. Rodney Collection, George Read II.

62. On boring, see depositions of George W. Bradley and Edward Simon, *Rump* v. *Williams*.

63. Crouding to Read, Mar. 19 and Apr. 12, 1798, R. S. Rodney Collection, George Read II, Mar. 20, 1800.

64. Bill, [Timothy?] Caldwell to George Fitzwater, ca. Oct. 1828, George Fitzwater, Folder 1800–1828, unprocessed manuscript material, University of Delaware Special Collections. "Bricks left from a previous year always command a higher price . . . if sold before the season opens"; deposition of George Snyder, *Huhn* v. *Huhn*.

65. Calculated from the MfrCen, Philadelphia Co., 1820, by deducting fuel costs (derived from number of bricks produced) and labor costs from "contingent expenses"; Affidavit of Henry Huhn, *Huhn* v. *Huhn* (1850); Affidavit of George W. Bradley, *Rump* v. *Williams*.

66. MfrCen, Philadelphia Co., 1820 and 1850.

67. Census categories for that year make it impossible to include black males in these calculations. In both brickmaking and bricklaying in Philadelphia, however, African-American men comprised a significant component of the labor force. MfrCen, Philadelphia Co., 1820 and 1850; Poulson's Scrapbooks, Nov. 28, 1849; *Hazard's Register of Pennsylvania* 8 (1831): 65–72.

68. An American cord is a "carefully stacked pile of wood 4 feet high, 4 feet wide and 8 feet long containing 128 cubic feet." Muntz, "Changing Geography," 97; MfrCen, Philadelphia Co., 1850; Poulson's scrapbooks, Nov. 28, 1849.

69. Townsend to Brown, Jan. 6, 1844; James Fox to Samuel Fox, Sep. 22, 1839, Samuel M. Fox, Correspondence.

70. Poulson's Scrapbooks, Nov. 28, 1849.

71. MfrCen, Philadelphia Co., 1820; on production in the county, see also Tench Coxe, *A Statement of the Arts and Manufactures of the United States for the Year 1810* (Philadelphia, 1814); *Hazard's Register of Pennsylvania* 11 (1833): 192.

72. Townsend to Brown, Jan. 6, 1844.

73. Calculated exclusive of the cost of capital invested. The yard of Matlock & Leeds, for example, earned $5,570 above expenses in raw materials, fuel and labor; MfrCen, Philadelphia Co., 1850.

74. O'Connor, "History of Brickmaking," 98–101; McKee, *Introduction to Early American Masonry*; see entries at "Brick Machine" and following, Leggett, *Subject Matter Index of Patents for Inventions*.

75. Brick press-maker Charles Carnell valued his inventory of twenty presses at $2,200 in 1850; MfrCen, Philadelphia Co., 1850. Carnall was successor to S. Beisel (see below); O'Brien, *Philadelphia Wholesale Business Directory and Circular for the Year 1850*, 243–45.

76. James C. Fox to Samuel M. Fox, Feb. 7, 1839, Samuel M. Fox, Correspondence.

77. For example, Matlock & Leeds, S. & G. Grimm, Jonathan Stevenson, H. & J. Grimm, Attey Davis, C. Mallen, David Reese, and Edward D. Martin, all located in Eighth Ward, Kensington. Yards in other wards did not distinguish the types of product, suggesting that the idiosyncracies of the individual enumerator might account for the more thorough information. MfrCen, Philadelphia Co., 1850.

78. O'Connor, "History of Brickmaking"; Samuel M. Fox, Correspondence, particularly 1838–1839; Bishir et al., *Architects and Builders*, 235.

79. Since the number of bricks was not recorded, I use value per worker as a proxy for bricks per worker. A clear case of diseconomies of scale is problematic,

however, since there were some yards of 16 and 25 in the lower end of value per worker, and two yards of 40 and 60 that fell above the median value produced per worker. It is possible, moreover, that given the diversity of the product, some yards concentrated on bulk rather than quality and made their profits by selling volume. Hence, using "value" could prove problematic. If large yards sold more brick at less price or value, however, this would suggest even greater diseconomies of scale. The average monthly yield of bricks per gang in 1850 was even slightly less than the 39,500 figure for 1820 production. The data were recorded somewhat differently, so exact statistics are elusive. MfrCen, Philadelphia Co., 1820 and 1850. (I used the Philadelphia Social History Project sorts at the University of Pennsylvania and confirmed specific examples with the manuscript census.) For 1850, I also compared capital invested with value of output, but found no clear relationship. More money spent on yard improvements did not increase production, though it may have improved the quality of the product and the price the brickmaker could command.

80. Hopkins, *Clay and Clay Industries*, 2: 47 finds that small yards in Philadelphia used mostly residual clay and implies that larger yards dug alluvial (purer and deeper) deposits.

81. *Rump* v. *Williams*, quotation in Deposition of George W. Bradley.

82. Family networks played a role, since other brickmakers shared surnames with those who rebounded. Docket, Federal Bankruptcy Cases, 1841–1843, USDC ED PA; Poulson's Scrapbook, Nov. 28, 1849; MfrCen, Philadelphia Co., 1850.

83. Edward W. Hocker, "Montgomery County History," *Bulletin of the Historical Society of Montgomery County, Pennsylvania* 12 (1959–61): 3–271, 91; Heinz J. Heineman, "The Farmar-Mather Mill: Its Owners and Its Times [1683–1745]," *Bulletin of the Historical Society of Montgomery County, Pennsylvania* 26 (Fall 1987): 41–75; Heineman, "The Lime Industry at Hope Lodge," typescript, undated, HSMC; J. P. Lesley, ed., *The Geology of Chester County*, vol. C4 (Harrisburg, Penn.: Second Geological Survey of Pennsylvania, 1883). Pure lime is calcium carbonate, a naturally occurring deposit, but the composition of most lime contains impurities (alumina or clay, silica, magnesia, sand, etc.). McKee, *Introduction to Early American Masonry*, 62–65; Kidder, *Building Construction*, 1: 93–97.

84. *Pennsylvania Gazette*, Oct. 11, 1750.

85. Quantities are derived from Neve, *The City and Country Purchaser*, and Nicholson, *Mechanical Exercises*. Tench Coxe, *A Statement of the Arts and Manufactures*; MfrCen, Montgomery Co., 1850; Watson, *Annals of Philadelphia*, 1: 257; John and Jacob Fitzwater, Ledger, 1813–1860. Lime was also transported by lime boats, but only (it appears) to regions north of Montgomery County. Josiah Albertson to Lewis S. Coryell, Nov. 11, 1836, Albertson Family Papers, University of Delaware Special Collections.

86. J. C. Aldred, Ledger, 1833, ChCHS; William Hellings, Ledger, [1827–1853?], HSMC; Perry Jamison, July 23, 1836, IPs and Bonds, ChCCCP.

87. Benjamin Albertson to Josiah Albertson, Oct. 10, 1837, and Feb. 3, 1838, Josiah Albertson Correspondence, Albertson Family Papers.

88. Hardness of the limestone in Upper Merion also added blasting costs to quarrying. In some deposits, the sum for powder was equal to fuel costs, though typically it entailed one fifth of that expense; MfrCen, Montgomery Co., 1850.

89. Articles of Agreement between Thomas Bull and others and Jacob Smith, Mar. 14, 1788, ChCHS; see also Memorandum of Agreement between William Deal and Christian Engle, Jan. 18, 1811, George Fitzwater, unprocessed manuscript material, University of Delaware Special Collections. Grantee Index, Deeds, Montgomery County Recorder of Deeds lists the many transactions of John, John Jr., Jacob, and Joseph Fitzwater; see also Alexander Crawford, Montgomery County Probate Records, RW8976 (1834), Montgomery County Records and Archives; *Norristown Free Press*, Dec. 16, 1836. All Norristown newspaper references come from Judith A. Meier, comp., *Advertisements and Notices of Interest from Norristown, Pennsylvania Newspapers* 6 vols. (Apollo, Penn., 1987–1992).

90. Eli Bowen, *The Pictorial Sketch-Book of Pennsylvania; or its scenery, internal improvements, resources, and agriculture* (Philadelphia, 1854), 46–48; George S. Havens and Mary Ely Havens, *In the Vicinity of Limeport* (New Hope, Penn., 1966); MfrCen, Montgomery Co., 1820; L. A. Toft, "Lime Burning on the Gower Peninsula's Limestone Belt," *Industrial Archaeology Review* 11 (Autumn 1988): 75–85.

91. McKee, *Introduction to Early American Masonry*, 62–65; Kidder, *Building Construction*, 1: 93–97; Nicholson, *Mechanical Exercises*, 223.

92. "[G]rain in the ground & . . . fencing" were important assets to a lime property. "Conditions of the present public vendue," Nov. 3, 1840, Josiah Albertson, Correspondence; Josiah Albertson, Day Book and Ledger, [1828–1836], Albertson Family Papers, University of Delaware Special Collections; MfrCen, Montgomery Co., 1820; Hocker, "Montgomery County History," 91.

93. Benjamin Albertson to Josiah Albertson, Oct. 10, 1837, and Mar. 23, 1838, Josiah Albertson Correspondence.

94. MfrCen, Montgomery Co., 1850.

95. Ibid.

96. In 1972 the company was acquired by an international corporation. Joseph L. Robertson, "Corson-Oldest Company in the Oldest Mineral Industry," *Rock Products* ([n.p.] rpt. July 1976). In 1997, however, Corson Lime Co. shut down. *Philadelphia Inquirer* (Western Suburbs edition), June 20, 1997.

97. Benjamin Albertson to Josiah Albertson, Feb. 23, 27, and Oct. 10, 1837, Josiah Albertson Correspondence.

98. Ibid., Nov. 11, 1837; [Draft, Benjamin Albertson to Josiah Albertson], Sep. 1, 1837, Josiah Albertson Correspondence.

99. Josiah Albertson, Day Book and Ledger.

100. Benjamin Albertson to Josiah Albertson, Mar. 23, 1838, Josiah Albertson Correspondence. Excess capacity of kilns was taken up by farmers and others who burned occasional batches or saw opportunity in long-term leasing. "Receipts of Lime Business of William Hellings [scrapbook]," HSMC; Heineman, "Lime Industry," App. (reprint of select entries, Samuel Morris, Ledger, 1741–1767).

101. For example, Report of E. Norney, Philadelphia, PA, vol. 1, p. 263, R. G. Dun & Co.

102. Report of Swartzengrover & McInnis, Philadelphia, PA, vol. 2, p. 331, R. G. Dun & Co.

103. Hocker, "Montgomery County History," 91; *Norristown Herald and Weekly Advertiser*, Mar. 24, 1824; Toft, "Lime Burning."

104. Like lumber merchants, from the earliest years of the colony limeburners lobbied aggressively to assist their vicinities. *Minutes of the Provincial Council* 1 (May 19, 1698), 536; Heineman, "The Farmar-Mather Mill"; Donald C. Jackson, "Turnpikes in Southeastern Pennsylvania in the Early Republic," in McGaw, ed., *Early American Technology*, 197–239. A cord of wood burns 66.6 bushels of lime, whereas a ton of anthracite coal burns 100 bushels. MfrCen, Montgomery Co., 1820 and 1850; Hocker, "Montgomery County History," 91.

105. John R. Thomas to Francis James, Mar. 26, 1835, ChCHS; see also William J. Buck, *History of Montgomery within the Schuylkill Valley*, 1859; Theodore W. Bean, ed., *History of Montgomery County* 2 vols. (Philadelphia, 1884); Jacob Whisler, Mar. 14, 1832, IP, ChCCCP.

106. Benjamin Albertson to Josiah Albertson, July 12, 1837, Josiah Albertson Correspondence; Bill in Equity, *Shultz v. Brown*.

107. Benjamin Albertson to Josiah Albertson, Sep. 27, 1837, Josiah Albertson Correspondence.

108. MfrCen, Montgomery Co., 1850.

109. George P. Merrill, *Stones for Building and Decoration*, 3rd ed. (New York, 1910), 222; Benjamin L. Miller, *Limestones of Pennsylvania* ([Harrisburg, Penn.]: Pennsylvania Topographic and Geologic Survey, 1925).

110. Development of railroad transportation in the 1830s and 1840s brought granite, as well as a higher grade of marble, into Philadelphia from New York and New England. In the construction of buildings, stone from these distant sources replaced Montgomery marble in all but the Norristown and King of Prussia markets. Merrill, *Stones*, 222–24.

111. The histories of the Hitner and Lentz quarries are reconstructed principally from Case of Abraham Weaver, OC 19967, Montgomery County Register of Wills and Orphans Court and Abraham Weaver, Montgomery County Probate Records, RW 6958.

112. M. Auge, *Lives of the Eminent Dead and Biographical Notices of Prominent Living Citizens of Montgomery County, Pennsylvania* (Norristown, Penn., 1877).

113. Abraham Weaver to William Weaver, Dec. 21, 1814; Deposition of Daniel Hitner, Aug. 18, 1821; Deposition of John White, June 12, 1837; Deposition of Jacob Holgate, Aug. 19, 1829, OC 19667; Charles B. Dew, *Bond of Iron: Master and Slave at Buffalo Forge* (New York, 1994).

114. *Wallace* v. *Lentz*, Answer of Defendants and Interrogatories, Feb. term 1845, no. 1, Equity Docket and Papers, MCCCP; Deposition of John White, June 12, 1837.

115. Depositions of John White, June 12, 1837, and Nov. 11, 1830; Deposition of Charles C. Beatty, June 9, 1837, OC 19667.

116. *Wallace* v. *Lentz*; John Lentz, OC 11484, Montgomery County Register of Wills and Orphans Court.

117. For example, in 1800 Thomas Moore, stonecutter, superintended a quarry, while his two partners, both marble cutters, ran dressing and marketing operations in Philadelphia. Thomas Moore, Montgomery County Probate Records, RW 4679; Deeds, 20: 47, 412, 33: 623, Montgomery County.

118. *Fritz* v. *Hocker*, 4 Rawle 370 (PA Sup Ct, 1834).

119. Deposition of Hitner, Aug. 18, 1821; Deposition of John White, June 12, 1837; see also Misc Bk 2: 442 (1826), 3: 51 (1827), Montgomery County, HSMC.

120. Deeds, 33: 623, Montgomery County. Hocker paid $7,400 in cash and executed a bond and mortgage for the balance of $8,000. The bond was a joint obligation of Hocker and Fritz. *Fritz* v. *Hocker*.

121. Deposition of George Coulter, Nov. 13, 1830, OC 19667.

122. Deposition of John White, Exhibits, June 21, 1823; Depositions of John White, June 12, 1837, and Nov. 11, 1830, OC 19667.

123. Deposition of John White, June 12, 1837; McKee, *Introduction to Early American Masonry*.

124. Allan Greenwell and J. Vincent Elsden, *Practical Stone Quarrying* (New York, 1913), 43–44, 80–81, 103–4; Merrill, *Stones*, 32–41.

125. Deposition of John White, June 12, 1837.

126. Deposition of John White, Nov. 11, 1830; *Wallace* v. *Lentz*; John Burgoyne, *A Treatise on the Blasting and Quarrying of Stone, for Building and Other Purposes*, 5th ed. (London, [1868]).

127. Depositions of John White, June 12, 1837, and Nov. 11, 1830.

128. All quotations from Deposition of John White, June 12, 1837. Appraisement of Personal Property, Mar. 19, 1817, RW 6958; Audit of Estate, Sep. 29, 1821, OC 19667. Hand-boring in crystalline limestone could be done at the approximate rate of thirty inches per hour; Greenwell, *Practical Stone Quarrying*, 219; McKee, *Early American Masonry*, 18. On accidents and the hazards of quarrying, see Samuel Ditterline, July 30, 1836, IP, ChCCCP; Robert Brown, Jan. 7, 1826, IP, DelCCCP; *Norristown Herald and Weekly Advertiser*, May 15, 1833; James Smith, May 13, 1833, Coroner's Inquests, Montgomery County, HSMC; *McDermott* v. *McCradon* [McCreedon], Mar. term 1846, no. 6, Equity Papers, PCCCP.

129. Deposition of John White, June 12, 1837; *Wallace* v. *Lentz*.

130. Audit of Estate, Sep. 29, 1821. The arrangement with Hitner also entailed less risk to Weaver, since one third of the proceeds was always relative to the sales by the quarry operator. The Lentz agreement, which obligated the operators to pay a flat fee for rent, was more risky to the tenants.

131. Jackson, "Turnpikes in Southeastern Pennsylvania," esp. 223–25.

132. Misc Bk 4: 60 (1834), Montgomery County; Andrew Trollinger, Sep. 25, 1823, IP, PCCCP.

133. "S. F. Jacoby & Co., Importers & Dealers in Foreign and Domestic Marble in All Their Varieties/ J. K. & M. Freedley," W. H. Rease (Artist), Printed P. S. Duval, ca. 1850, LCP; see also Nicholas Wainwright, *Philadelphia in the Romantic Age of Lithography* (Philadelphia, 1958). On lime boats, see Benjamin Albertson to Josiah Albertson, Sep. 27, 1837, Box 1, Josiah Albertson Correspondence 1800–1849.

134. McKee, "Brick and Stone, 74–95; C. Stegnani to Stephen Girard, "Bill," June 8, 1825, Stephen Girard Papers.

135. Deeds, 43: 110, Montgomery County; see also *Norristown Herald and Weekly Advertiser*, Feb. 12, 1802, and Jan. 18, 1826; *Wolf* v. *Traquair*, May term 1822, no. 84, Continuance Docket and Papers, MCCCP.

136. *Norristown Weekly Register*, July 15, 1829, and Aug. 23, 1826.

137. *Hazard's Register of Pennsylvania* 5 (1830): 256; *Norristown Herald and Weekly Advertiser*, July 15, 1829; Bean, ed., *History of Montgomery County*, 1: 762.

138. Account, Feb. 7, 1829, Peter Fritz and Christopher Hocker, Hocker Family File, GHS.

139. *Norristown Herald and Weekly Advertiser*, May 3, 1826; Bean, *History of Montgomery County*, 1: 762; Deeds, 41: 465, Montgomery County; PopCen, Northumberland Co., 1850.

140. Deeds, 99: 116, Montgomery County; Auge, *Lives of the Eminent Dead*.

141. Auge, *Lives of the Eminent Dead*.

142. McKee, "Bricks and Stone"; Merrill, *Stones*; MfrCen, Montgomery Co., 1850; Auge, *Lives of the Eminent Dead*.

143. Report on Pennsylvania Land & Marble Co., Philadelphia, PA, vol. 1, p. 338, R. G. Dun & Co.

144. MfrCen, Montgomery Co., 1850. His son and successor Channing Potts, for example, erected a large steam marble-sawing works that produced up to 30,000 cubic feet of marble annually.

145. Hitner also owned an iron furnace capitalized at $20,000. MfrCen, Montgomery Co., 1850; "Montgomery County Residents from the Population Census of 1850," *Bulletin of the Historical Society of Montgomery County, Pennsylvania* 16 (Fall 1967–Spring 1968): 333–65.

146. Report on Pennsylvania Land & Marble Co., R. G. Dun & Co.

147. Bill of Complaint, *Tennant* v. *Highlands*, Dec. term 1837, no. 8, Equity Papers, PCCCP; R. G. Dun & Co. Reports on J. K. Freedley, Philadelphia, PA, vol. 2, p. 54; John Baird, Philadelphia, PA, vol. 2, p. 121; see also John Rice, Philadelphia, PA, vol. 3, p. 172.

148. "S. F. Jacoby & Co., Importers & Dealers in Foreign and Domestic Marble."

Chapter 5. *"Windows Sashes & Sundry Other Light Things"*

1. The following account of Sharples's activities is reconstructed largely from J. Sharples, Account and Day Book.

2. Ibid.; Minutes of the Concord Monthly Meeting for June 8, 1796, and Removals issued, 1779–1865, Concord Monthly Meeting, Society of Friends, Friends Historical Collection; see also Bart Anderson, ed., *The Sharples-Sharpless Family*, 3 vols. (West Chester, Penn., 1966), 1: 103.

3. J. Sharples, Account and Day Book.

4. Moxon described joinery as "an Art Manual, whereby several Pieces of Wood are so fitted and join'd together by Straight-line, Squares, Miters or any Bevel, that they shall seem one intire Piece"; Moxon, *Mechanick Exercises*, 63–109; quotation 63.

5. In 1806 Sharples engaged a shop belonging to John Lancaster, who was then in partnership with cousin Moses Lancaster. The pair probably consolidated production under the roof of Moses, leaving John's shop available for a tenant. J. Sharples, Account and Day Book.

6. J. Sharples, Account and Day Book; Deeds, EF24: 203.

7. Although a master craftsman, Sharples remained single until 1808; Marriages, 1772–1907, Northern District Monthly Meeting, GSP; Hinshaw Card Index, Philadelphia Northern District Meeting, Friends Historical Collection.

8. *Democratic Press*, Apr. 6 and June 20, 1827; Charles F. Hummel, *With Hammer in Hand: The Dominy Craftsmen of East Hampton, New York* (Charlottesville, Va., 1968).

9. *Democratic Press*, April 21, 1827; *Bailey's Franklin Almanac, for . . . 1827* (Philadelphia, [1826]); *Pennsylvania Almanac, for the year of our Lord 1827 . . . containing The Rising, Setting . . . of the Sun . . . carefully calculated for the Latitude and Meridian of Philadelphia* (Philadelphia, [1826]). In his study of northern England, Donald Woodward suggests that early modern "workshop based" craftsmen often continued labor after dark. Donald Woodward, *Men at Work: Labourers and Building Craftsmen in the Towns of Northern England, 1450–1750* (Cambridge, England, 1995), 137. For a bookbinder's work by candlelight, see Rock, ed., *New York City Artisan*, 192–93.

10. Indenture of Thomas Whitesel, 1806, Mayor, Apprentice, and Redemptioner Indentures.

11. John and Moses Lancaster, Account Book, 1812–1820; J. Sharples, Account and Day Book. When work was available, journeymen labored six days a week for months at a time, rarely absenting themselves from construction; William Wagner, "Account Book N° 3, Journemans Wages, 1809[–1812]," GHS.

12. J. Sharples, Account and Day Book.

13. John and Moses Lancaster, Account Book; see also Franks and Wagner, Receipt Book, 1824–1839.

14. John and Moses Lancaster, Account Book.

15. William Irvine to Callender Irvine, Dec. 11, 1792, Papers of General William Irvine, HSP. Judith Ridner generously provided me with this reference.

16. Mechanics described these pursuits as suffering "in open buildings without fire." *Pennsylvanian*, Mar. 21, 1836.

17. J. Sharples, Account and Day Book; John and Moses Lancaster, Account Book.

18. Linda Clarke, *Building Capitalism: Historical Change and the Labour Process in the Production of the Built Environment* (London, 1992), 52–53, 57–58, 81, 101. New York City was an exception to the measurement system until the early 1800s. The city's General Society of Journeymen House-Carpenters argued that "the method long in use in the principal cities in the United States, and also in Europe, of working by Measure and Value, would be a general benefit to the City, and particularly all concerned in Building." General Society of Journeymen House-Carpenters, New York, "List of prices" (New York, 1810), Shaw & Shoemaker Microprint 20574; see also the Company of Master Builders, "House carpenters' book of prices . . . with rules of measuring and valuing all their different kinds of work" (New York, 1802), Shaw & Shoemaker Microprint 2059; Rock, *Artisans of the New Republic*, 248. For additional comparisons to British trades, see James Ayres, *Building the Georgian City* (New Haven, 1998).

19. J. Sharples, Account and Day Book.

20. *American Daily Advertiser*, May 16, 1791; Commons et al., *History of Labour*, 1: 69–70, 110. A Marxist interpretation holds that day rates signaled the complete commodification of labor; in this case, however, it is journeymen who argue in support of daily wages, in preference to measure and value compensation. See Linda Clarke, *Building Capitalism*; Lubow, "Artisans in Transition."

21. *Pennsylvanian*, Mar. 21, 1836.

22. Wagner, "Account Book N° 3, Journemans Wages."

23. *Pennsylvanian*, Mar. 17, 1836.

24. *Pennsylvanian*, Mar. 21, 1836; "Isaac Ashtons Bill," Feb. 12, 1798, Ashton Papers.

25. Moses Lancaster, Receipts (6/16/1829); *M'Intyre* v. *Carver*, 2 W & S 392 (PA Sup Ct, 1841).

26. *American Daily Advertiser*, May 16, 1791; Commons et al., *History of Labour*, 1: 70.

27. M'Intyre shaped piecework in his cellar for the same master who engaged him by the day at outdoor building. *M'Intyre* v. *Carver*.

28. Moses Lancaster, Receipts (11/23/1816); for the underlying rationale of piece rates, see the times estimated for carpentry and joinery tasks, *General rules of work for house-wrights, in Newburyport* (Newburyport, Mass., 1805), Shaw & Shoemaker, Microprint 8508.

29. *M'Intyre* v. *Carver*; Moses Lancaster, Receipts (4/11, 5/9, 5/23, and 10/3/1829).

30. J. Sharples, Account and Day Book; Wagner, "Account Book N° 3, Journemans Wages"; John and Moses Lancaster, Account Book. In the 1830s journeymen recorded their average daily wage at $1.25 from the first of April until the first of November, and $1.12 during the remaining months; *Pennsylvanian*, Mar. 17 and Mar. 21, 1836.

31. *Pennsylvanian*, Mar. 17 and 21, 1836.

32. Bishir et al., *Architects and Builders*, 187. On summer-winter wage differentials in areas of northern England and in London, see Woodward, *Men at Work*, 138–41.

33. J. Sharples, Account and Day Book. Isaac Shunk, who worked from December 1805 to August 1806, earned more than $220.

34. Average annual income for these eleven cases was $286. Wagner, "Account Book N° 3, Journemans Wages." Compare journeymen house carpenters' own estimates of 1809 income (and expenses) in Rock, ed., *New York City Artisan*, 233–34.

35. Sharples noted that his boarding cost $3 each week in 1804 and 1805, which was also the amount indicated in an 1815 source. Rockwell to Blundell, Oct. 15, 1815, Rockwell Letters.

36. Laurie, *Working People of Philadelphia*; Herbert G. Gutman, "Work, Culture, and Society in Industrializing America, 1815–1919," in *Work, Culture, and Society in Industrializing America* (New York, 1976), 3–78; Wilentz, *Chants Democratic*; Northrup, "Decomposition and Reconstitution"; Lubow, "Artisans in Transition".

37. [Anonymous], *Memoirs and Autobiography of Some of the Wealthy Citizens*. Baker's identity is clarified in Jacob Franks and William Wagner, Receipt Book, 1810–1817 (gift of Louise B. Beardwood to the author).

38. Perhaps John Barron (by 1810) and Joseph Smith (by 1811) were married and headed independent households (as their appearance in city directories may suggest). Robinson, *Philadelphia Directory for 1810*; Jane Aitken, *Census Directory for 1811* (Philadelphia, 1811). Joshua Sharples spent slightly more than $10 for one year's washing in 1803.

39. I am assuming that Rubincam and Shunk shared the income credited to their account equally. On that basis, each man earned $330 in 1810, and $549 in 1811. In April or May of 1812, Rubincam teamed up with another journeyman, and Rubincam's income totaled $335. Shunk thereafter appears to have worked on his own and earned $312 in 1812. Average yearly income for 1810–1812 for Rubincam was $405, and for Shunk, $397. Average amounts are more useful, since Wagner made some payments in large sums, after settlement of accounts or completion of a portion of a job.

40. Averaging the 1811 and 1812 data from Table 1 shows that a man could have expected to earn $269 at day rates. In late 1811 Moore teamed up with Little, but simultaneously continued to work with Rittenhouse. I calculated total income in this case by assuming that Rittenhouse got the bulk of money for labor done during Moore's concurrent work with Little.

41. A visitor to America in the second decade of the nineteenth century estimated starting capital costs for carpenter shops in New York City at $500; evidence for Philadelphia, however, testifies to a considerably lower threshold. Henry Fearon, *Sketches of America* (London, 1819; New York and London, 1969), 24–25, 30–33; Richard B. Stott, *Workers in the Metropolis: Class, Ethnicity, and Youth in Antebellum New York City* (Ithaca, N.Y., 1990), 36–37.

42. *Hinchman* v. *Graham*, 2 S & R 170 (PA Sup Ct, 1815); *Wallace* v. *Melchior*, 2 Browne 104 (DCCCP, 1811); J. Sharples, Account and Day Book.

43. John and Moses Lancaster, Lumber Day Book; see also *Perigo* v. *Vanhorn*, 2 Miles 359 (DCCCP, 1840).

44. IP, PCCCP: Michael Barron, Mar. 13, 1835; Philip Justus, June 16, 1835; William Clayton, Sep. 29, 1815; James Shaw, June 14, 1830; James Traquair [to George Read], May 15, 1799, R. S. Rodney Collection, George Read II; Jacob Franks, 1828, no. 117, Will and Inventory, Registrar of Wills, Philadelphia County; U.S. Direct Tax of 1798, Philadelphia, West Northern Liberties, Inner Part, Form A and Form B, and South Ward, Form B; Misc Bk, IC1: 70 (1813); Misc Bk, GWR1: 305 (1825); DSB, Sep. term 1829, no. 44, PCCCP. Philadelphia's noted Federal artist William Birch depicted the relocation of a frame building in his view of "Walnut Street Gaol"; S. Robert Teitelman, ed., *Birch's Views of Philadelphia: A Reduced Facsimile of "The City of Philadelphia . . . As it Appeared in the Year 1800"* (Philadelphia, 1982).

45. Justus, IP; *Democratic Press*, Apr. 21, 1827; J. Sharples, Account and Day Book; Misc Bk, MR1: 274 (1817); Misc Bk, IH1: 100 (1821); PopCen, 1820.

46. On various sources of tools, see Hummel, *With Hammer*, 53–55; Paul B. Kebabian, *American Woodworking Tools* (Boston, 1978), 48–54, 83–89; Diane Lind-

strom, *Economic Development*, 44; Geoffrey Tweedale, *Sheffield Steel and America: A Century of Technological Interdependence, 1830–1930* (Cambridge, England, 1987); Harry C. Silcox, *A Place to Live and Work: The Henry Disston Saw Works and the Tacony Community of Philadelphia* (University Park, Penn., 1994); Misc Bk, AM1: 552 (1833).

47. Indenture of George Cunningham, Guardians of the Poor, Almshouse Indentures, 1804–1812; Moses Clement, Dec. 14, 1815, IP, PCCCP; see also DSB, June term 1829, no. 301, DCCCP.

48. John and Moses Lancaster, Account Book; J. Sharples, Account and Day Book.

49. *Pennsylvanian*, Mar. 17 and 21, 1836; Eyre, Diaries, 2/2/1849 and 8/28/1849.

50. Barron, Mar. 13, 1835, and Apr. 12, 1837, IPs; J. Sharples, Account and Day Book.

51. Isaac C. Neall, June 5, 1837, IP, PCCCP; see also John Binley, Dec. 15, 1836, IP, PCCCP.

52. *American Daily Advertiser*, May 16, 1791; Commons et al., *History of Labour*, 1: 69–71; Indenture of Whitesel; Walter Thompson, June 22, 1837, IP, PCCCP; Journeymen House Carpenters' Association of the City and County of Philadelphia, *Constitution & By-Laws* (Philadelphia, 1837).

53. Benjamin F. Hannis, Mar. 19, 1836, IP, PCCCP; *Desilver's Philadelphia Directory and Stranger's Guide for 1835 & 1836*; *A. M'Elroy's Philadelphia Directory for 1839* (Philadelphia, 1839) and *A. M'Elroy's Philadelphia Directory for 1840*; PopCen, 1840.

54. Evan Lloyd, Deposition, May 24, 1803, Case of Evan Lloyd, Bankruptcy Cases, 1800–1806, USDC ED PA; Thompson, IP. Michael Barron, who attained master status before the age of twenty-five, calculated building costs with his "own work as a Carpenter included." Barron, Mar. 13, 1835, IP.

55. William Clark, June 5, 1822, IP, PCCCP; J. Sharples, Account and Day Book; Wagner, "Account Book Nº 3, Journemans Wages."

56. Peter Crouding to George Read, Dec. 1, 1797, R. S. Rodney Collection, George Read II.

57. See, for example J. Sharples, Account and Day Book; G. Reade to John Reade, Mar. 9, 1805, George Ross Reade Collection.

58. Peter Crouding to George Read, Dec. 28, 1797; "Memorandum of Mr. G. Read's juniors Account" [Apr./May 1798?], R. S. Rodney Collection, George Read II.

59. *Pennsylvanian*, Mar. 21, 1836.

60. Jackson, *Formation of Craft Labor Markets*, quotation 7; Richard Price, *Masters, Unions, and Men: Work Control in Building and the Rise of Labour, 1830–1914* (Cambridge and New York, 1980), 29–34.

61. Whereas major colonial cities might have supported some specialized crafts, beyond American population centers, artisans combined house carpentry and joinery to make a living. See, for example, Cooke, *Making Furniture in Preindustrial America*, 13–32; Carl Bridenbaugh, *The Colonial Craftsman* (New York, 1950), 65–69ff; Robert Blair St. George, "Fathers, Sons, and Identity: Woodworking Artisans in Southeastern New England, 1620–1700," in Ian M. G. Quimby, ed., *The Craftsman in Early America* (New York, 1984), 89–125; Bishir et al., *Architects and Builders*.

In seventeenth- and eighteenth-century England, house carpentry and joinery were separate trades, but common expertise engendered frequent disputes over territory. Woodward, *Men at Work*, 17–19; see also Peterson, ed., *The Carpenters' Company of the City and County of Philadelphia 1786 Rule Book*, xix, n. 13.

62. Scharf and Westcott, *History of Philadelphia* 3: 1762, estimate the number of dwelling houses and inhabitants of the city and county for the period. Their "Careful Estimates" are suspicious. Their data show perfect parity in population growth and increase in the number of dwellings in the county between 1810 and 1850. (Dwellings increased 267 percent, as did inhabitants of Philadelphia County.) The authors may have estimated early figures for dwellings using proportions derived from later statistics. See also Elizabeth M. Geffen, "Industrial Development and Social Crisis, 1841–1854," in Russell F. Weigley, ed., *Philadelphia: A 300-Year History* (New York, 1982), 307–62, 309; Glynn R. deV. Barratt, "A Russian View of Philadelphia, 1795–1796: From the Journal of Lieutenant Iurii Lisianskii," *Pennsylvania History* 65 (Winter 1998): 62–86, quotation 75; *Journal of the Select Council of the City of Philadelphia, 1850–51*, App. 7, 57.

63. Paint colors also reflected the interest in light interiors; Lapsansky, "South Street Philadelphia," 70–79, 97; Talbot Hamlin, *Greek Revival Architecture in America* (New York, 1944), 10–12; Arnold Nicholson et al., "Notes on the Design and Architectural Detail of Philadelphia Row Houses, 1740–1850," ["compiled from material in the archives of the Philadelphia Historical Commission and published by the old Philadelphia Development Corporation"], (n.p., n.d.).

64. Blumin, *Emergence of the Middle Class*, 146–63; Richard Bushman, *The Refinement of America: Persons, Houses, Cities* (New York, 1992); Lapsansky, "South Street Philadelphia," 76; Warner, *Private City*. See a later refrain of "dispersion of taste" in "Practical Carpentry and Joinery," *Architectural Review and American Builders' Journal* 1 (Aug. 1868): 140–43.

65. Scranton, *Proprietary Capitalism*; Pierre Claude Reynard, "Manufacturing Strategies in the Eighteenth Century: Subcontracting for Growth among Papermakers in the Auvergne," *Journal of Economic History* 58 (Mar. 1998): 155–82. On shifting journeymen among shops, note overlapping personnel in the accounts of Joshua Sharples, and Moses and John Lancaster.

66. Michael V. Kennedy, "Working Agreements: The Use of Subcontracting in the Pennsylvania Iron Industry 1725–1789," *Pennsylvania History* 65 (Autumn 1998): 492–508, 503–4.

67. Kennedy, "Working Agreements," 501. The instance Kennedy cites follows a typical division of task, since the jobbing carpenters did the inside work after the contracting master had framed the structures.

68. *A general description of all trades: digested in alphabetical order . . .* (London, 1747); see also Charles E. Peterson, "Carpenters' Hall," *Transactions of the American Philosophical Society*, vol. 43, pt. 1 (1953): 96–128, 97 and n. 9. On jobbing in northern England, see Woodward, *Men at Work*, 30.

69. See Chapter 2 for incidence of insolvency in building.

70. *M'Intyre* v. *Carver*.

71. Wills and administration records capture inventory estates after many decedents have disposed of significant productive property. Chattel mortgages and

bills of sale are a better indication of the belongings of a mechanic in midcareer. Nonetheless, the latter group of documents does have its biases, particularly when fiscal stress underlay the reason for sale or mortgage. Chattel mortgages and bills of sale are recorded in the Miscellaneous Book series, PCA. For the usefulness of tool inventories for charting specialties, see also Cooke, *Making Furniture in Pre-industrial America*, 15–18. For a comparable trend in England, see Ayres, *Building the Georgian City*, 150–168.

72. Misc Bk, ICi: 204 (1814); see also Misc Bk, GWR2:418 (1829) and IHi: 358 (1823). The following sources were consulted throughout my discussion of tools: R. A. Salaman, *A Dictionary of Tools Used in the Woodworking and Allied Trades* (London, 1975); Graham Blackburn, *The Illustrated Encyclopedia of Woodworking Handtools, Instruments, and Devices* (New York, 1974); Hummel, *With Hammer in Hand*.

73. Misc Bk, AMi: 113 (1831); PopCen, 1830 and 1850.

74. Misc Book, AMi: 360 (1832).

75. Bills, Ashton Papers: David Jones, Apr. 8, 1795; Richard Robison, Nov. 18, 1795; Jacob Seniff, July 27, 1796.

76. Claim, DSB, Dec. term 1812, no. 128; see also DSB, Mar. term 1835, nos. 32 and 71, and Dec. term 1829, nos. 348 and 349; John and Moses Lancaster, Lumber Day Book.

77. John and Moses Lancaster, Account Book; DSB, Mar. Term 1829, no. 291; see also Mechanics' Lien and City Claims, Mar. term 1837, no. 8, PCCCP.

78. John and Moses Lancaster, Account Book; *Moroney* v. *Copeland*.

79. My suggestion here—that subcontracting is often a cyclical response to periods of highly speculative activity characterized by a large influx of capital—contrasts with that of Wilentz, who sees subcontracting in the building trades as growing during the 1820s (a period of relative economic dirth). Wilentz, *Chants Democratic*, 132–34. The years 1824-25 and 1828-29 were somewhat speculative periods, which could have given a general face to the decade consistent with either argument.

80. DSB, Dec. term 1812, no. 182; Edward Burd, Folder 7, Am 03494, HSP; "Survey of Edward Burd's Lots on 11th & Spruce, & Locust," Sixth Survey Division, no. 134, PCA; Execution Docket, Mar. 1813, no. 161, June term 1813, no. 15, June Term 1815, nos. 33, 238, and 256, Sep. term 1815, no. 185, DCCCP.

81. When journeymen house carpenters joined together in 1791 to protest various craft practices, they offered carpentry work to the public at 25 percent below the prices of masters. The explanation was intended to discredit master employers, but given the trouble of superintendence, the risk of building, and the expense of tools, the masters regarded the charge as just compensation. *American Daily Advertiser*, May 11, 1791; Commons et al., *History of Labour*, 1: 127–28.

82. Amos Yarnall, Deposition, Mar. 21, 1796, *Jordan* v. *Wetherill & Son*.

83. DSB, Dec. Term 1812, no. 176; Mar. term 1813, nos. 42, 43, and 78; Practical House Carpenters' Society, *The Constitution*.

84. DSB, June term 1813, no. 21; John and Moses Lancaster, Account Book. Estimates are based on price and wage data from several sources: Bezanson et al., *Wholesale Prices in Philadelphia*; U.S. Department of Labor, Bureau of Labor Statistics, *History of Wages in the United States*; Adams, *Wage Rates in Philadelphia*; Donald

R. Adams, Jr., "Residential Construction Industry in the Early Nineteenth Century," *Journal of Economic History* 35 (1975): 794–816.

85. For example, DSB, Mar. term 1829, no. 291, Dec. term 1828, no. 197, Jan. term 1829, no. 32, Mar. term 1835, no. 32, and Sep. term 35, no. 85.

86. Practical House Carpenters' Society, *The Constitution; Insolvent Register for the Last Five Years.*

87. *Morton* v. *Sibley.*

88. PopCen, 1860; *Philadelphia Wholesale Business Directory . . . for 1850*; The Massachusetts census of 1830 enumerated four men by the name of "Abel Reed"; three lived in Worcester County, but none was a certain match. On the importance of the Worcester region to woodworking technology, see Clancey, "The Cylinder Planing Machine."

89. *Desilver's Philadelphia Directory and Stranger's Guide for 1837* (Philadelphia, 1837) identifies two men by the name of Abel Reed, both at the same dwelling. The second was a carpenter, suggesting either that Reed was listed twice—once by a former(?) occupation—or that a male relative (presumably his father) had also relocated to Philadelphia. Either possibility points to the craft background of many early sash and door manufacturers.

90. Report of Abel Reed, Philadelphia, PA, vol. 2, p. 363, R. G. Dun & Co.

91. *Philadelphia Wholesale Business Directory . . . for 1850.*

92. Rights to construct, use, and vend Josiah Fay's tenoning machine, which Reed had in his factory by 1850, were assigned in March 1833 to Mark Richards, John Hemphill, and John Inslee (men also involved in buying Woodworth rights for Philadelphia). I could find no patent assignment for the other machines Reed ran in his shop in 1850. Digest of Assignments, F-1, p. 8, U.S. Patent Office, RG 241, NARA, Washington, D.C.; *Philadelphia Wholesale Business Directory . . . for 1850*; Cooper, "A Patent Transformation."

93. William Read to George Read, June 11, 1802, R. S. Rodney Collection; Eliza Wolcott, "George Read (II) and His House" (M.A. thesis, University of Delaware, 1971), 59.

94. *Croskey* v. *Coryell.*

95. *M'Intyre* v. *Carver.*

96. Kenneth Sokoloff, "Was the Transition from Artisanal Shop to the Non-mechanized Factory Associated with Gains in Efficiency?" *Explorations in Economic History* 21 (1984): 351–82; Salaman, *Dictionary of Tools.* House carpenter John A. Miskey used a "mortice" machine in his shop in the 1830s, but it might have been steampowered; Miskey, IP.

97. Catherine Bishir and others find the first steampowered sash and blind factories in North Carolina dating from 1848. Bishir et al., *Architects and Builders*, 155–59, 212–19. Elsewhere, waterpower was a less costly and more convenient option than steampower; Johnson, *Shopkeeper's Millennium*, 41.

98. Clancey, "Cylinder Planing Machine," 23. Clancey suggests that Woodworth had not so much solved the mechanical aspects of planing lumber by machine, but, rather, had brought together "labor talent and money" to make a marketable innovation (32).

99. Cooper, "Patent Transformation," esp. 293–304.

100. Clancey, "Cylinder Planing Machine," 51–52; DSB, Mar. term 1830, no. 295; DSB, Mar. term 1835, no. 61. On competing innovations, see Carolyn Cooper, "A Patent Transformation," 305–6; Leggett, *Subject Matter Index of Patents*; Inventory, James M. Patton, Federal Bankruptcy Cases, 1841–1843.

101. Quoted in Clancey, "Cylinder Planing Machine," 30.

102. John and Moses Lancaster, Account Book. Calculations based on rates proposed by Clancey, "Cylinder Planing Machine," 36; see also Cooper, "A Patent Transformation," 293.

103. Eyre, Diaries, 8/15/1849; see also 6/8, 6/9, and 6/19/1849.

104. Cooper, "Patent Transformation"; "Proceedings of a Mass Meeting of the Citizens of the City and County of Philadelphia in favor of a repeal of the present extension of the Woodworth Planing Machine and opposed to the further extension," April 6, 1850, Records of the Committee on Patents and the Patent Office, U.S. Senate, SEN 31A-H14, NARA, Washington, D.C.

105. Clancey, "Cylinder Planing Machine," 172–73.

106. *Philadelphia Wholesale Business Directory . . . for 1850*.

107. *Philadelphia Wholesale Business Directory . . . for 1850*; MfrCen, Philadelphia Co., 1850 and 1860; Report of Reed, R. G. Dun & Co. A contemporary report suggests that the loss estimated by the credit reporter was somewhat exaggerated; Eyre, Diaries, 1/30/1854.

108. See also returns of Jonathan Naglee's sash and door manufactory and of the Philadelphia Wood Moulding, Planing & Manufacturing Co., MfrCen, Philadelphia Co. (Middle Ward and Northern Liberties, Seventh Ward), PA, 1850; Report of Philadelphia Wood Moulding, Planing and Manufacturing Co., Philadelphia, PA, vol. 3, p. 294, R. G. Dun & Co. The Philadelphia Social History Project (PSHP) archives at the University of Pennsylvania was particularly helpful for drawing together information on the industry (see the "Sort by Business" for MfrCen, Philadelphia Co., 1850).

109. Misc Bk, AM 2: 483 (1837); MfrCen, Philadelphia Co., 1850 (Fourth Ward, Kensington); see also return of Light & White, Second Ward, Southwark.

110. By 1860, most sash and door manufactories operated with at least 15-horsepower steam engines; MfrCen, Philadelphia Co., 1860. John Richards, *A treatise on the construction and operation of wood-working machines* (London, 1872), 34; see also Nathan Rosenberg, "America's Rise to Woodworking Leadership," in *America's Wooden Age: Aspects of Its Early Technology*, edited by Brooke Hindle (Tarrytown, N.Y., 1975), 37–62.

111. *Philadelphia Wholesale Business Directory . . . for 1850*. Bishir and coauthors suggest that well into the mid-nineteenth century, northern factories sent sash, blinds, etc. to southern markets—joinery that, nonetheless, was made from southern lumber. Bishir et al., *Architects and Builders*, 214–15. On effects of the integration of regional and national markets on craftsmen, see Commons et al., *History of Labour*, 1:102–6.

112. *Philadelphia Wholesale Business Directory . . . for 1850*; McElroy's Business Directory, 1857 (Philadelphia, 1857).

113. On hours and seasons of operation in a similar concern (a mahogany sawmill) see Deposition of John B. Moses, *Vandyke v. McFadden*.

114. I am talking here about relative wages (comparisons among groups of earners), not real wages (comparisons to the cost of living).

115. The U.S. Census of Manufactures, notwithstanding numerous problems, is one of the few gauges available to measure workers' earnings in this period. I have calculated median daily wages from the PSHP "Sort by Business" of the 1850 census, using the following method: I divided average monthly wages by the number of men (equivalent to number of employees) to find an average monthly wage per man; then divided that amount by twenty-six days, a constant that I used as an average number of days worked at full employment; the result was an average daily wage per employee. I then found the median wage of each group (sash and door workers; carpenters; and house carpenters combined with builders).

"Carpenters" in the 1850 census subsumed a variety of occupations and specialties ranging from bedstead makers to specialized joinery shops. By contrasting workers in sash and door manufactories with these more general carpenters, I do not mean to imply that carpenters were absent from sash and door enterprises.

Using median wage within sash and door manufactories is not a perfect measure of economic opportunities of the trade. A mechanized workshop may well have employed a greater range of labor—skilled and high-priced, on the one hand, and unskilled and cheap, on the other—than a typical carpentry shop.

116. Eyre, Diaries, for example 8/10 and 10/26/1850, 5/29/1851, and 3/26/1853.

117. As an engineer-machinist, of course, Richards was interested in elevating the importance of skill; see Richards, *Treatise on Construction*, 282–83. Qualitative evidence is scarce, but suggests that men operating sawing and woodworking machinery apprenticed to the trade in their youths, and accumulated years of experience useful in running, repairing, and modifying ever-changing equipment; Depositions of Henry Ecker, John B. Moses, David B. Thomas and others, *Vandyke* v. *McFadden*. Bob Reckman concurs that mechanization did not deskill carpenters, but rather changed skill factors. Bob Reckman, "Carpentry: The Craft and Trade," in Andrew Zimbalist, ed., *Case Studies on the Labor process* (London, 1979), 73–102.

118. "Report of the Committee on the Machinery of the United States," in Nathan Rosenberg, ed., *The American System of Manufactures* (Edinburgh, 1969), 167. On modifying by hand items that were produced by machine, see Robert B. Gordon, "Who Turned the Mechanical Ideal into Mechanical Reality?" *Technology and Culture* 29 (1988): 744–78.

119. Richards, *Treatise on Construction*, 282–83; "Report of the Committee on the Machinery of the United States," 171.

120. Deposition of William G. Probasco, in John Northrop, no. 828, Federal Bankruptcy Cases, 1841–1843, USDC ED PA.

121. "Report of the Committee on the Machinery of the United States," 171, 167. On estimates for time involved in production by hand, see *General rules of work for house-wrights, in Newburyport*.

122. Reed claimed that his machine could do "Mortising, either in hard or soft wood," but he might have exaggerated its ability; compare to "Practical Carpentry and Joinery."

123. Returns for F. R. Gatchell and John G. Thum, MfrCen, Philadelphia Co., 1860.

124. Eyre followed the same system with moldings, preparing lumber in the shop when he had manpower, but having it worked at a planing mill when he did not. Eyre, Diary, 2/2, 2/8, 4/12, 7/11, 10/26, 10/27, and 12/27/49; 3/23, 8/8, 8/10, and 12/18/1850; 3/6, 4/24, and 6/5/1851; 6/9/1855; 2/14/1857. Eyre continued to buy joinery from Reed, even though he owned a "Morticing Machine"; labor time, not machinery, was Eyre's principal criterium in ordering from Reed.

125. *Morton v. Sibley*; see also Eyre, Diary, 2/27, 6/11, and 6/25/1849.

126. MfrCen, Philadelphia Co., Fourteenth Ward, Second Division; Fifteenth Ward, 1860; Eyre, Diaries, 5/4/1855. Joseph Whitworth, author of the "Report of the Committee on the Machinery of the United States," suggests that staircase manufactory was mechanized, but all Philadelphia operations surveyed for the 1860 census were run by "hand," not steampower.

127. MfrCen, Philadelphia Co., Sixth Ward, 1860. Census enumerators complicated occupational designations further by their individual perspectives, which led to sobriquets that varied by ward. Compare, for example, in amount of detail as well as differences of titles (for likely the same business), First Division, Sixth and Ninth Wards, with Fourteenth Ward.

128. "Report of the Committee on the Machinery of the United States," 171.

129. Laurie, *Working People*, 184. Cooper has shown that the anger of building tradesmen and lumber merchants was fueled by monopolistic pricing practices, not mechanization; Cooper, "Patent Transformation," 314–16. Of course, "[a]t times, such as in 1840 and in 1857, real estate became absolutely stagnant," but generally from about 1843 to 1857, economic, demographic, and geographic growth kept demand for building steady; [E. M.], "The Vitality of Real Estate," *Architectural Review and American Builders' Journal* 2 (June 1870): 734–36, quotation 735.

Chapter 6. Final Assembly

1. Laurie, *Working People*, 48–49; Scharf and Westcott, *History of Philadelphia*, 3: 2255; *Cadwalader* v. *Montgomery*, Case Papers, 1849–1852, Judge John Cadwalader, Legal.

2. Commons et al., *History of Labour*, 1: 564–65; Thorp et al., *Business Annals*, 76; Geffen, "Industrial Development and Social Crisis," 318.

3. PopCen, 1860; *Moroney's Appeal*.

4. *Cadwalader* v. *Montgomery*.

5. Much has been claimed for structural innovations in construction known as "balloon framing." The system, "invented" in the midwest in the 1840s, used lumber of widths and depths significantly slighter than that used for timber (braced) frames. The house derived its strength from a greater number of pieces, secured together by nails. Thus, it eliminated the need for mortise and tenon joints, and presumably decreased the skill required to construct a house. Paul E. Sprague, "Chicago Balloon Frame," in H. Ward Jandl, ed., *The Technology of Historic American Buildings: Studies of the Materials, Craft Processes, and the Mechanization of Building Construction,* (Washington, D.C., 1983), 35–61. I find no evidence to suggest that balloon framing had any impact on brick row construction in Philadelphia in the pre-1850

period. The system applies more logically to changes in wooden houses, and might have been important at midcentury in neighborhoods beyond the city's core (West Philadelphia and Chestnut Hill, for example). Other scholars question the impact of balloon framing on wooden buildings in the northeastern region of the country anytime before 1870. See Clancey, "The Cylinder Planing Machine," 3–4.

6. Bill, Apr. 1815, Samuel B. Morris-Morris Family Papers. The vault was probably used for storage; see *Harker v. Conrad*.

7. Eyre, Diaries, 2/23/1850; see also 4/23/1849.

8. Minutes of the Common Council, June 13, 1833, in *Hazard's Register of Pennsylvania* 12 (1833): 27.

9. Eyre, Diaries, 2/25/1850; see also 10/1/1849.

10. Since no permit was required for the laying of building materials in private yards and streets, rosters of permits can only loosely be used to calculate the number of houses built. Commissioners of the District of Spring Garden, Ordinance of Apr. 16, 1827, in *A Digest of the Acts of Assembly and of the Ordinances of the Inhabitants and Commissioners of the District of Spring Garden* (Philadelphia, 1841); Spring Garden District, Stubs, Permits to Place Building Materials in Public Streets, August 24, 1849, permits 278 and 279, PCA; ibid., *Journal of the Select Council of the City of Philadelphia* (Philadelphia, 1848), app. 9; ibid., (Philadelphia, 1849), app. 31.

11. Pennsylvania Abolition Society and Society of Friends, Manuscript Census Schedule of Coloured Persons, 1847, Philadelphia Social History Project; Franks and Wagner, Receipt Book, 1824–1839.

12. *Philadelphia Gazette & Daily Advertiser*, Oct. 2, 1802. To make room for the Bank of the United States in 1818, its building committee put "[a]ll the building materials, as they now stand, (except the brick and foundation stone)" up for sale. *American Centinel and Mercantile Advertiser*, June 27, 1818.

13. *Cadwalader v. Montgomery*; see also deposition of Jacob L. Gardner, in *Pollock v. Moroney*.

14. Eyre, Diaries, 4/15/1840; 2/19 and 7/16/1850; 4/26/1849, 3/8 and 3/7/1850.

15. Eyre, Diaries, 7/5/1852; *Ellmaker v. Britton* [Mar. 1841], Cadwalader Papers, Judge John Cadwalader, Legal; John and Moses Lancaster, Account Book; Eyre, Diaries, 3/13/1851.

16. Peterson, ed., *The Carpenters' Company of the City and County of Philadelphia 1786 Rule Book*; *Wray v. Devlin*, June term 1848, no. 7, Equity Cases, PCCCP; Eyre, Diaries, 10/16, 12/8, and 12/10/1849.

17. Eyre, Diaries, 10/6/1849; 4/26 and 4/28/1849.

18. *Democratic Press*, May 25, 1827; Isaac Townsend, Dec. 20, 1823, IP, PCCCP; Eyre, Diaries, 11/8/1850. Contemporaries had also begun to suspect occupational health hazards from long-term exposure to substances such as lead (among painters and plumbers); Mathew Carey, *A Plea for the Poor* (Philadelphia, 1837), 10.

19. Eyre, Diaries, 3/1/1850; 10/26/1855; 10/10/1849; 4/28/1849; 5/2/1854.

20. Nicholson, *Mechanical Exercises*; Neve, *The City and Country Purchaser*; Eyre, Diaries, 12/18/1855.

21. Bills of Earl Shinn, June 25, 1832, and January 31, 1848, Samuel B. Morris —Morris Family Papers; for a more contentious instance, see *Mingle v. Ingram*, Bill in Equity, Mar. term 1846, no. 2, Equity Cases, PCCCP.

22. Eyre, Diaries, 3/12/1849; 2/27, 3/3, and 10/17/1851; 4/7, 4/8, and 4/10, 1851; 7/4/1850; 7/8/1851; 5/2/1849.

23. Kebabian, *American Woodworking Tools*, 103–14; Moxon, *Mechanick Exercises*, Nicholson, *Mechanical Exercises*; Eyre, Diaries, 5/25/1849. On double tusking, see Peterson, ed., *Carpenters' Company of the City and County of Philadelphia 1786 Rule Book*.

24. Eyre, Diaries, 4/11/1850; 3/15, 3/27, 4/5, and 4/24/1849; 4/18/1850; 5/5/1849.

25. Eyre, Diaries, 6/24 and 7/15/1853; Hugh Brown, June 8, 1815, IP, PCCCP; *MFP*, June 14, 1828.

26. *Cadwalader* v. *Montgomery*; *Ellmaker* v. *Britton*.

27. Eyre, Diaries, 12/6, 5/30, and 6/1/1849.

28. Ibid., 6/2/1849; 9/17/1853.

29. William Ingram to the Building Committee [for Founders Hall, Haverford College], Feb. 28, 1832, RG 910A, Haverford College Library; William Strickland to Lewis S. Coryell, May 7, 1819, LSCC; *Evans* v. *Hindman*, Mechanics' Lien Claims, Nov. 8, 1834, ChCCCP; Eyre, Diaries, 3/12/50. A putlock is "one of the short horizontal timbers of a scaffolding on which the scaffold-boards rest"; *Oxford English Dictionary*, 2nd ed. (Oxford, 1989). The term can also mean the hole in the (brick) wall used to support the scaffolding; Steven J. Phillips, *Old House Dictionary: An Illustrated Guide to American Domestic Architecture, 1600 to 1940* (Washington, D.C., 1992).

30. John Nisbet, Deposition, Dec. 21, 1805, and Matthew Duncan, Deposition, Dec. 3, 1805, *Duncan* v. *Wray* (PA Sup Ct, Dec. term, n.d. [1805?]), PSA; Eyre, Diaries, 6/1/1849; 6/17/1840, and 5/26/1849. The craftsman might even fasten a roof temporarily, securing it the next spring when building resumed. *Stevenson* v. *Stonehill*.

31. Eyre, Diaries, 5/8/1840; 12/8/1849; 1/12/1852.

32. Report of Warren & Burnham [1854, 1856], Philadelphia, PA, 2: 551, R. G. Dun & Co; *Philadelphia Merchants' and Manufacturers' Business Directory for 1856-57* (Philadelphia [1856]).

33. Eyre, Diaries, 10/13/1854 and 11/30/1855; *Cadwalader* v. *Montgomery*.

34. Eyre, Diaries, 3/11/1850.

35. Nicholson, *Mechanical Exercises*; Neve, *The City and Country Purchaser*; Nicholson, *The Carpenter's New Guide*; Margaret B. Tinkcom, "Cliveden: The Building of a Philadelphia Countryseat, 1763–1767," *PMHB* 88 (Jan. 1964): 3–36; Kidder, *Building Construction*, 1: 189–90, 200; McKee, *Introduction to Early American Masonry*; Hawkes, "Economical Painting"; William Haber, *Industrial Relations in the Building Industry* (Cambridge, Mass., 1930), 44–45, 110–15; James Hopkins, Mar. 15, 1832, IP, PCCCP.

36. IPs, PCCCP: Thomas B. Hazzard, July 2, 1835; Isaac S. Britton, Mar. 27, 1837.

37. Eyre, Diaries, 2/22/1851; 4/26/1852; 11/15/1853; 12/28/1855.

38. Moxon, *Mechanick Exercises*, 149–53; *Harker* v. *Conrad*; Eyre, Diaries, 6/8, 6/9, 6/19, and 8/15/1849.

39. Moxon, *Mechanick Exercises*; Nicholson, *Mechanical Exercises*; McKee,

Introduction to Early American Masonry, 81–87; Kidder, *Building Construction*, 1: 327–30; Eyre, Diaries, 11/2 and 11/4/1850. On the availability of gypsum, see *Niles' Weekly Register*, Mar. 7, 1812, Aug. 12, 1813, Feb. 25, 1815; June 28, July 5 and 19, 1817; Misc Bk, AM1: 263 (1832).

40. Eyre, Diaries, 11/3/1849; 10/31/1849.

41. *Savoy v. Jones*, 2 Rawle 342 (PA Sup Ct, 1830); see also Articles of Agreement between Esau Cox and William Kirk, on the one part, and William Seal et al., Feb. 2, 1816, Building Committee Papers, Wilmington Monthly Meeting, Friends Historical Collection, Swarthmore College; Eyre, Diaries, 1/30/1854; Deposition of John H. James, *Twelves v. Krumhaar*, June term 1838, no. 13, Equity Cases, PCCCP.

42. Moxon, *Mechanick Exercises*; Nicholson, *Mechanical Exercises*; *Hopkins v. Conrad*; *Ellmaker v. Britton*; Eyre, Diaries, 4/24/1856; Hawkes, "Economical Painting."

43. Christian Johns, Mar. 6, 1817, IP, PCCCP; DSB, Dec. term 1812, no. 177, DCCCP; "Paxton's Philadelphia Annual Advertiser," in James Paxton, ed., *The Philadelphia Directory and Register for 1818*; Beatrice B. Garvan, *Federal Philadelphia, 1785–1825: The Athens of the Western World* (Philadelphia, 1987); Eyre, Diaries, 11/27/1854.

44. McKee, "Brick and Stone"; C. Stegnani to Stephen Girard, "Bill," June 8, 1825, Stephen Girard Papers; George and Franklin Lee, Ledger; *Hazard's Register of Pennsylvania* 5 (1830): 256; Eyre, Diaries, 8/10/1850.

45. Maureen Ogle, *All the Modern Conveniences: American Household Plumbing, 1840–1890* (Baltimore, 1996), 8–19; Wainwright, ed., *A Philadelphia Perspective: The Diary of Sidney George Fisher*, 239–41; For bathhouses in residences after the late 1830s, see for example, *U.S. Gazette*, July 31, 1838, Nov. 27, 1845; Franklin Fire Insurance Survey, no. 1989 (1837), HSP; Eyre, Diaries, 6/1/1840 and 11/15/1849.

46. John L. Cotter suggests that Philadelphia ordinances regulated the depth of privies so that human waste did not mix with the groundwater; Eyre's procedures, then, are confounding. Although his diggers "reached water at the distance of 27 feet," for instance, they made the privy hole 28 feet deep. Cotter, et al., *The Buried Past: An Archaeological History of Philadelphia* (Philadelphia, 1992), 117, 136, 158, 305–6; Eyre, Diaries, 2/13 and 2/14/1851; on depth, see also Claim, *Croskey v. English*, June 1828, no. 5, DCCCP.

47. *Journal of the Select Council, 1850–51*, app. 7.

48. Quoted in Mathew Carey, *Plea for the Poor*, 15; Isaac Parrish, "Report on the Sanitary Condition of Philadelphia, *American Medical Association Transactions* 2 (1849): 459–86, 464.

49. For example, *U.S. Gazette*, Nov. 27, 1845.

50. Eyre, Diaries, 11/17, 9/14, and 6/7/1849; 12/22/1854; *Ellmaker v. Britton*.

51. Eyre, Diaries, 7/15 and 9/27/1850.

52. IPs, PCCCP: Strickler; see also Jacob Bachman, Mar. 27, 837.

53. *Pennsylvanian*, Mar. 17, 1836.

54. Laurie, *Working People*, 183; Geffen, "Industrial Development and Social Crisis," 335; Jackson, *The Formation of Craft Labor Markets*, 105–10; Commons et al., *History of Labour*, 1: 575. Eyre's employees might have won some concessions. A week later, Eyre began to pay his employees on Friday, a day earlier than customary,

to "enable them to have the advantage of Marketing" on Saturdays. Eyre, Diaries, 5/7 and 5/16/1851.

55. Parsons, ed., *Extracts from the Diary of Jacob Hiltzheimer*, April 7, 1786; see also Nov. 2 and 29, 1792, and July 9, 1796.

56. Kebabian, *American Woodworking Tools*; John and Moses Lancaster, Account Book; Trotter, "Account of Cost of New House"; Bill, "Expences at the Raising of the Friends Meeting House," Aug. 9, 1816, Building Committee Papers, Wilmington Monthly Meeting; Misc Bk, AM2: 631 (1837).

57. Eyre, Diaries, 6/1/1849; see also 3/30/1850: "had a little repast for the men at the building in the form of a raising supper."

58. Eyre, Diaries, 5/31/1854; 9/2/1865; 5/5/1867; 2/12/1850.

59. *Philadelphia Gazette & Daily Advertiser*, May 19, 1803.

60. DSB, Dec. term 1812, no. 105, DCCCP; See also Glenn, September 5, 1835, IP; Eyre, Diaries, 9/17/1856.

61. *U.S. Gazette*, Sep. 12, 1845.

62. *U.S. Gazette*, Dec. 9, 1845.

63. Root, Dec. 22, 1840, IP.

64. George Hunter, Deposition, Aug. 22, 1795, *Lessee of Girard* v. *Denn* (PA Sup Ct, n.d.), PSA; see also Bonsall, Day Book, 1815 to 1831.

65. *U.S. Gazette*, Sep. 12, 1845.

66. James Carmall to Isaac Worrell, n.d., and Worrell to Carmall, Dec. 4, 1819, [Folder Llewellyn Phipps], Society Collection, HSP.

67. "Release of Liens," Jonathan P. Smith and George Justice and others, Dec. 8, 1819, Society Collection.

68. Henry J. Sergeant, *A Treatise on the Lien of Mechanics and Material Men*, 2nd ed. (Philadelphia, 1856).

69. I am drawing here on having looked extensively at the DSB Dockets and Claims, DCCCP, for 1811 through 1836; see also Eyre, Diaries, 1/29, 10/15, and 10/16/1849, and 2/6/1851.

70. See, for example, DSB, June term 1851, nos. 14, 27, and 49, DCCCP.

Conclusion

1. Nicholson, *A Treatise on the Law Relating to Real Estate in Pennsylvania*, 62, 66–67, 74–76, 121–23.

2. *Architectural Review and American Builders' Journal*, 1 (Feb. 1869): 521–24.

Primary Sources

Philadelphia City Archives and Records

Cemetery Returns, Board of Health
Deeds, Philadelphia County
Appearance Docket, DCCCP
Execution Docket, DCCCP
Sheriff's Deeds, DCCCP
DSB Docket and Claims, DCCCP
Guardians of the Poor, Almshouse Indentures
Insolvent Bonds and Petitions
Kensington District, Third Division, District Plan
Kensington District, Paving Assessment Ledger
Mayor, Apprentice and Redemption Indentures
Miscellaneous Books, Philadelphia County
Mortgages, Philadelphia County
Naturalization Petitions and Declarations, Philadelphia Court of Quarter Sessions
Equity Papers, PCCCP
Mechanics' Lien and City Claims, PCCCP
Miscellaneous Docket, PCCCP
Miscellaneous Papers, PCCCP
Sheriff's Deeds, PCCCP
Road Petitions, Philadelphia Court of Quarter Sessions
Scott Legacy, Account and Day Books
Stubs, Permits to Place Building Materials in Public Streets, Spring Garden District
Surveys and Property Books
County Tax Assessment Ledgers
State Tax Assessment Ledgers

Historical Society of Pennsylvania, Philadelphia

Apprentices Library Company Papers
Isaac Bedford Papers
William Bell Papers, Society Small Collection
John Bonsall, Day Book, Brinton Collection
Bricklayers Company of Philadelphia Papers
Buchanan Papers

Josiah Bunting, Business Accounts
Edward Shippen Burd, Real Estate Papers and Society Collection
Edward Burd Papers
Cadwalader Papers
Judge John Cadwalader, Legal, Cadwalader Collection
Cemetery Returns, Board of Health
Mark Clement, Account Books
Lewis S. Coryell, Correspondence
John and Jacob Fitzwater, Business Accounts
William H. Foust and David P. Weaver, Business Accounts
Samuel M. Fox, Correspondence
Franklin Fire Insurance Surveys
Jacob Franks and William Wagner, Business Accounts
Edward Carey Gardiner Collection
Jacob Graff, Receipt Book
Griffith MSS, Murray Family Collection
History of the Fifth Street Methodist Episcopal Church, 1882
William Irvine Papers
Jones, Clark & Cresson, Receipt Books
Moses Lancaster, Receipt Books, 1812–1836, 1828–1844
John and Moses Lancaster, Business Accounts
Franklin Lee Papers
Benjamin Lehman, Account Book
Logan Collection
Maitland Family Papers
Meredith Papers
William F. Miskey, Autobiography
Morris Family Papers—Samuel B. Morris
Penn Estate, Correspondence
Derrick Peterson, Ledger
Provincial Delegate Papers
Reliance Fire Company Papers
Joseph Reed and Warnet Myers, Real Estate Accounts
Rockwell Letters, Society Collection
Thomas Savery, Account Book
Joshua Sharples, Account and Day Book
Shippen Family Papers
Society Collection
Society Miscellaneous Collection
Society Small Collection
Alexander Steel, Business Accounts
William Tilghman, Rent Book
Joseph Trotter, Accounts
Isaac H. Whyte, Receipt Book
Map Collection

American Philosophical Society, Philadelphia

Carpenters' Company of the City and County of Philadelphia Papers, on deposit at
  the APS
Franklin Legacy Bond Books
Stephen Girard Papers
Plat Book of Northern Liberties, property of Roy E. Goodman, on deposit at the
  APS
Eli K. Price Papers

National Archives and Records Administration, Mid-Atlantic Branch, Philadelphia

Bankruptcy Cases, 1800–1806, U.S. District Court, Eastern District of Pennsylvania
Bankruptcy Cases, 1841–1843, U.S. District Court, Eastern District of Pennsylvania
U.S. Census of Manufactures, 1820, 1850, and 1860
Law and Appellate Cases, U.S. Circuit Court, Eastern District of Pennsylvania
U.S. Decennial Censuses, Population Schedules, 1790, 1800, 1810, 1820, 1830, 1840,
  1850, 1860, 1870
Revolutionary War, Pension Bounty-Land Applications
U.S. Direct Tax of 1798, Philadelphia

National Archives and Records Administration, Washington, D.C.

Digest of Assignments, U.S. Patent Office
Historic American Buildings Survey, Philadelphia, National Parks Service, Depart-
  ment of the Interior
Records of the Committee on Patents and the Patent Office, U.S. Senate

Genealogical Society of Pennsylvania, Philadelphia

Horatio L. Melchior and Elenor Burk Files

Library Company of Philadelphia

Print Collection
Poulson's Scrapbooks

Third Survey District Office, City of Philadelphia

Joseph Siddall, Plat Book

Philadelphia County Recorder of Wills

Administrations
Estate Records, Orphans Court
Wills

Wagner Free Institute, Philadelphia

William Wagner Papers

University of Pennsylvania, Philadelphia

Committee of Finance Papers, University Archives
General Collection, University Archives
John Haviland Papers, Special Collections
Philadelphia Social History Project

Bucks County Historical Society, Doylestown, Pennsylvania

Deeds, Bucks County
Mechanics' Lien Claims, Bucks Country Court of Common Pleas
Daniel Parry, Account Book
Tax Lists, Newtown Borough

Chester County Archives and Records, West Chester, Pennsylvania

Affidavits, Depositions and Interrogatories, Court of Common Pleas
Insolvent Bonds and Petitions
Continuance Dockets
Mechanics' Lien Claims, Court of Common Pleas

Chester County Historical Society, West Chester, Pennsylvania

J. C. Aldred, Business Accounts
Industry-Brickmaking File
Townsend Papers

Delaware County Court of Common Pleas Archives, Lima, Pennsylvania

Affidavits, Depositions, and Interrogatories
Insolvent Bonds and Petitions

Germantown Historical Society, Germantown, Pennsylvania

Hocker Family File
William Wagner, Business Accounts

Montgomery County Archives, Norristown, Pennsylvania

Register of Wills and Orphans Court Files
Probate Records
Deeds

Montgomery County Court of Common Pleas, Norristown, Pennsylvania

Equity Docket and Papers
Continuance Docket and Papers
Mechanics' Lien Claims

Historical Society of Montgomery County, Norristown, Pennsylvania

William Hellings, Business Accounts
Miscellaneous Books
Coroner's Inquests

Friends Historical Collection, Swarthmore College, Swarthmore, Pennsylvania

Nathan Sharples, Day Book
Joseph Watson and Josiah Bunting, Receipt Book
Religious Society of Friends, Monthly Meeting Minutes, Membership Rolls, Removals, and Marriages
William Eyre Papers
Building Committee Papers, Wilmington Monthly Meeting
Hinshaw Card Index

Quaker Special Collections, Haverford College, Haverford, Pennsylvania

Founders' Hall Building Committee Papers

Pennsylvania State Archives, Harrisburg

Insolvent Debtor Papers
Pennsylvania Supreme Court Records
Pennsylvania Septennial Census, 1800
Petitions to Extinguish Ground Rent

University of Delaware Special Collections, Newark

George Fitzwater (unprocessed manuscript material)
Albertson Family Papers

Historical Society of Delaware, Wilmington

R. S. Rodney Collection
George Ross Reade Collection
Robinson-Elliot Papers

Winterthur Museum and Library, Winterthur, Delaware

Ashton Papers
Robert Blackwell Papers
Jacob Graff, Account Book, Joseph Downs Collection
Alexander Ramsey, Receipt Book, Joseph Downs Collection

Cornell University, Ithaca, New York

Hulce Family Papers, George M. Lauman Collection

Baker Library, Harvard Business School, Boston, Massachusetts

R. G. Dun & Company Collection

Index

Acknowledgments

In the process of completing this study, I have incurred many debts. Walter Licht generously read portions of the manuscript. Bruce H. Mann urged me through the writing process, reassuring me that (whether for good or for ill) I had conquered the obscurities of nineteenth-century real estate transactions. Throughout revisions I have been particularly grateful for his encouragement and humor.

Beginning in my first semester at Penn, Richard S. Dunn welcomed me into the fold of scholars at the McNeil (Philadelphia) Center for Early American Studies; in later years, the Center provided me with office space, a forum to present my work, and funding. The Center was both an institutional and intellectual anchor and I owe an incalculable debt to Richard and the community he has drawn there. I benefited especially from the unparalleled generosity of Susan E. Klepp, who read the entire manuscript not once but twice; the final version is far better for her questions and insights. Rosalind Beiler has been friend, colleague, and fellow traveler, and has endured more prolonged discussion of the structure, arguments, and frustrations connected with this book than any other person. Maurice Bric, James Farley, Michael Kennedy, Simon Newman, George Rappaport, Rosalind Remer, and Anne Verplanck read parts of the manuscript and helped me to shape my ideas and prose more clearly. John Bezis-Selfa, Liam Riordan, Judith Ridner, and Billy G. Smith directed me to worthwhile sources and shared their own research with me.

Scholars farther afield have also responded to my questions and read drafts as the work progressed. Thomas K. McCraw, Takashi Hikino, Alfred D. Chandler, and Julio Rotemberg patiently explained relevant economic theory, taught me much about business history, and saved me from technical land mines. The Business History faculty at Harvard Business School may have been at a bit of a loss to know what to do with me—a historian working on small businessmen in the an age before the railroad—but they were no less hospitable. My sojourn there also gave me the opportunity to present my work to the Economic History Seminar at Harvard University. I am grateful to its participants for a characteristically lively exchange that aided me in refining my discussion of real estate financing. During my residence in the Boston area, Gregory Clancey, David Hancock, Marc Stern, and Martha Burns extended good company and good food.

Without the assistance and generosity of James Duffin, I never could have mined Philadelphia archival material with such lucrative results. Thomas Heinrich shared my interest in small producers but prodded me always to look at the big picture. Carolyn Cooper has repeatedly shared her enthusiasm and knowledge about woodworking technology and entrepreneurs. John J. McCusker forced me to wrestle with concepts of entrepreneurship and speculation; in the end, however, I am responsible for my own intractability. Gary Kornblith, John Lauritz Larson, Lisa Lubow, Philip Scranton, and Alfred Young commented on early drafts of chapters and asked probing questions. Howard Rock graciously answered several pleas for assistance. Warren Sanderson, Ned Landsman, Ruth Schwartz Cowan and Chris Sellers have been solicitous and sympathetic colleagues who devoted time and energy to see this project completed.

My research has brought me to diverse archives where I have been assisted by many individuals. A few stand out for the lengths they went to track down elusive citations, cart filthy boxes from remote storage, or explain byzantine court filing systems. I cannot adequately thank Jefferson Moak for his assistance over the many years that I used the records of the Philadelphia City Archives. Louise Jones and Linda Stanley, both formerly of the Manuscripts Division of the Historical Society of Pennsylvania, shared their knowledge of the collection to steer me to fruitful sources. Jeffrey A. Cohen offered to bail me out when illustrations failed to materialize, though Erika Piola and Jenny Ambrose of the Library Company of Philadelphia were able to come to speedy aid. Ruth O'Brien of The Carpenters' Company of the City and County of Philadelphia graciously gave me all manner of help in tapping the Company's resources.

Dun & Bradstreet & Company, through the mediation of the Baker Library, granted permission to quote from its early agency reports, and the Historical Society of Delaware allowed me to quote from the R.D. Rodney Collection. *Pennsylvania History* granted permission to print material that appeared in the journal.

I have been fortunate to receive funding from several sources. A Charles E. Peterson Research Fellowship in Early American Architecture and Building Technology through The Athenaeum of Philadelphia, as well as an Early American Industries Association Grant-in-Aid, supported work in regional archives. This research coalesced into the discussion of building materials that appears in Chapter 4. A Harvard-Newcomen Postdoctoral Research Fellowship provided me with that element invaluable to academic authors, time to write. A Nuala McCann Drescher Affirmative Action Leave Award/ United University Professions and a semester's leave from the Department of History, State University of New York at Stony Brook enabled me to complete final revisions.

Richard Dunn and Robert Lockhart shepherded the manuscript through to completion. Noreen O'Connor, Cory Stephenson, and behind-the-scenes individuals at the press who struggled with state-of-the art-graphics technology shaped this work into a much better book than I could have imagined.

Louise B. Beardwood introduced me to many secrets of Philadelphia and never lacked for enthusiasm about my work, even if it did seem to take a dreadfully long time to come to light. Michael Pillinger, a scholar despite his denials, deserves special thanks for his care in reading and commenting on the entire manuscript, for suggesting alternative wording, and for attempting to teach me about language. One could not ask for a more gentle and thorough critic, and I only wish that the final product does justice to his efforts. Judy Goldman, Randy Sheinberg, and Nina Tisch have had faith in this project for a very long time. Gerry Krieg made numerous revisions to the maps that appear in this book; in countless ways, he has been my polestar.